HOME OF THE GAME

HOME *of* *the* GAME

The Story of Camden Yards

Thom Loverro

Foreword by George F. Will

TAYLOR PUBLISHING / Dallas, Texas

Published by Taylor Publishing Company
1550 West Mockingbird Lane
Dallas, Texas 75235
www.taylorpub.com

Library of Congress Cataloging-in-Publication Data

Loverro, Tom
       Home of the game : the story of Camden Yards / Thom Loverro.
       p.   cm.
       ISBN 0-87833-222-7
       1. Oriole Park at Camden Yards (Baltimore, Md.)—History.
2. Stadiums—Social aspects—Maryland—Baltimore. 3. Stadiums—
Economic aspects—Maryland—Baltimore. I. Title. II. Title:
Story of Camden Yards.
GV416.B356L68   1998
796.357'06'87526—dc21   99–12020
                                                     CIP

Printed in the United States of America
10 9 8 7 6 5 4 3 2 1

*To my wife, Liz, who is my life's source;
my sons, Rocco and Nick, who are my life's
pride; and to my parents, Andy and Irene,
who taught me the simple but
valuable lesson to enjoy life.*

Contents

Acknowledgments

Many people have been key players in the development of Oriole Park at Camden Yards and the events that have taken place there since its opening in 1992, and therefore many people were key players in chronicling that development and those events for this book.

I'd like to thank Larry Lucchino, Herb Belgrad, William Donald Schaefer, Janet Marie Smith, and others for their help in trying to sort out the history of how the ballpark evolved into such a success, and Joe Foss, Peter Angelos, Pat Gillick, Cal Ripken, John Maroon, and others who helped in giving perspective to the impact of the ballpark and the dramas that have played out at Camden Yards since its opening.

I would also like to thank my sports editor at *The Washington Times*, Gary Hopkins, and my agent and friend, Jake Elwell, and also Mike Emmerich and all the people at Taylor Publishing for their support.

Foreword

by George F. Will

Do not underestimate the power of architecture. It has been well said that we make our buildings, and then the buildings make us. The physical environment that we make matters. About this, the men and women of major league baseball have become believers. They have come to understand that intelligently designed baseball parks do not just please fans, they make fans. This discovery has been made in the nick of time.

In the 1960s and 1970s the National Football League rose to prominence. In the 1970s and 1980s the National Basketball Association seized the nation's imagination. Major league baseball, facing fresh competition from these sports, and suffering some self-inflicted wounds, seemed to experience a crisis of confidence. The question was how to give baseball an infusion of new energy. The answer was in an old song.

The song says, "Take me out to the ball game, take me out with the crowd." Bingo!

For baseball fans, more than for fans in America's two other great team sports, much of the enjoyment of the game derives from sharing the experience with other fans. NFL football and NBA basketball are spectacles; baseball is a habit. Baseball—players thinly dispersed on an eye-soothing green expanse—is a more observable game than football for the fan in the stands. Unlike basketball, which is a game of flow, baseball is a game of episodes. This encourages reflection and conversation, which nourish the crowd's sense of a common involvement in an unfolding narrative.

Hence the importance of Oriole Park at Camden Yards. And the importance of Thom Loverro's book about this ballyard—the Yard which has had, and continues to have, a radiating influence on the game. Loverro knows the innards of the Yard (including its twenty miles of beer pipes), and he knows the inside story of the events that produced the Yard.

Inevitably, this book is a broth of both sports reporting and business reporting. But sports fans are used to this—used to doing an occasional double take and wondering: Am I reading the sports page of my local paper, or the *Wall Street Journal*?

Yes, baseball is a business, even one engaged in interstate commerce—a fact that in 1922 eluded the Supreme Court, with lasting consequences. A sports columnist, the late Jim Murray, once said that if baseball is not a business, then General Motors is a sport. Loverro knows that the business side of baseball can be as interesting as the game on the field, because what goes on on the field reflects what has already gone on in the front offices. The world of major league baseball is not a sentimental world; it should not be seen through a gauze of sentiment. Loverro sees it steadily and sees it whole.

Like any writer worth his salt, Loverro has strong views and does not flinch from making interpretations and coming to conclusions. You may not—I do not—agree with all of them. But that does not detract from the enjoyment of what Loverro has written—a baseball book for grownups.

Introduction

The title of this book, *Home of the Game: The Story of Camden Yards*, may seem fairly presumptuous to some, especially those fans who frequent Wrigley Field, Fenway Park, or Yankee Stadium—all historic and cherished ballparks in their own right. But the game of baseball has changed dramatically over the past twenty-five years, and for ballparks, the biggest change took place in Baltimore on April 6, 1992, the day that Oriole Park at Camden Yards opened. Major league baseball commissioner Bud Selig said this may have been "the most dramatic event in sports in the past twenty-five years." The opening of Oriole Park certainly has been among the most influential. It has spawned a series of ballparks modeled on Camden Yards—a traditional, old-fashioned ballpark with modern amenities, located in an urban setting—with more to come.

If you consider baseball to be sports theater, a drama played out in green cathedrals, then Camden Yards has become the stage for the game, the new theater that draws people in record numbers. "I think it's the best baseball facility in the United States," said former Orioles general manager Pat Gillick. "I know it's a good place because I've talked to the managers not only in the American League, but the National League managers as well that have come in here. All of them genuinely say it's the best park in baseball. It's a great place to come to see a game."

So are Jacobs Field in Cleveland and Coors Field in Denver—and the new ballparks in San Francisco and Seattle are expected to be as well. But when you are watching the drama of baseball unfold at those ballparks, you are seeing Camden Yards. "Baltimore's success at Oriole Park," wrote *The Baltimore Sun* in a March 8, 1997, editorial, "practically overnight caused America to rethink its view of stadiums as more than just big bowls where athletes clash."

Many people were involved in the success of Camden Yards and the birth of the new ballparks, but one person in particular, former Orioles president Larry Lucchino, was the driving force behind the vision from beginning to end. The road he traveled to arrive at such a fateful place in sports history and his role in developing the Camden Yards blueprint form an important piece of any examination of the impact of this ballpark.

The Camden Yards stage has seen its share of high drama in its short history, and perhaps there has been no greater drama in the game in this decade than that of the night of September 6, 1995, when Orioles shortstop Cal Ripken broke Yankees legend Lou Gehrig's consecutive-game streak of 2,130 games. It came at a time when baseball was at an all-time low, still suffering the bitter effects of the baseball strike, and all eyes were on Camden Yards that night for an event that helped to lift the game out of its grave. Ripken is one of several main characters in dramas that unfolded both on and off the field at Camden Yards. Just as Lucchino was the main player in creating the stage, Baltimore Orioles owner Peter Angelos has been the featured player in many of the Camden Yards' performances, and his role in those events is also part of the story of the ballpark.

I have had a chance to see firsthand many of these events, having attended close to 500 games at Camden Yards. I've been privileged to be in the press box the night Ripken broke Gehrig's record and watch the most cynical of sportswriters touched by the power of the event. I've seen some great players come through, like Ken Griffey, Jr., Mo Vaughn, and Juan Gonzalez, who left their mark on the ballpark with memorable home runs. I've seen Kenny Lofton rise over the center-field fence to rob home runs. I've seen Roberto Alomar make plays at second base that sometimes made him seem like the best baseball player on earth. I've sat in the stands and watched Mike Mussina come within two outs of pitching a perfect game. And I've seen the skies open up and the rain pour down on the field on the last game before the 1994 strike began.

I've seen 48,000 people come to Camden Yards to watch game after game since the ballpark opened in 1992, and there is no end in sight. They are doing it in Cleveland and Denver and will likely do it in San Francisco, Pittsburgh, and the other communities that have embraced the concept of Camden Yards—Home of the Game.

PART ONE

The Stage

CHAPTER ONE

Changing the Game

I t was a night of glitter and glamour. Some of the biggest names in the worlds of sports and entertainment showed up for the grand opening of the biggest sports restaurant in America, the ESPN Zone, the first one of its kind by the Disney Corporation, owners of the ESPN network. But the highest-profile sports restaurant in the country wasn't making its big splash in a media center like New York or Los Angeles. This was Baltimore.

That is perhaps the most remarkable aspect of the ESPN Zone as you look around at all the glitz, all the games, features, and sports memorabilia on display—this place is in Baltimore. Ten years ago, Baltimore would have been an unlikely place for such a sports palace. After all, while the city's Inner Harbor was a national tourist attraction, the city was hardly a sports mecca. It had no National Football League (NFL) franchise, as the storied Baltimore Colts had fled to Indianapolis in 1984, and the once-proud Baltimore Orioles franchise had fallen on hard times, a losing team playing in an antiquated stadium.

But that was Baltimore B.C.—Before Camden, as in Yards, the ballpark that transformed not just the city of Baltimore, but all of baseball and the entire professional sports industry. "It changed the economics of stadiums and teams much more than any of us understood at the time," said major league baseball commissioner Bud Selig. "It was huge."

Disney never would have considered coming to Baltimore to open its first ESPN Zone restaurant if Camden Yards had never been built. The impact of the heralded ballpark is far-reaching in the city and the country, as sports franchises, in one form or another, have copied the Camden Yards plan—a traditional, old-fashioned ballpark that incorporates modern amenities and is located in an urban setting.

"Camden Yards has changed the thinking of stadium construction," said former Maryland governor William Donald Schaefer. "The thinking now is how can we benefit the city?" Schaefer believes Camden Yards influenced Abe Pollin, owner of the Washington Wizards National Basketball Association (NBA) team and the Washington Capitals National Hockey League (NHL) franchise, in his decision to build an urban stadium. "Abe Pollin built the MCI Center right in downtown Washington," Schaefer noted. "I don't think that gets built down there if Camden Yards doesn't work."

Orioles owner Peter Angelos, who purchased the franchise at a bankruptcy auction for a record $173 million in August 1993, has been reaping the rewards of the ballpark and knows firsthand what Camden Yards has done, not just for Baltimore but for other cities faced with stadium issues. "The real impact of Camden Yards is that other cities have come here, and they have looked at and watched the Orioles franchise in operation and have gone back to their communities to put the same plan in place there. Now you are seeing Camden Yards–type facilities in the works in Detroit and other places, and they were all here in full force. Camden Yards has pointed the way."

Detroit Tigers president John McHale said all of the new ballparks—including the one being built in Detroit—can trace their roots to Camden Yards (which, of course, traces its roots to such historic ballparks as Ebbets Field and Wrigley Field). "Most everything I know is either an adaptation or a refinement or embellishment of what was done at Oriole Park at Camden Yards," McHale said. "The blast furnace of Maryland politics and the Orioles and the Maryland Stadium Authority and all of the players that went into producing that ballpark, they found such a valid template that it has struck a chord every place it has been tried. They really found some fundamental values and taught people the importance, not just of replicating what they were able to do, but looking at the fundamental values that guided them in the development process. Camden Yards kicked off a new era in all kinds of ways."

This new era continued in Cleveland, where Jacobs Field has been every bit as successful for the Indians and the city of Cleveland as Camden Yards has been for the Orioles and Baltimore. "Camden Yards had a strong influence on us," said Indians vice president Bob DiBiasio. The San Francisco Giants hope to match the Camden Yards success with their new ballpark under construction. "We wanted an intimate downtown ballpark that we called Camden Yards meets Wrigley Field," said Giants chief operating officer Larry Barr. "We wanted a ballpark that had the modern conveniences and the charm of Camden Yards, and the old-fashioned nostalgia of Camden Yards, married to the really incredible intimacy of Wrigley Field."

These and other baseball executives have paraded through Camden Yards with visions of their own to take home. George Steinbrenner plays in the House that Ruth built, one of the most storied ballparks in baseball, Yankee Stadium. Yet Steinbrenner and New York city officials came to Camden Yards on an official fact-finding tour to see how they could implement the Camden Yards plan in New York.

Some of the tours of ballpark hopefuls that have come through Camden Yards have an ironic connection to the ballpark. One of the offspring of Camden Yards is Coors Field in Denver, the home of the Colorado Rockies. "The success of Camden Yards clearly had an impact on our plans," said Rockies owner Jerry McMorris. "It was the model we were looking at. If it had not been successful, I think baseball would be different today. Franchises would have to rethink what they were going to do."

A group of government officials and business leaders wanting to build a ballpark in Northern Virginia, and seeking a franchise that would compete in the Orioles market, traveled to Coors Field for its own fact-finding tour. So one of the ballparks that Camden Yards spawned was being used to garner support for a ballpark in Northern Virginia that would compete against Camden Yards. Last year a group of Montreal government and business leaders came to Camden Yards to meet with Orioles officials to hear about their success and to tour the ballpark. This was part of the group's own campaign to raise support for its proposed ballpark in downtown Montreal for the Expos because it faced losing the team to out-of-town buyers from where? Northern Virginia. The web of Camden Yards is woven deeply in baseball.

Former Orioles assistant general manager Kevin Malone, now the Los Angeles Dodgers general manager, knows what it is like to play in a facility so cold that it keeps people away, which was his experience when he was general manager of the Expos. This franchise has suffered from its Olympic Stadium home in Montreal. After three years of looking out of the window of his office at the B&O Warehouse onto Camden Yards, Malone has an acute appreciation for the impact of the ballpark. "Once this ballpark was built and people saw what it did for the Orioles franchise and the city, I think everyone began evaluating their situations and started the thought process that these kind of ballparks do draw people. It has taken baseball to the next level as far as generating resources. But there is an atmosphere here that has still not been equaled by the other ballparks. Maybe it's because it is the first one, or maybe because of the warehouse; I don't know why. But there is something special about this place."

Baseball fans back up that claim. There is little argument that Wrigley Field and Fenway Park—the real thing—are still the crown jewels of baseball and are what Camden Yards and most of the other ballparks have tried to replicate. But in 1997 a *Baseball America* reader's survey found that the most popular ballpark, after Fenway and Wrigley, was Camden Yards. The atmosphere that the ballpark creates and some of the memorable events that have taken place there in its short history, such as the night Cal Ripken broke Lou Gehrig's consecutive-game record, have given Camden Yards the unofficial title of the "Home of the Game."

It is not only fans who rank Camden Yards at the top of the new wave of ballparks. Players do as well. "From a player's standpoint, everyone who comes in here believes this is the greatest place to play, the way the ballpark is set in the city and how alive it is," said Ripken, who had played for ten years at Memorial Stadium before coming to Camden Yards. "When you go to Camden Yards and start playing there, you quickly forget about Memorial Stadium, which I didn't expect at all."

Camden Yards literally sold pitcher Rick Sutcliffe on joining the Orioles before it even opened. Sutcliffe, a free agent, came to Baltimore with his agent Barry Axelrod in the winter of 1991, when construction of the ballpark was in its final stages. They conducted talks with team president Larry Lucchino and general manager Roland Hemond on tables set up under the ballpark in a storage area for beer kegs. Sutcliffe insisted on going on the field, and he walked through a little bit of snow to the mound and looked around. He spoke to Axelrod after that and soon signed a two-year contract. "He told his agent that we were taking advantage of them, that they couldn't say no after seeing this place," Hemond said. "That was his reaction to the beauty of Camden Yards." Sutcliffe, appropriately enough, would start the first game at the ballpark—opening day, April 6, 1992—and come away with a 2–0 win.

Beauty, though, is in the eye of the beholder. Economists and social scientists have conducted studies and debated about the true, quantifiable merits of Camden Yards and other ballparks.

Government officials' claims about the revenue that such facilities bring in are often inflated, and opponents often fail to take into account the immeasurable psychological impact of a successful sports franchise on the business community and the mental well-being of the population at large. The numbers can be crunched to fit any argument, and no one can say for sure what sort of ego benefit a community reaps from a ballpark.

But the sort of evidence that you see with your eyes is sometimes all you can really go on, and there is no denying the impact of Camden Yards when 48,000 people converge on Baltimore for more than eighty games a year, and beyond that. You see it when the ESPN Zone and the Hard Rock Cafe have lines outside. You also see it when the Inner Harbor becomes revitalized, reminiscent of its early days when it made Baltimore a tourist destination in the late 1970s and early 1980s.

"If Baltimore hadn't pulled the Orioles downtown, and then pulled the Ravens downtown, the Inner Harbor would be like a sick shopping mall," said former Orioles vice president Janet Marie Smith, a key architectural advisor for the ball club during the design and construction of Camden Yards. "Any developer will tell you that you have to renew any kind of development periodically. They don't just sit. They have lives and need to be fed and cared for."

Camden Yards fed and cared for the whole waterfront area of Baltimore, if you believe your eyes. Governor Schaefer saw that in his visions when he insisted on the Camden Yards site for the new ballpark. "I wanted it downtown," he said. "Every night there are now more than 40,000 people downtown, and the impact on businesses is tremendous."

The ballpark has helped to give a city with an inferiority complex a real sense of civic pride. When *Monday Night Football* broadcasts its pre-game show, it comes from the ESPN Zone in Baltimore. That's a remarkable ego boost for a city that didn't even have a football team ten years ago. "The real positives, the good things that have happened, may not have been things you could have put down on paper and planned," said former Maryland Stadium Authority chairman Herb Belgrad. "They just happened spontaneously."

Some things were put down on paper, though—such as the Camden Yards football stadium that opened in August 1998. Originally the plans called for a multi-purpose ballpark for both football and baseball, but the Orioles lobbied hard for a baseball-only facility. "We looked around and saw that the franchises that were most successful, the ones that were truly great, all had baseball-only facilities," former Orioles president Larry Lucchino said. So the stadium authority agreed to plan for a ballpark and a football stadium, with the funding for the football stadium tied up until the state could secure a team. With the success of Camden Yards—sold-out crowds on display and rave reviews from the national media—it was only a matter of time before an NFL franchise would move to Baltimore. Camden Yards made it too good to ignore. That, and the sweetheart deal the state offered Art Modell to move his Cleveland Browns to Baltimore.

The move of the Browns to Baltimore to become the Baltimore Ravens is another powerful testament to the power of Camden Yards. The football stadium that was built next to the ballpark would likely never have seen the light of day if it wasn't for the continuing success of the Orioles ballpark. The money for the football stadium was locked up until an NFL franchise could be secured. Time and time again, the stadium authority failed to attract a team, despite being teased by the Cardinals, who moved from St. Louis to Phoenix; the Rams, who moved from Los Angeles to St. Louis; and the Tampa Bay Buccaneers, who stayed at home. Also, Baltimore was jilted by the NFL in expansion, passed over in favor of Jacksonville and Carolina. Patience was running out in the state legislature to keep the funding intact. What elected officials saw at Camden Yards made it more difficult for them to give up. Finally it would pay off. After the Ravens played for two years at Memorial Stadium, the Camden Yards football stadium would open, first with an exhibition game on

August 9, 1998, then later for the regular season opener. Like its sister baseball park, it was a glowing success.

A football stadium will never call upon the same level of nostalgia or the intimacy of a baseball park. So the Camden Yards football stadium is not a traditional, old-fashioned ballpark. The $220 million stadium does complement the look of the baseball park with its brick and glass façade—all part of another Helmuth, Obata & Kassabaum (HOK) design. The inside, though, is much like Ericsson Stadium in Charlotte, with the latest in high-tech amenities. It has two SmartVision scoreboards, which can split into sixteen images. The 69,426-purple-seated stadium (purple is the Ravens' color) has open corners. This feature gives it a greater sense of intimacy than is found in Jack Kent Cooke (JKC) Stadium, the other new Maryland football stadium that opened the year before in Landover in suburban Maryland.

The Ravens stadium stands out as another gem when it is compared to JKC Stadium, a large, cavernous facility with no character standing alone in the suburbs while nearly every other major sports facility built in the 1990s followed the path Camden Yards blazed to the cities. JKC Stadium is the legacy of Redskins owner Jack Kent Cooke. Unlike the Ravens stadium, JKC was built by the owner, using private funds. However, about $90 million in state money was used for infrastructure costs, such as roads. The Redskins had played at RFK Stadium since 1961, when it opened as D.C. Stadium, but Cooke ran into problems trying to make a deal to build his new stadium in the District. He then went to the suburbs but had similar problems in Alexandria, and the aging owner was running out of time when he went to Prince George's County in Maryland to get the stadium built. It sits next to the Washington Beltway in Landover, ironically, a stone's throw from the old USAir Arena, where the Washington Wizards and Capitals used to play until they moved to downtown Washington and the MCI Center in the fall of 1997. Now JKC Stadium is a brand new dinosaur, sitting out there like a sore thumb in the Washington suburbs, while the Ravens stadium enhances an already thriving Baltimore waterfront area.

More than 53,000 people purchased personal seat licenses to get their place at the new football stadium, ranging in price from $250 to $2,900, plus their season tickets. It has 108 luxury suites, 102 of which were sold by the first game, at prices ranging from $50,000 to $200,000 annually. Within a ten-year period, Baltimore had gone from having no NFL franchise and an antiquated baseball stadium to having two of the premiere sports facilities in the country. This change truly hit home when the Ravens had a Sunday night game on ESPN early in the 1998 season, and the entire nation saw how Baltimore had become a city of sports palaces. "You can't buy that kind of coverage," said Governor Schaefer. "It puts Baltimore in the forefront."

Schaefer was the line that legislators who wanted to do away with the football-stadium funding wouldn't cross. He insisted on keeping the lottery-and-bond financing plan intact despite all the disappointments. Although the Ravens came to Baltimore on successor governor Parris Glendening's watch, Schaefer enjoys seeing the attention that came to the city with the baseball park continue with the football stadium. "It's a great compliment to Camden Yards," he said. "It's much bigger, but it is not out of place. The whole downtown is going to benefit and beyond that. Hotels will be booked for people coming to the stadium from out of town. They are still giving the governor trouble about building the stadium, but when you add up all the things that are going to be beneficial, it's going to be a big difference."

The funding and construction of the Ravens stadium and the money that also went for infrastructure for JKC Stadium did become a big political issue during the 1998 elections. Again, like the debate before Camden Yards was built, the arguments revolve around how much a community really needs a football stadium compared to more pressing needs like education, health care, and social services, and why spend money to fill the pockets of the rich men who own these teams. Make no mistake about it, these ballparks and stadiums are money in the bank for the owners of the teams that play in them. University of Dallas economics professor Gerald Scully has estimated that a new park adds $50 million to $75 million to a baseball franchise in increased value and first-year revenue. The Orioles themselves were sold for $70 million in 1988 and, after less than two years in Camden Yards, the sales price was $173 million. Modell's pockets were stuffed with cash by the state for bringing his team to Baltimore. He gets to keep all the money from luxury seating, concessions, parking and advertising—which amounts to more than $25 million—as well as an estimated $70 million from the sale of personal seat licenses. Modell's deal brought howls of criticism from those who believed the state had given up too much to the owner.

These are legitimate questions, and the rational answer is that it is no contest; the state should be using the funds for something other than building sports facilities that enrich team owners. But the reality is that community egos are often measured by the arts and entertainment offered, professional sports included. Perhaps nowhere in America, save for Green Bay, did a football team mean more to a community than the Colts did to Baltimore. This team was the NFL's version of the Brooklyn Dodgers, a beloved team that during its heyday, with great players like Johnny Unitas and John Mackey, defined the city of Baltimore. When Robert Irsay took the team to Indianapolis, he tore out a piece of the fabric of the city that could not be dismissed as merely a sports team. The Ravens did not necessarily replace that—it would be impossible to recreate the relationship between the city and the old Colts—but for many who grew up in Baltimore, there was a hole in the city that was not filled until they got the team that would become the Ravens. This culminated in the opening of the Camden Yards football stadium.

All of the goodwill that the baseball park and football stadium created is not shared by some longtime fans, who long for the days when sports writers called Memorial Stadium "the world's largest outdoor insane asylum" during the passionate Colt days,

or the times when a more working-class crowd would attend
Orioles games. To some critics, Camden Yards is a yuppie palace
full of Washington lawyers and bankers with cell phones, snobs
who don't share the same passion for the game that those who
went to Memorial Stadium did. One *New York Daily News*
columnist said it was "the best Bennigan's I've ever seen."

That is a touchy subject for the Orioles brass, particularly one
former Washington banker, club vice chairman Joe Foss, who had
no problem defending the rights of the wine-and-cheese crowd.
"The cynics of this game talk about real fans and who is here and
who isn't here, this whole issue of the wine-and-cheese crowd and
the cell phones and all that," Foss said. "I find that whole thing
fairly amusing on the one hand and disgusting on the other. First
of all, by implication, they are saying people who drink wine and
[eat] cheese, the sophisticates as it were, the people who presum-
ably might have more money, can't enjoy baseball. I think that
is preposterous."

Camden Yards and the other new traditional, old-fashioned
ballparks may have called upon the likes of Ebbets Field and
Forbes Field for their design and inspiration, but this isn't
Brooklyn in 1955. For better or worse, the economics of baseball
and all of professional sports have changed dramatically, and
Camden Yards played a huge role in that as well. Expectations are
higher for everyone involved. Sellouts have become the norm, not
the exception, and when the Tampa Bay Devil Rays drew 2.5 million in their first season—an average of 31,000 per game—they
were considered a box-office failure. The Orioles drew 3.7 million, an average of 15,500 per game. The Indians drew 3.5 million, an average of 43,000 per game. The Rockies drew 3.8
million, an average of 47,000 per game. The Rangers drew 3 million, an average of 36,000 per game. All play in new ballparks. If
any of them dropped to 2.5 million, it would send shock waves
through the organization.

Also, the economics of the game, new ballparks included, has
driven up the cost of a ticket, in all sports, to the exclusion of the
average fan. The fan that is catered to is the one whose name ends

in Inc. As far as the average fans are concerned, owners are satisfied with their occasional appearance at the ballpark, as long as they watch their product on television and spend their money on the team's merchandise.

Also, the actual design of these new old traditional ballparks may simply give the illusion of intimacy, according to architectural critic John Pastier. In an interview with *The Cincinnati Enquirer*, Pastier said a study he conducted of ballparks showed that the distance from the top deck—the diagonal viewing distance straight back from home plate to a point in the upper deck, one-third of the way back from the front row—was greater at Camden Yards and Jacobs Field than the ballparks they replaced (182 feet at Camden Yards, 161 feet at Memorial Stadium; 195 feet at Jacobs Field, 148 feet at Cleveland Stadium).

None of these criticisms, though, blunts the impact of Camden Yards. Critics may not like the direction of baseball and other professional sports driven by the success of Camden Yards, but they can't deny it.

According to Orioles owner Peter Angelos, Camden Yards and its followers only serve to feed the beast—the beast being escalating players' salaries. "Nobody is making any money," Angelos said. "Maybe the New York Yankees because of their huge television contract and their deal with Adidas. But those deals aren't available to every franchise. I think what they [the new ballparks] are doing is energizing the game of baseball, but not generating any real profits. The money is going to the players and their agents. The escalating salaries is in part made possible by the greater attendance. You can't get something that is not there. Camden Yards has allowed us to put a better team on the field and to pay our mortgage. We have a mortgage. We bought this team five years ago. Contrast that to the Yankees, who were purchased twenty-five years ago for $10 million and have no mortgage. That is why there is probably a profit there. Not a great profit."

Many team owners would trade places with Angelos, though, Selig among them. "In the early 1980s, when Edward Bennett

Williams and I started a financial consortium trading information, the Orioles and the Brewers were two peas in a pod," Selig said. "Our expenses and revenues were identical. Camden Yards changed all that." Selig—technically Selig's daughter, Wendy Selig-Prieb, who took over ownership of the team when Selig was officially named commissioner—hopes to match the Orioles revenues with the new Brewers ballpark, Miller Park.

Many baseball fans who find themselves priced out of major league baseball in Baltimore have turned to minor league baseball. One more impact of Camden Yards on a local level is how it fueled the growth of minor league baseball in the state. Maryland had two minor league teams B.C.—Before Camden. Both were Orioles affiliates, a Class AA team in Hagerstown in the western part of the state, and a Class A team in Frederick that had begun play only in 1989. Both were owned by the same group, Maryland Baseball, and the Frederick team opened a new ballpark in 1991, one year before Camden Yards opened.

The growth would continue rapidly. The Class AA team would move to suburban Washington, in Bowie, Maryland, and would play in another new ballpark. Soon after, a Class A team was established on Maryland's Eastern Shore, also playing in a new ballpark. All three of these teams are Orioles affiliates, owned by Maryland Baseball, which plans a fourth team with yet another new ballpark for Aberdeen, Cal Ripken's hometown. A Class A team that replaced the one that left Hagerstown, a Toronto Blue Jays affiliate, has plans in the works for a new ballpark there. Ten years ago, there was one minor league team in Maryland that drew just over 100,000 people. Now there are four, drawing a total of 1.3 million, with another in the works. Twenty years ago, the Orioles drew just a little more than one million at Memorial Stadium. "All of those ballparks are offshoots of Camden Yards, and are important to the economies of their communities," Governor Schaefer said.

What will the Camden Yards world of sports be like twenty years from now? What will ballparks of the future look like? Will

Camden Yards finally be old enough to be called an old old-fashioned traditional ballpark? The sport went from lively urban palaces, to sterile concrete monstrosities, back to replica lively urban palaces. Whatever shape it may take, the success of Camden Yards has raised the awareness level of the importance of the ballpark as the stage on which the drama of the game is played.

CHAPTER TWO

Bricks and Steel

When Peter Ueberroth ran the Los Angeles Olympic Committee in 1984, he was called a genius, a visionary. Major league baseball owners believed so, too, and hired him to be their commissioner. He had a vision all right—a vision of what the ballpark of the future should be like. It wasn't anything like Camden Yards. Ueberroth hired the Bechtel Corporation to build a prototype model for what he believed all baseball parks should be in the future. In January 1988, he was pushing his plans for a generic, two-deck, 36,000-seat ballpark for the future home of the Baltimore Orioles. "It had a very antiseptic look to it," said then Orioles vice president Larry Lucchino.

If the Orioles did not have their own vision in mind—one of a "traditional, old-fashioned ballpark with modern amenities"—Ueberroth Stadium very well could have been the Orioles new ballpark. Not Ueberroth Stadium? Then how about Comiskey Park east? Helmuth, Obata & Kassabaum (HOK) came to the Orioles with plans that were similar to those of the most recent ballpark they had designed—Chicago's new Comiskey Park, which opened the year before Camden Yards did to horrible reviews. It is a sterile ballpark that sticks out like a sore thumb among the Camden Yards offspring that followed in the 1990s. "We said we don't want that kind of facility," Lucchino recalled. "We don't want that design. We want to do something that is distinctive, that is more like a traditional, old ballpark and not Comiskey Stadium."

Lucchino was theatric in making his point about what the Orioles wanted for their new home. At a February 1988 meeting in Washington, D.C., Lucchino passed out Yugo brochures to everyone in attendance. "While I was driving to the meeting, I stopped at a Yugo dealership and picked up some brochures," he recalled. "I had them at everyone's place for the meeting, and I said, 'We want to make it clear. We don't drive Yugos, and we're not going to play in a Yugo.'"

But perhaps Lucchino's most infamous display of commitment of vision was when the architects brought a model of new Comiskey to a meeting with the Orioles. "We just ripped one piece of it after another," he said. "We said, 'We don't want this, we don't want that.' One of the architects said, 'Larry, do you have any idea how much these models cost?' I said, 'No, but we're trying to make a point here.'"

That point proved to be vital for the future of baseball, for without the success of Camden Yards, the wave of ballparks that followed that have drawn in record numbers of fans may never have been built, or at least built in the fan-friendly style they have been.

The success of Camden Yards had many stages to pass through, but much of the spotlight in the past has focused on the construction stage. Nevertheless, it's important to note that the seed for the architectural success of the ballpark was planted at two critical stages of the development of Camden Yards: during the decision to build a traditional, old-fashioned ballpark and during the choice of its location. There are no design touches from Ebbets Field or Shibe Park if Ueberroth Stadium or some other generic version is agreed to early on in the process. Also, there will be no urban feel—no draw to the city—if the Baltimore ballpark is built someplace besides Camden Yards. You can have all the old-fashioned design touches that you want, but if stadium construction continued to follow the flight to the suburbs, you wind up with The Ballpark in Arlington, a suburban baseball theme park more than a ballpark. Camden Yards showed the way back to the city.

Ueberroth had ideas about what Camden Yards should look like. His predecessor, Bowie Kuhn, had ideas about where the Orioles new ballpark should be. He suggested somewhere between Baltimore and Washington because the District had not had a major league baseball team since the Washington Senators moved to Arlington, Texas, after the 1971 season. "Kuhn was talking to Ed [Williams] about putting the ballpark between Baltimore and Washington," Lucchino said.

In fact, just a few days after Edward Bennett Williams purchased the team in August 1979, he pulled Lucchino away from a Martha's Vineyard vacation to start looking at sites for a new ballpark. "I was flying around in a helicopter looking for places to put a ballpark," Lucchino said. Williams also owned the Washington Redskins with Jack Kent Cooke, and the two men were considering the idea of building a multi-purpose stadium between Baltimore and Washington for the two teams to use. They looked at sites in Columbia and Laurel along Interstate 95 and a site at the intersection of Route 175 and the Baltimore-Washington Parkway.

There had been talk of a new ballpark for many years before Camden Yards opened in 1992. There was talk when Jerry Hoffberger owned the team before Williams, and discussions of possible sites included the Camden Yards industrial area location, two blocks from the city's main attraction, Inner Harbor. But the momentum for a new ballpark picked up dramatically when Bob Irsay had the Mayflower vans packed at midnight and took the beloved Colts from Baltimore to Indianapolis. William Donald

Schaefer, mayor of Baltimore at the time, appointed a task force to look at possible sites for a new ballpark. Another committee appointed by the Baltimore City Council examined the possibility of renovating Memorial Stadium to attract another NFL franchise. But fixing up Memorial was not going to be an option. The NFL privately told state officials that they would never get a franchise to come to Baltimore if all they offered was a renovated Memorial Stadium.

While Schaefer's group, aided by HOK, the dominating architectural firm in stadium construction, looked at thirty-three sites in the city, the Manekin Commission, another study committee, looked at possible locations both in and out of the city. The Schaefer group recommended Camden Yards. The Manekin Commission selected a place south of the city in Lansdowne.

Schaefer would become governor the following year, and that sealed the Camden Yards location. It was a pivotal moment in baseball history. It set the stage for the return of not only baseball, but professional sports facilities to the city; it also dictated the design of the ballpark by forcing architects to come up with a ballpark that would fit inside a tight urban area, particularly after the decision was made to save the B&O Warehouse (another important moment in the development of Camden Yards).

Schaefer deserves the credit for driving home Camden Yards as the ballpark location. "The selection of the site was so important to the success of the ballpark," said Janet Marie Smith, who was the Orioles vice president of planning and development and who was the design point person on the ballpark. "It wouldn't have been Camden Yards if it hadn't been downtown, and Governor Schaefer saw that."

Schaefer was convinced that the ballpark would have the greatest effect in the city. "It wouldn't have helped anybody in Lansdowne," he said. "They didn't want a ballpark there. Where you really wanted it was where it could have a real impact." Camden Yards was "the ideal spot, and you can see that now," Schaefer said. "Every night there is a game, there are more than

40,000 people downtown, and the impact on businesses there is tremendous." According to Lucchino, Schaefer convinced Williams to accept the Camden Yards location. "Williams started this process with a bias towards being someplace between the two cities," Lucchino said. "It was Schaefer who persuaded Williams that Camden Yards was the site."

"At first Williams didn't even want to consider Camden Yards because it had a school in the middle of it," Lucchino recalled. "He said, 'I am not going to knock down a school to build a ballpark.' I said, 'Ed, the mayor says they are going to close that school anyway. Very few kids go there now, and the school board is going to close it.' Only then did he consider it."

"From our point of view, it was appealing," Lucchino said, "because instead of being in the far northeast quadrant of Baltimore, which was hard to get in and out of and hard to park, this was a more prominent and easier-to-find location, particularly for people coming from the south in Maryland and Washington and that area. It seemed like a way to appease the people in Baltimore by keeping it in Baltimore, but also making it as convenient as possible to the people in the south, particularly Washington."

Williams made the final decision on Camden Yards during a phone call with Schaefer. After Williams put down the phone, he turned to Lucchino and said, "Larry, sometimes in life you've got to make a decision. It's like trying to build a house halfway between your wife and your girlfriend. You've just got to make a commitment."

At that moment, Williams committed to Baltimore, but the Camden Yards site had its share of critics. With Inner Harbor so close, many believed that there was already too much traffic in the area and that people coming in there for games would create monumental traffic jams. So perhaps the most remarkable facet of the April 6, 1992, opening day at Camden Yards was the surprising ease with which people were able to reach the ballpark and leave. "One of the reasons the site works so well is because people get there and are in a good mood because they don't have a lot of traffic to deal with," Herb Belgrad said.

The next consideration was the whole concept of building a baseball-only facility. The idea of a traditional, old-fashioned ballpark is moot if a multi-purpose facility is built. The initial decision, at least from the Maryland Stadium Authority's point of view, was to build a combination football-baseball facility. Lucchino went into this believing that a baseball-only facility was needed, and he convinced Williams to push for one. "I told Ed that we looked around at all the best baseball teams in the country, and the ones that have been the most stable, the most storied, the most competitive and prosperous have one thing in common—they play in a baseball-only park," Lucchino recalled. "I said the Red Sox, and he had a real weakness for the Red Sox. If he could own one franchise, he wanted to own the Red Sox. I cited the Red Sox, the Yankees, the Dodgers, and the Cubs as successful franchises that all had traditional, baseball-only facilities, and the ballpark is part of the appeal. I said to him, 'We should talk about a baseball-only facility and not just one stadium. We should be talking about two.'

"He looked at me like I was speaking Greek," Lucchino continued. "He said, 'Are you crazy? Two? You go out and talk about it, and when you get crucified, don't mention my name.'"

Belgrad, after visiting Kansas City's dual stadiums, was intrigued as well by the idea and asked architects, for example's sake, if one stadium costs $5 million, would two cost $10 million? "They said no," Belgrad related. "Then I asked them if you could put two stadiums in the Camden Yards area, and they said they would look into it. What they came back with shocked me. What they told us essentially is that it would cost just about $16.5 million more to build two stadiums than it would to build one multi-purpose stadium. Now this was with stadiums that were no frills, that didn't have everything they have now at Camden Yards. But the way it worked out was that the costs to build a multi-purpose stadium to use for both baseball and football would be high because you have to build a super-structure, plus additional parking and other facilities that would incur tremendously greater costs than if they would build just a baseball stadium for baseball."

Belgrad then pitched the idea to Governor Schaefer, who looked at Belgrad sort of the way Williams had looked at Lucchino. "It would take a lot of convincing for me to approve two stadiums, rather than a single stadium," Schaefer said. But the combination of the Orioles lobbying for a traditional showcase ballpark and the conviction that the city had no chance of getting an NFL franchise with a multi-purpose facility convinced Schaefer and the other decision makers. The caveat was that funds set aside for the football stadium would not be spent until a franchise was locked up. After the city was jilted by the NFL in the expansion process in 1993, the two-stadium concept finally reaped its full reward when the Cleveland Browns moved to Baltimore in 1996 and became the Baltimore Ravens. Two years later, the new football stadium opened up at Camden Yards to glowing reviews.

The baseball-only concept opened the door for Lucchino to push for the concept of an old-fashioned, traditional ballpark that would include modern amenities. This turned into a battle between the Orioles, who weren't paying for a ballpark that would be a revolutionary baseball palace, and the members of the Maryland Stadium Authority, who were feeling the pressure of trying to contain the costs of a project with a lot of political baggage attached to it.

The lease negotiations would be the battlefield between both sides on the debate over what kind of ballpark would be built, as well as the design. The stadium authority wanted the Orioles to commit to a thirty-year lease, but the Orioles weren't going to sign a lease until they knew what sort of ballpark they would be moving into. "You don't do a deal to buy a house without knowing what the house looks like," Lucchino said. "These guys wanted to sit down and negotiate a lease. First let's talk about what it is going to look like before we talk about how much rent we are going to pay. We're not going to talk about the length of the lease, the amount of the rent, the terms of the agreement, until we know what the ballpark looks like. That got us into something that was known as the minimum requirements document. We insisted on drafting that first and simultaneously, so I guess it got done at the same time that the lease got done. So while the state wanted to talk to us about whether or not the lease would be twenty years or thirty years, and what percentage of this or that we would pay, we wanted to talk about how many people is it going to hold? What is it going to be made of? We were operating to some degree on two different tracks."

The two factions were doing battle in the political arena as well. The state planned to fund the ballparks through lottery money and bonds sales, which was bringing out the sharp knives from some members of the General Assembly during the 1987 session, who were opposed to the state paying the entire freight for the ballpark. All along, Schaefer had said he would handle the politics of the ballpark. But now it was crunch time, and he needed to call on Williams, the preeminent courtroom orator of his time, to come to Annapolis to convince state legislators not to block the ballpark financing. So Schaefer announced in a press conference that Williams would address a joint session of the House and Senate Judiciary Committees on March 4.

The problem was, nobody had told Williams. "I get this call from Lucchino saying whose idea was this? Where did this come from?" Belgrad said. "I told him I hadn't been consulted, and Larry told me that Williams was scheduled to be in Boston that morning for his chemotherapy treatment." Williams's condition was worsening. He would be dead within fifteen months. But he agreed to be there.

"I picked him up at the airport that day after he came from his chemotherapy in Baltimore," Belgrad said. "Now, being a lawyer, I hold Edward Bennett Williams in awe. I tell him that he will be sitting next to me, and if he would get tired, he could give me some kind of signal and I'd do something. He looked at me in the most hostile way and said, 'Young man, I make my living practicing law. If the word went out that I'm not 100 percent, I wouldn't have any clients tomorrow. I don't need anybody to stand there and defend me.'"

Williams and Belgrad headed to Williams's Washington law offices, and then left for Annapolis with Lucchino, who told Williams that he heard the Ripken family—Cal senior, Cal junior, and Billy, all now on the Orioles major league roster—was on the cover of the latest issue of *Sports Illustrated*. "We are scrambling around Washington trying to find a copy, and we stop at this newsstand on K Street and I run in and find a copy of the issue with the Ripkens on the cover." Belgrad brought it out to Williams in the car. "Now this is a visual aid," Williams said. He would bring it with him to the hearing and wave it around for everyone to see, declaring, "The family Ripken is all over America, and the Orioles and Baltimore are all over America. This is important."

Williams didn't need any visual aids. He called upon his courtroom and people skills to come up with testimony that would prove to be pivotal in getting the financial commitment needed to move ahead with the ballpark. Among other things, he told legislators, "We're going into a loss situation at Memorial Stadium, and much quicker than I had projected. And I'm not rich enough to operate a major league baseball team in the red. I'm not rich enough to build a stadium."

Williams's appearance shifted the momentum in favor of stadium funding. "What was so brilliant about his performance was that he did it in a very different gear than most people would have," Lucchino said. "Most people would think you would have to be forceful and assertive and make clear exactly what you want. Williams was ready for all that, but at the last minute he dropped it into a much lower gear. He was much more deferential, much less aggressive or assertive than another sports owner might have been. They expected a warrior, and they got a guy who was thoughtful and reflective in his responses, and he won them over."

As negotiations for the lease and memorandum of understanding continued, two significant issues would turn out to play huge roles in the success of Camden Yards: what kind of material would be used to build the ballpark, and whether or not to keep the B&O Warehouse.

The debate on materials was one of steel versus concrete, and the Orioles were adamant about the importance of constructing this ballpark with steel to give it the traditional, old-fashioned look they wanted. That was how the old ballparks were built. If you don't think this issue was important, the next time you go to Camden Yards or Coors Field or one of the other new old-fashioned traditional ballparks, look up at the steel tresses you see throughout the interior of the ballpark. Next, imagine what the ballpark would look like without them, with concrete columns surrounding you instead.

Leading the fight for the Orioles on this issue was Janet Marie Smith, who had been the coordinator of architecture and design at Battery Park City in New York but was not an architect. Smith became the Orioles' voice on design issues concerning the ballpark in order to make sure that the vision Lucchino and others had stayed on course. HOK, the architects, worked with the urban design firm of RTKL; the landscape architecture firm of Wallace, Roberts and Todd; and several engineering firms. But they all worked for the stadium authority.

Smith was the Orioles' answer to the state's architectural design team, and she filled that role very well. She helped find architectural and artistic details that would be critical to the charm of the ballpark. "I would say during the off season between 1988 and 1989 that there was no more important acquisition that we made than hiring Janet Marie Smith, because she helped give detail and reality to the visions and the concepts," Lucchino said. "Eli Jacobs, on at least four occasions, wanted me to fire her, and I refused to do so. He didn't like some of the decisions we were making or the way this was unfolding." Smith also saw the need for steel to see the vision through. "She was a very forceful advocate for steel versus concrete," Lucchino said. "She would say, 'Larry, if you want what you want, we cannot compromise on the issue of steel.' She was very assertive about steel."

But this ballpark project was hemorrhaging financially. In June 1989, Belgrad discovered that the costs were skyrocketing way over budget, particularly for land acquisition. What they believed would cost $50 million would actually cost closer to $100 million, and the entire project was about $100 million over budget. When it was all over, land acquisition wound up costing the state $100 million, $40 million more than had been anticipated, and the ballpark came in at $105 million, nearly $30 million more than the original estimates. Belgrad was faced with the prospect of telling Governor Schaefer the bad news. Schaefer was in Ocean City at a Maryland Association of Counties convention, and Belgrad drove to the beach to meet with him. "He was the first one I was going to tell," Belgrad said. "I assured him that we could trim $50 million or more from that figure. You can imagine his shock, this being his pet project, and we're $100 million over budget. It was clear I had pulled the rug out from under him, but he expressed full confidence in us in that meeting."

Schaefer told Belgrad that he would have to call an emergency meeting of the legislative leadership within twenty-four hours, and Belgrad immediately went to work on cutting costs that would change Camden Yards. If those costs were not cut, Camden Yards might have had 52,000 seats instead of the 48,188 they have now, and this much of a difference could have changed the intimacy of the ballpark.

"In our original memorandum of understanding, Edward Bennett Williams had absolutely insisted that we have around 52,000 seats in the ballpark," Belgrad said. "There was no justification for it because we had all the attendance figures for the past ten years, and they hadn't sold out on more than five days in any season. Some years they only sold out one day, and that was opening day. We felt that it was prudent for supply and demand purposes, not for cost purposes only, to have a stadium that would be in demand, rather than one with so many seats that people didn't need to buy season tickets. We were trying to come down to a figure closer to 45,000, but again, Edward Bennett Williams pretty much got his way because he had the team, and he had the leverage. So we agreed to 52,000."

"But now with these budget problems," Belgrad continued, "I went to Larry and told him that we had to kick in together to cut this down, and that's when we agreed to the size of the ballpark to between 47,000 and 48,000." That, combined with reducing the amount of land they were seeking for parking, helped to bring the costs down.

In this atmosphere, however, the Orioles were asking for steel, which the stadium authority's consultants said would cost $11 million more than concrete. "That was $11 million we didn't have," Belgrad said. "It was a major piece of our budget." The Orioles, though, were relentless in their fight for steel and came back with their own consultant's estimate, just about $1 million more than concrete, which was far less than the stadium authority's figure. "It turned out there were a lot of faults with our consultants, and we ended up terminating them and hiring the Orioles firm," Belgrad said. The Orioles agreed to pay for half of the annual maintenance of the steel, and that would create the framework, literally, for the design success of Camden Yards.

The other significant aspect of the development of Camden Yards is the one part of the blueprint that all the other ballparks that have followed the plan have not been able to duplicate: the B&O Warehouse beyond the right field wall on the other side of Eutaw Street. Built between 1898 and 1905, the B&O Warehouse is the longest building on the East Coast—1,016 feet. Once part of a thriving railway operation, it fell into disrepair and remained vacant, despite being considered for a variety of uses, including condominium units. The warehouse was still vacant when the state was trying to figure out how, if at all, it would fit into the ballpark's plans.

"Some of the leading business leaders in the city were very much opposed to saving the warehouse," Governor Schaefer said. "I don't think they could see that the place could be fixed up and become an attractive building. It was a tough decision. They said it would divide the city. But that didn't happen."

Who first decided to save the warehouse is one of the most debated issues in the history of the development of Camden Yards. According to Peter Richmond's book *Ballpark*, an architectural student named Eric Moss was the first one to build a model of the ballpark that included the warehouse, an idea apparently picked up by HOK without credit to Moss. "The student was the first time I saw a rendering or model that saved most of it," Lucchino recollected. "But even he cut out a substantial part of the middle, sort of an arch. But he was the first guy to talk about saving all of it instead of bits and pieces of it. Various architects took stabs at trying to preserve it. HOK cut it in half."

Belgrad said he didn't believe that the idea of saving the warehouse grew from the Moss model. "It's my recollection that HOK came up with the design of the ballpark with the warehouse independently," Belgrad said. "The warehouse was there. You had to either decide whether it would stay or go, and in their discussions with us, that was an option they presented. Their option was the entire warehouse, but that was subject to modification. I did like that model," Belgrad commented about the Moss structure, "but I don't think it was the source for the decision on the warehouse."

Smith also downplayed the impact of the Moss model. "I wouldn't call it a turning point," she said. "There was a lot of support for the warehouse from a lot of camps. HOK looked at it very carefully when they were first asked to study the site. They proposed cutting the warehouse off, but they still proposed saving it. There are some issues that you can give to a person, and there are others that have a lot of support from a lot of different camps, and concerns from a lot of different camps."

The Orioles didn't want to save the warehouse. They weren't opposed to it, per se, but didn't like the stadium authority's plan to save it, which included putting the Orioles offices in the warehouse instead of in the ballpark. "The debate over the warehouse was less about the value of the building from a preservationist standpoint," said Smith. "I think everyone always thought it was a cool old building. The issue was could you make it work."

The Orioles wanted their offices in the home-plate area of the ballpark, the traditional location for team offices in a ballpark. But the stadium authority couldn't afford to acquire and rehabilitate the warehouse unless the Orioles were going to use it. To build offices for the team within the ballpark would have cost another $9 million, Belgrad said. The Orioles relented, provided that an additional 1,000 square feet of office space was set aside in the home-plate area of the ballpark itself for the Orioles to use as game-days offices. As it turned out, conducting business from the warehouse was not a problem, and the team has never used that space in the ballpark for offices.

There was even talk of adding to the warehouse to make it more economically feasible. That brought about "the Wart"—a bubble-like addition proposed for the south end of the building. "There was a possible deal with the Maryland Department of Transportation, which was looking to centralize its headquarters in that area," Belgrad said. "But they needed more space than what was in the south end of the warehouse, and there was a proposal to add on space for the Department of Transportation." It was not a popular architectural addition, to say the least, but the pressure was strong to house the state agency. The decision ultimately was up to Schaefer. "There was heavy pressure on me to add the addition," Schaefer said. "It was a good location, and the idea of putting the transportation department there seemed like a good idea. But I took a couple of walks down there and felt the building would have lost some of its character. I told them no."

Lucchino credits Belgrad as the champion for the cause of saving the warehouse. "Herb Belgrad saw the preservationist value in preserving the warehouse," he said. The total cost to purchase and renovate the structure was $18 million. Today, in addition to the Orioles offices, the south end houses the team store, restaurants, and Waverly Press.

"It was a building that was there, it had a lot of history and tradition, and if we could keep it, we should," Belgrad said. "The warehouse lends itself to the feeling that we were trying to build into the whole architectural design, to make something old fashioned and traditional. The warehouse is something that is for real because it was built at the same time the great ballparks were built at the turn of the century. The warehouse is an identification mark of the ballpark. I don't think the ballpark would have attracted the same kind of recognition as it has if it wasn't for the warehouse."

Belgrad nearly didn't play any role in Camden Yards. When he was first approached to take the position as chairman of the newly created Maryland Stadium Authority, he declined. "I had been chairman of the state ethics commission for eight years, and from 1985 to 1986, I was president of the Maryland State Bar Association," Belgrad said. "I had a meeting with Governor [Harry] Hughes, and he said I've got a new job for you, chairman of the state authority. I told him I don't know anything about that, but I would be interested in something like social services, something I could make a contribution to. I left it at that and went on vacation. I got another call about it at the end of August and said I would give it some thought. This was about two weeks away from the primary election, with two serious candidates [Schaefer and attorney general Steve Sachs], and those two had to be approached about it. Each of them would have to agree that they would want me appointed if they were elected, because I wasn't going to serve for two or three months and walk away. Both candidates said they would accept it, and I was appointed in September 1986."

It's difficult to imagine Camden Yards without its distinctive warehouse. "The foresight to have left this warehouse as a backdrop really sets the visual dimension to this facility that without it would have been a missing component of the success here," said club vice chairman Joe Foss. "It's worked well for our offices and for other commercial businesses."

The warehouse led to the creation of the Eutaw Street corridor, the walkway between the warehouse that houses Boog's Barbecue and other stands and places where people like to congregate. "Eutaw Street gave us a chance to bring people closer to the ballpark," Smith said. "Ballparks today are so big and so secure, and gone are the days when the fences were literally on the outfield. This was a way for fans to come and pay homage to the ballpark without buying a ticket, and also make it part of the downtown."

The corridor is open to the public except several hours before a game, when it is then open to only those fans who have tickets for that day's game. It was born out of the RTKL November 1988 master plan, which saw Eutaw Street as a "unique pedestrian environment between the warehouse and the ballpark, in the spirit of streets adjacent to Fenway Park in Boston."

All of these other issues would be moot, though, if the Orioles and the stadium authority could not agree on a lease. It was getting down to the wire, and both sides were very close to an agreement. Williams and Schaefer wanted to be able to announce on May 2, 1988—which was designated "Fantastic Fans Night" at Memorial Stadium, in honor of the Orioles fans who stood by the team during their disastrous 0–21 start that season—that the team had signed a thirty-year lease. The dramatic announcement nearly didn't come off.

"We had made some significant progress, but we were far apart on some major issues," Belgrad said. "We decided to work round the clock to resolve those issues. The season was opening on a Monday, and Saturday was Jewish Passover, and Sunday was Easter Sunday. So we decided to meet at a motel that was halfway between Baltimore and Washington on the Baltimore-Washington Parkway. We met Saturday and took some breaks so people could observe their religious observances, and we met Sunday. But it became clear that it just wasn't going to work."

They all took a break for several days, then went back into negotiations. On May 2, Fantastic Fans Day, they met at 9 A.M. at the Washington offices of Williams & Connolly. "We hadn't seen Edward Bennett Williams in months," Belgrad said. "We go to his office, and he sits at the head of the conference table. He buttons his jacket to his coat, and his jacket slides off his shoulders because he lost so much weight. It was a very emotional moment. You couldn't say anything, but everyone sort of felt the same way. He was clearly weak."

Nevertheless, Belgrad recalled, Williams took control of the meeting. "I want to know where we are apart and what we are going to do," Williams says. They go over the issues point by point until about 2 P.M., when Williams has to leave for Memorial Stadium for that night's festivities. "Assuming we are going to reach an agreement, I want to be there for the announcement," Williams tells them.

Lucchino stays behind to work out the final details with Belgrad. Someone suddenly realizes that it's five o'clock, and if they don't catch the 6 P.M. Amtrak Metroliner, they won't make the game in time. The group—still finalizing a lease—rushes to pack up their stuff and run down to the Metro stop to catch the subway to Union Station. They are minutes from missing the train to Baltimore.

"The Metroliner is about to pull out, and we don't have any tickets," Belgrad recalled. "Gene Feinblatt, our general counsel, goes downstairs to the platform and puts one foot on the train and the other on the platform, and he won't let it leave until we all get down there."

They all pile into the club car and are on their way to Baltimore—still no lease. As Belgrad recalled it, "Finally, we finish the language on the back of a menu." Lucchino calls Williams to get final approval on the details. When they arrive at Memorial Stadium, they have a deal on the back of a menu. Williams is ready to announce it before the game when Schaefer pulls Belgrad aside. "I want this in writing, signed, before I go out there and make an announcement," he says.

They announce the lease before 50,000 fans that night, but problems remain. They spend the next day debating more issues, such as parking spaces. The state Board of Public Works is meeting Thursday, and the contracts have to be ready for approval at that meeting. The night before the meeting, Belgrad gets a call at home from American League president Dr. Bobby Brown. "I just want you to know that we have a very firm policy, and your lease, just like every other lease of every team, is subject to the approval of major league baseball, and you have to provide for 5,000 spaces," he tells Belgrad. The final issues had been worked out, though, and at two o'clock Thursday morning, a state trooper came to Belgrad's house with the lease agreements for him to sign. They were approved that morning at the Board of Public Works meeting.

Williams passed away three months later, and Eli Jacobs purchased the team from the Williams estate in December 1988. Six months later, demolition on the Camden Yards site began. Work continued while the Orioles played their final two years at Memorial Stadium. As construction wound down, one final issue had to be dealt with—the name of the ballpark. Jacobs wanted Oriole Park. Schaefer wanted Camden Yards, and both were adamant. They didn't even talk to each other for months. Schaefer had enjoyed the sparring with Williams. They were cut from the same mold. Jacobs was the opposite, an introverted, unsociable man. "He was entirely different from Mr. Williams," Schaefer said. "He wasn't a friendly man. But I wasn't going to give in, and neither was he."

Finally, Lucchino and Belgrad set up a lunch for the two men at the Polo Grill in Baltimore. After about an hour, they all came up with "Oriole Park at Camden Yards," but not without a little paranoid theatrics from Schaefer. At one point, he began yelling, "I'm not going to agree to that!" Jacobs looked at him in shock and asked, "What are you talking about? I thought we just had an agreement." Schaefer shot back. "No, I'm not going to do it!" Then a waiter who had been near the table left, and Schaefer smiled at Jacobs, saying, "That was a show. I don't know what he was listening to, and we don't want this to get out until we're ready to announce it."

When the gates opened at Camden Yards on April 6, 1992, for the first game—which the Orioles won 2–0 against the Cleveland Indians—the name across the top of the ballpark at the home-plate entrance was Oriole Park at Camden Yards. But Camden Yards would eventually win out as the primary name for the ballpark, the one that most people use when referring to it.

Some changes had to be made, however, in the final months before the ballpark opened. The dugouts had to be redone because they blocked some sightlines. Just days before the ballpark opened, a new foul screen had to be found and installed so that the view from the press box wasn't obstructed. Also, it turned out that a whole section of seats forced people to turn their heads to get a view of the action at home plate. (Those seats wouldn't be fixed until the following season.) One other change had to be made, and this was done by an Orioles player.

At a luncheon several days after the ballpark opened, Cal Ripken told the crowd that everything about the new ballpark was great except for the showers. Ripken didn't like the shower heads in the clubhouse, so he went to a hardware store and spent $110 for a new one. He and clubhouse manager Jimmy Tyler installed Ripken's new shower head at one pipe in the showers. As a result, all of his teammates were lining up to use Ripken's shower. When Belgrad heard this, he had all new shower heads installed while the Orioles went on their first road trip to Toronto and Boston. When Ripken got back, sitting in his locker was the shower head he and Tyler had installed themselves.

Except for the water problem, Ripken was surprisingly pleased with what he found when he took the field on opening day. After all, he was the conscience of the Orioles, the bridge between the old and the new. He was a worthy judge of the merits of Camden Yards and how it measured up to the only other home the Orioles had ever known, Memorial Stadium, where he broke in ten years earlier, in 1982, as a rookie.

"I was worried that when we went to Camden Yards, we would lose the old Orioles history, the feeling of playing in a place that was special for baseball," he said. "But when we got on the field at Camden Yards and started playing there, it seemed like it was a place where baseball had been played before. Intellectually, you knew it was brand new and no baseball had been played there until we got there. But when you walked into the place, it was a ballpark. It represented so many things and brought up some deep feelings about the game."

About the Orioles' former ballpark, "I don't miss Memorial Stadium," Ripken said. "You are thankful that you played there. You are thankful that you had a lot of great experiences there. But as a stadium, you don't miss it. If the design of Camden Yards was different, perhaps more sterile an atmosphere, then maybe you actually would cling to the comfort and security of Memorial Stadium. It's so well done and cozy and baseball oriented, and it provides such good entertainment."

The accolades that rained down on Camden Yards when it opened—and still do today—create some bitter feelings about credit for the success of the project. It became a very touchy issue. When Peter Richmond's book *Ballpark* came out, much of the way the story of the ballpark unfolded gave credit to Jacobs and Smith. This angered Belgrad and Lucchino so much that they issued a joint press release criticizing the book. "It was a revisionist view," Lucchino said. "Belgrad and I and several other people labored in the vineyards for a lot of years, and to see this story come out, which was a complete rewrite of what happened, was offensive to us."

A month earlier, an article in *The New York Times* had given the impression that Smith was the architect of the Camden Yards project. There was no mention of Joe Spear, the chief HOK architect of the ballpark. This omission caused a stir. "As the article was written, Janet Marie took a lot of credit for herself, which no one else, even the Orioles, I believe, thought she was entitled to, and it was a tense situation," Belgrad said. "I was having a dinner party that night, and Joe Spear didn't want to come. I told him he was invited as my social guest to my house, and I would personally resent it if he and his people were not there." The HOK people came to the party, and the Orioles showed up with Camden Green jackets and autographed balls, and the situation was diffused for that night.

The role of HOK in the development of Camden Yards remains in dispute. The Kansas City architectural firm had been and is still the preeminent sports-facility design company. It has been involved in 450 arena and stadium projects, working for thirty of the thirty-one NFL franchises and twenty-two of the thirty major league teams. Included among those projects were Jacobs Field, Coors Field, and the football stadium at Camden Yards. There is no denying that HOK has dominated and influenced the wave of new ballpark design and construction. "We call Joe Spear the Rembrandt of ballpark construction," said Larry Barr, vice president of the San Francisco Giants, whose new ballpark was an HOK design.

But although HOK had designed a minor league ballpark in Buffalo with an exterior reminiscent of old ballparks, it also designed the outcast of the 1990 ballparks, new Comiskey, which had served as HOK's template for its initial plan for Camden Yards—a plan that Lucchino literally tore apart. Spear said the demands of the project created a tension that caused some bad feelings. "Expectations were very high, and there were tensions between all of the parties, as you might imagine anytime you have that kind of an undertaking," he said. "But the project turned out well. Everyone felt like they were instrumental in that success story, and I think that they were."

As architect Spear pointed out, "There was a lot of heated debate about what the design should be or what the place should feel like or look like or be. But I think in the end everyone was trying to make it as good as it could be. I think everyone felt that it would have been a different project if they hadn't individually been involved, and it's probably true."

Smith is still smarting from the bruises over the credit disagreements. "Credit for this project was a real sore point," she said. "There is an old adage that credit is cheap, and I really subscribe to that. There were so many people who played such a significant role in making it happen, and it culminated in something really wonderful, and to suggest that each of these decisions was a singular inspiration of any one person or that they didn't happen without a whole team of people working to make it happen is misguided.

"The exceptions were the leadership of Schaefer, and Larry, who had this idea whose time had come," Smith added. "He was in the right place at the right time with the right idea."

CHAPTER THREE

A Tour of the Ballpark

Two presidents have visited Camden Yards for games: George Bush, who threw out the first pitch on opening day in 1992, and Bill Clinton, who has been to the ballpark four times over five years. But the allure of Camden Yards goes far beyond that of simply a place to see baseball. It pulls people in when no one is running the bases, and no balls are being pitched or hit—almost like a baseball museum. In fact, Camden Station, next to the B&O Warehouse, will soon be home to one of the biggest baseball museums in the country, the Babe Ruth Baseball Center, thanks to a $1 million donation from Orioles owner Peter Angelos to refurbish the station for the museum. It will feature a full-size theatre, virtual-reality exhibits, and hands-on children's learning areas. The Babe Ruth Museum and Birthplace on nearby Emory Street has already gained a reputation as the best baseball museum in America outside of Cooperstown, New York, and it is expanding to Camden Station. Babe Ruth left from Camden Station to join the Boston Red Sox as a major league player, and the Orioles arrived at Camden Station to open their inaugural 1954 season.

The ballpark already attracts people as a museum-like site. More than 70,000 people a year tour Camden Yards when no games are scheduled. "That is the highest compliment to our ballpark," Cal Ripken said. "How many people go to a ballpark with no game going on? They do it in our ballpark." Although the ballpark has been around only since 1992, the site and the accompanying B&O Warehouse have a storied history.

The earliest recorded history of the site is 1781, when French General Comte de Rochambeau and his troops camped there on their way to and from Yorktown, Virginia, where they fought alongside George Washington against the British in the final battle of the Revolutionary War. In 1828, the site's railroad legacy began when the B&O Railroad started building a rail line that would head west over the Allegheny Mountains to the Ohio Valley. But twenty-four years would pass before the rail line, running from Baltimore to Wheeling, West Virginia, was finished. The same year, 1852, the construction of Camden Station began. When it opened five years later, it was the largest railroad depot in the world.

Camden Station played a historic part in the Civil War. A battle between 225 Union soldiers and a group of Southern supporters took place as the troops were trying to enter the depot to travel to Washington. After an attack on Fort Sumter, President Abraham Lincoln ordered some troops to Washington to protect the Capital. The clash resulted in the death of four soldiers and twelve civilians—the first casualties of the Civil War.

Camden Station was also part of the Underground Railroad, and part of the route of three historic trips that Lincoln made. On the first trip, Lincoln was on his way to Washington for his inaugural, and he went through the station earlier than expected to avoid large crowds after an assassination plot was uncovered in 1861. He also went to Camden Station on his way to and back from Gettysburg, where he dedicated the battlefield cemetery in 1863. His final trip came when his funeral train stopped, and his casket was moved to the rotunda at the Merchant's Exchange

Building, where his body lay in state before continuing the trip to bring him back home to Springfield, Illinois.

The area continued to grow as a transportation and shipping center, and in 1898 construction began on the B&O Warehouse. It was finished in 1905, a 1,016-foot-long structure (but just 51 feet wide) that remains the longest building on the East Coast. The decline of trains and the increase of car use after World War II hit the warehouse hard, closing the building in 1974. These changes eventually limited Camden Station to handling just a few commuter trains between Baltimore and Washington. The station and warehouse have received new life thanks to the building of the ballpark—the station in its development as a baseball museum, and the warehouse as an office, shops, and restaurant complex.

The location of the ballpark itself has some remarkable history. Ruth's Cafe, the tavern Babe Ruth's father operated, was located where center field is now at Camden Yards, which was once the corner of Conway Street and Little Paca. Archeologists found the remains of the saloon building with the help of Ruth's then ninety-year-old sister, Mary Ruth Moberly. It was one of five saloons George Herman Ruth, Sr., managed in the Camden Yards area at one time or another.

Years from now, baseball historians will look back on a new era of history at Camden Yards, starting with opening day on April 6, 1992, against the Cleveland Indians. Here are some of the facts they will find:

The first pitch at Camden Yards, ball one, was thrown by Rick Sutcliffe at 3:20 P.M. on a sunny 63-degree day. Sutcliffe signed as a free agent with the Orioles after the 1991 season while sitting at a makeshift table beneath Camden Yards, which was in the final stages of construction. He signed after standing out on the mound and then telling his agent that he wanted to pitch in this ballpark. Sutcliffe was a fiery competitor who would go on to win twenty-six games in two seasons with Baltimore. He was also a strong clubhouse leader.

The first batter was Indians center fielder Kenny Lofton, who flied out to right fielder Joe Orsulak. Lofton would go on to make some of the most memorable catches of his career in center field at Camden Yards. Cleveland first baseman Paul Sorrento got the first hit, a single to left center field with one out in the top of the second. Mark Whiten had the first strikeout at the ballpark.

Ironically, the first Orioles hit came in the bottom of the second, a single to center by, of all people, Glenn Earl Davis. This may have been the only memorable hit he made during his three seasons with Baltimore, and he remains the single worst trade in the history of the franchise. Davis was once one of the best home-run hitters in the National League, hitting 166 home runs for the Houston Astros from 1985 to 1990. The Orioles were desperately in need of a power hitter, and they mortgaged their future to get Davis from the Astros on January 10, 1991, in a trade for pitcher Pete Harnisch, Curt Schilling, and outfielder Steve Finley.

This was the mother of bad trades. Davis became the poster boy for the disabled list, playing in just forty-nine games in 1991 and just 106 games in 1992. He was healthy in 1993 but couldn't play anymore, batting just .177 with one home run in thirty games. He was sent down to the team's Class AAA club in Rochester. While on a road trip to Norfolk, Davis and several teammates were involved in a fight at a nightclub, and Davis's jaw was broken. He came back up to the Orioles several weeks later and, while sitting in the dugout during a game, nearly got hit in the face with a foul ball. When he finally healed, Davis had the nerve to walk into manager Johnny Oates's office and demand to know why he was playing behind Mike Pagliarulo at first base. Oates went ballistic, coming out of his office, his face beet red, screaming at the top of his lungs to Davis's friend Rick Sutcliffe, "Get him out of here Sut! Get him out of here!" The next day, Davis was released.

All three of the players the Orioles gave up—Finley, Harnisch, and Schilling—went on to become All-Star players. That, and the first Orioles hit at Camden Yards, is Glenn Earl Davis's legacy in Baltimore.

The first Orioles run was scored in the bottom of the fifth inning, when Sam Horn walked, went to second base on a single by Leo Gomez, and scored on a double by Chris Hoiles. Again, like Davis, Horn is one of the more infamous Orioles. A 6-foot-5, 250-pound lefthanded slugger, Horn swung—and acted—as if he was the next coming of Willie McCovey. Although never reaching that level of the game, he was one of the more entertaining players to ever wear an Orioles uniform. He tied the record for the most consecutive strikeouts in one game, striking out six straight times in a fifteen-inning game on July 17, 1991, against Kansas City, but was the first non-pitcher to do so. He often declared during the 1992 season that he would be the first one to hit the warehouse with a home run, but he never did, and was gone from Baltimore after 1992. Horn went over to play baseball in Japan, where he declared he would become a "Yenyionaire." He never did, and he was last seen playing baseball in Taiwan.

Hoiles's double was the first one at the ballpark and also the first run batted in (RBI). Sorrento hit the first home run there two days later, on April 8, off Bob Milacki. The next day, Mike Devereaux hit the first Orioles home run, leading off the top of the fourth against Jack Armstrong. Cleveland's Mark Lewis stole the first base at the ballpark in the third inning on April 9, and Baltimore's Randy Milligan hit the first grand slam on April 17 against Detroit in the seventh inning off Les Lancaster. Cal Ripken hit the first triple there, in the sixth inning on April 17 off Detroit's Scott Aldred. Gregg Olson recorded the ballpark's first save on April 19 in a 3–2 win over the Tigers. The first inside-the-park home run came on August 22, 1993, when Texas outfielder Butch Davis hit one off Arthur Rhodes. The Orioles won ten of their first eleven games at Camden Yards, the best start ever for a team in a new ballpark. After the 1998 season, the Orioles had a record of 286–246 at Camden Yards.

The history of Camden Yards, from its previous lives to its current place in history as one of the important and popular ballparks in the world, is all part of the tours that take place there daily. Before we embark on one with our tour guide, it is important to pay tribute first to the ballpark the Orioles left behind, Memorial Stadium.

This ballpark was home to the Orioles for thirty-eight years and hosted some of the club's finest moments. It was also the site of five World Series and many other memorable events, including the glory days of the Baltimore Colts. Memorial Stadium was built on the site of the old Municipal Stadium at a cost of $6 million. Its capacity in the Orioles' final days there was 53,273. It was 309 feet down the left and right field lines and 405 feet in straight-away center. Memorial Stadium was functional when the Orioles left in 1991, but it was not one of the ballparks that will go down in history as a design masterpiece. Its place in the hearts of Orioles fans is because of what they witnessed there and the memories created there. Cal Ripken played for ten years at Memorial Stadium, and he loves Camden Yards. But when he was on the field at Memorial Stadium for a football game in 1996—the first time since his last game there at third base on October 6, 1991—he felt all of those memories coming back in the old surroundings. "I found myself standing on the sidelines, looking around for places in the stadium that were familiar," he said. "I was looking around for where the overhang was. I remembered my first grand slam hit off there."

After the Orioles left, Memorial Stadium had a life as the home for the Baltimore Stallions in the Canadian Football League and then served for two years as the home of the Cleveland Browns when they moved to Baltimore and became the Ravens. But now, with the new Ravens stadium at Camden Yards, it appears that Memorial Stadium is on its way to becoming nothing more than a memory.

Before the tour of Camden Yards begins, it may be important to learn the ground rules:

1. Foul poles (transported from Memorial Stadium) with screens attached are outside of playing field.
2. Thrown or fairly batted ball that remains behind or under the canvas or canvas holder: two bases. Ball rebounding in playing field: in play.
3. Ball striking surfaces, pillars, or facings surrounding the dugout: in dugout.
4. Ball striking railings around photographers' booths: in play.
5. Fair-bounding ball striking railings above cement wall down right-field line: out of play.
6. Foul ball hitting ground-crew shed roof in right field and bouncing back into play: home run.

Now that we know the rules, we can follow our Camden Yards guide as he begins his tour on Eutaw Street, standing near Boog's Barbecue. "In 1989, they broke ground here to build this ballpark," the guide tells the group touring Camden Yards this summer day. "This is a ballpark. Do not call this a stadium. We only had one other event here other than a baseball game, and that was when a gentleman came from Rome, Italy, and spoke out here before 50,000 people," the guide says, referring to the time Pope John Paul II appeared at Camden Yards in 1994.

Standing near the B&O Warehouse, the guide tells the crowd that it took $20 million to renovate the warehouse. "They had to clean all 3 million bricks by hand. They could not use any machinery because the mortar was so brittle between the bricks. They replaced every one of the 898 windows in the building. It's the longest building east of the Mississippi River. If you turned it on its side, it would be two stories lower than the Empire State Building."

Eutaw Street—the walkway between the ballpark and the warehouse—is open to the public all year long for people to walk through, sit down in, eat their lunches, and look out on the ballpark. But about four hours before the start of a game, the gates on each end of the street are closed. The gates reopen for ticket holders two hours before game time. Eutaw Street is then filled with fans milling about or waiting on line to get food at Boog's or some of the other concession stands that line the street during a game.

Boog's remains one of the biggest non-game attractions at Camden Yards, thanks to its namesake, the keeper of the barbecue and Oriole flame, Boog Powell. The one-time Oriole first baseman, who played thirteen seasons for Baltimore, including on two World Championship teams (in 1966 and 1970), was one of the best home-run hitters of his time, slamming 337 career home runs and driving in 1,187 runs. Powell was a fan favorite in Baltimore not just because of his hitting, but also because of his colorful personality and ability to connect with fans. He has parlayed that into Boog's Barbecue. Before every Orioles home game, fans line up at his stand for barbecue and a chance to meet Boog, who is out there before every game talking with people and signing autographs.

In 1997, Powell went through some difficult times. The same year that Eric Davis was diagnosed with colon cancer, Powell was, too. Like Davis, though, he caught the cancer early enough to undergo successful surgery and treatment. He has since recovered and is still a fixture on Eutaw Street at Camden Yards.

Not far from Boog's barbecue is the Orioles Hall of Fame, located at the north end of the warehouse on the wall at the base of the scoreboard. The wall holds plaques, similar to those enshrined in Cooperstown, of members of the club's Hall of Fame, such as Paul Blair, Al Bumbry, and Mike Flanagan.

Just outside of Eutaw Street, at the north end of the warehouse, are 4-foot monuments honoring the Orioles with retired numbers: Brooks Robinson (5), Jim Palmer (22), Frank Robinson (20), Earl Weaver (4), and Eddie Murray (33). More honors are on display at the south end of Eutaw Street, where the Maryland Athletic Hall of Fame is located. Here, native Marylanders, such as Al Kaline and Jimmy Foxx, represent twenty-seven different sports. Also on view are plaques mounted along the street for the Mid-Atlantic Scouts Hall of Fame.

As we continue down Eutaw Street, our guide points out some of the many features in the ballpark that push our nostalgia buttons. "They wanted to incorporate old Baltimore into the ballpark, and these cobblestones here, you'll see them throughout the ballpark." The tour stops at the place on Eutaw Street where six home runs landed and are marked by brass plates embedded in the sidewalk, giving the hitter's name, the team logo, the distance the ball traveled, and the date it was hit. Nineteen balls have landed on Eutaw Street; plans to mark the others are in the works. Baltimore first baseman Rafael Palmeiro has the most, with three. The following players have launched shots onto Eutaw Street since Camden Yards opened in 1992:

April 20, 1992—Mickey Tettleton (former Oriole), Detroit Tigers, off Bob Milacki, 432 feet.

May 5, 1992—Kevin Reimer, Texas Rangers, off Jose Mesa, 443 feet.

May 23, 1992—Lee Stevens, California Angels, off Rick Sutcliffe, 430 feet.

April 24, 1994—Ken Griffey, Jr., Seattle Mariners, off Brad Pennington, 424 feet.

June 8, 1995—Kevin Bass, Orioles, off Solomon Torres, 409 feet.

April 3, 1996—Rafael Palmeiro, Orioles, off Mark Gubicza, 412 feet.

April 27, 1996—Brady Anderson, Orioles, off Bobby Witt, 380 feet.

April 30, 1996—Paul O'Neill, New York Yankees, off Arthur Rhodes, 431 feet.

July 7, 1996—Mo Vaughn, Boston Red Sox, off Scott Erickson, 419 feet.

July 26, 1996—Jim Thome, Cleveland Indians, off Mike Mussina, 440 feet.

August 14, 1996—Eddie Murray, Orioles, off Jeff D'Amico, 384 feet.

September 8, 1996—Bobby Bonilla, Orioles, off Jose Lima, 405 feet.

April 11, 1997—Palmeiro, off Eric Gunderson, 411 feet.

April 11, 1997—Palmeiro, off Ed Vosberg, 408 feet.

June 17, 1997—Henry Rodriguez, Montreal Expos, off Scott Kamieniecki, 443 feet.

May 13, 1998—Anderson, off Chad Ogea, 405 feet.

May 30, 1998—Lee Stevens, Texas Rangers, off Sidney Ponson, 415 feet.

June 21, 1998—Carlos Delgago, Toronto Blue Jays, off Sidney Ponson, 415 feet.

July 24, 1998—Palmeiro, off Bill Swift, 413 feet.

No one has yet hit the warehouse during a game, though Griffey hit it during the home-run hitting contest at the 1993 All-Star Game workout day event. A plaque marked the spot of the Griffey home run, but it was stolen off the warehouse. Also, the windows of the building were not as shatterproof as they were supposed to be. When the Orioles' Kevin Bass hit one that landed on Eutaw Street on June 8, 1995, it bounced and smashed through a second-floor window.

Off Eutaw Street in right field, above the electronic scoreboard on the right-field wall, is the flagpole area, where many fans stand and watch the game, often waiting for a home run to come their way. Three rows of flagpoles represent the three divisions of the American League. Each day during the season, the flags on the three poles are arranged according to the standings in each division in the league for that day.

The tour then walks down through the stands, past the seats on the lower level. There are 18,000 box seats between the foul poles. Below the lower boxes are 6,800 terrace box seats. The upper deck has 25 rows of seats, 1,850 bleacher seats, and 275 standing-room-only (SRO) locations that go on sale two hours before game time. Every aisle seat has a reproduction of the logo used by the Baltimore Orioles of the 1890s, a National League team that won consecutive pennants in 1894, 1895, and 1896. In all, the official capacity of Camden Yards is 48,876. What is amusing is that the twenty-five biggest crowds in the history of the ballpark all occurred after Peter Angelos purchased the team. Former owner Eli Jacobs and others in the former administration gave away many more tickets to friends and associates.

There are not very many giveaways now. The prices for Orioles tickets in 1998 were as follows: $35 for club box; $30, field box; $22, lower box and left-field club seats; $18, upper box and left-field lower box; $14, left-field upper box; $13, upper and lower reserve; $11, left-field upper reserve; $9, center-field bleachers; $7, standing room only.

Two seats in the ballpark are specially marked red seats. The one in the lower box in left field marks where Cal Ripken's 278th career home run landed, a new record for major league short-stops, breaking Ernie Banks's number. Ripken hit it on July 15, 1993, in a 5–3 win over the Minnesota Twins, off Twins starter Scott Erickson, who would become Ripken's teammate two years later. The other noteworthy seat is located in the right-field bleachers, the landing place when Eddie Murray hit his 500th career home run (the fifteenth player in baseball history to reach that mark), coming off Detroit's Felipe Lira on September 6, 1996—exactly one year to the day that his friend Ripken broke Lou Gehrig's record with his 2,131st consecutive game.

The tour reaches the field, but everyone is strongly reminded over and over again to stay on the track around the field and not walk on the grass. Groundskeeper Paul Zwaska is legendary for his tenacity in protecting the playing surface at the ballpark. The field is 16 feet below street level and is made up of Prescription Athletic Turf, an irrigation and drainage system below the natural grass turf. This system removes as much as 75,000 gallons of water from the field in an hour. The turf has been effective in cutting down the number of rainouts for the Orioles. But other drainage components at Camden Yards are all wet, such as those in the dugout, which turn into small swimming pools during a heavy rainstorm. Once, in fact, the Orioles clubhouse filled up with backed-up water from the drainage system that went all the way into the manager's office.

Before leaving the field, the tour stops at home plate, one of the links with the Orioles' past at Memorial Stadium. On the final day of the 1991 season, the last Orioles game at Memorial Stadium, in a memorable, stirring event, home plate was dug up in a ceremony, transported in a white stretch limousine to Camden Yards, which was still under construction, and put in the new ballpark.

Heading down the tunnel behind home plate under Camden Yards, the guide points out the stool near the wall where Ernie Tyler, the real "Iron Man" for the Orioles, sits. The umpire's attendant has not missed an Orioles home game since opening day 1960, a streak of 3,076 regular season games entering the 1999 season. He sits on the stool during games and brings home-plate umpires new baseballs. Tyler helps prepare these balls by rubbing Delaware River mud on them to condition the rawhide. Sixty baseballs are prepared before every game. Tyler's presence is another unique aspect of Camden Yards: he is the only umpire's attendant in baseball who prepares the balls; at the other ball-parks, umpires do this job.

Tyler has gotten an up-close-and-personal view of some of the greatest players in the game from his seat. He recalls talking to New York Yankees Mickey Mantle and Roger Maris during rain-outs and had Los Angeles Angels pitcher Bo Belinsky over to his house to play pool. He counts Eddie Murray as one of his closest friends. "Eddie once bought me a new pair of shoes because the ones I had were getting a little old," he revealed.

The Tyler presence at Camden Yards is not limited to seventy-four-year-old Ernie. His two sons, Jim and Fred, are clubhouse managers at the ballpark. Jim is in charge of the Orioles club-house. This is his thirty-eighth season with the ball club, having started as a clubhouse boy in 1962. Fred has been in charge of the visitors' clubhouse for fifteen years, and he has another connection to the Orioles. He was a standpoint baseball player at Bel Air High School, and as a senior, he hit a single to drive in the winning run to beat Aberdeen High School and its pitcher—Cal Ripken, Jr. That year, Fred was the All Harford County pick for shortstop. Ripken was named to the All-Star team as a pitcher.

Beneath the ballpark are the arteries and stomachs that Camden Yards runs on: twenty miles of beer pipes, plus loading docks where thousands of pounds of food and other beverages are unloaded and stored to satisfy 48,000 people for more than eighty games a year.

The tour moves up two floors to the lower press box, where dozens of reporters sit every game and report for their newspapers and other media outlets. It can accommodate up to 110 reporters. An old-time, open-air press box, it is closer to the action than those in most other ballparks. Just before Camden Yards opened, a screen ran all the way up to the press box to stop foul balls from going back deep into the crowd. But the screen blocked the view from the press box, and reporters' complaints resulted in the Orioles taking down the fence and putting up a smaller screen that protects fans seated in the seats immediately behind home plate, but a number of balls come flying back into the crowd.

The official scorer also sits in the press box, and Camden Yards has its own unique way of letting the crowd know if the scorer ruled a play as a hit or an error. A clock on top of the center-field scoreboard advertises a Baltimore newspaper in large characters: "THE SUN." When a play needs the official scorer's interpretation, the "H" lights up for a hit, and the "E" lights up for an error.

The tour stops at one particular location in the press box where a plaque commemorates someone else who made Camden Yards a unique place for the game: public address announcer Rex Barney, who passed away on August 11, 1997. Once a promising, young, fireballing pitcher with the Brooklyn Dodgers, Barney played with Jackie Robinson in 1947 and pitched a no-hitter against the rival New York Giants at the Polo Grounds in 1948. He never realized his potential as a player, though, because he suffered from control problems and retired after six seasons with a record of 35–31. Barney went into broadcasting and came to Baltimore in 1954. He began working as a part-time public-address announcer for the Orioles in the late 1960s and early 1970s, and he became the full-time announcer for the club in 1974.

Barney developed several trademark calls that became part of the language for anyone who followed the Orioles. After making an address to fans, he would end it with a "Thank yoouuuu" that became legendary. Whenever a fan made a great catch of a foul ball, the crowd waited to hear Barney's "Give that fan a contract." For an Orioles fan, that was better than catching the ball itself. In this age of high-tech ballpark attractions and effects, Rex Barney was the real deal.

But it wasn't just Barney's calls that made him so special to Baltimore fans. He connected with them, displaying a gentle nature with people at a time when anger and cynicism had come into vogue in sports. He was a commodity that baseball could ill afford to lose. "He had a genuine love for the game and for people, and that came through," said Orioles bullpen coach Elrod Hendricks, who knew Barney. Hall of Fame pitcher Jim Palmer commented, "He was a wonderful man. He loved baseball and had a great passion for it."

There was no public-address announcer on August 13, the first game after Barney's passing. The Orioles used substitutes for the rest of the year, but no one sat in Barney's seat in the press box. Perhaps the best illustration of how Barney connected with Orioles fans is that the most frequently asked question from fans who came up to the press box was, "Where does Rex Barney sit?"

On the third floor of Camden Yards is the upper press box, where the broadcast facilities are. There are 286 miles of broadcast cable and telephone wires that run through the ballpark. Also upstairs is the communications room, where all the audio and video seen and heard throughout the ballpark originates: for example, birthday greetings on the Sony JumboTron, music when a pitching change is made, and the electronic cheerleading to stir up fans in the ballpark.

This became a sore point at Camden Yards after the 1996 season. Some players felt the fans weren't animated enough. Furthermore, Orioles owner Peter Angelos, after hearing the raucous noise created not just by Yankee fans at Yankee Stadium, but also artificially induced by an aggressive sound-system program, put the orders out for those in the communications room to raise the level of music and use loud noise to ignite Camden Yards fans. Some critics argued that Orioles fans were simply good baseball fans who didn't respond blindly to any action on the field. But the game was changing, becoming more and more the definition of entertainment as much as sport. The philosophy at Camden Yards, as well as through much of baseball now, is that the ballpark is an entertainment destination, and to keep it filled for more than eighty games a year, fans needed to entertained by more than balls, strikes, and singles. The equipment in the communications room, the center-field JumboTron, the right-field scoreboard, and the other auxiliary scoreboards represent an $11.5 million investment (nearly three times as much as it cost to build Memorial Stadium) in entertainment, not baseball.

Next the tour moves up to the fourth floor, the money floor, where seventy-two luxury boxes can be leased for a three-year minimum term for between $75,000 and $175,000 annually, depending on the box. Corporations are on the waiting list to lease them. These boxes seat ten to fourteen people and have their own bathrooms, refrigerators, videocassette recorders, indoor and outdoor televisions—and even waiters and waitresses.

Along the tile walkway behind the luxury boxes are exclusive restaurants, bars, and several concierges, who, according to the tour guide, will get you "anything you can get at a very expensive hotel." Displayed in one of those bars is a bizarre replica of Camden Yards built with trading cards. Ironically, none of them is a baseball card.

Each of the three large party rooms holds up to sixty people. The rooms are named after three Orioles greats: Brooks Robinson, Frank Robinson, and Jim Palmer, all three enshrined in the National Baseball Hall of Fame in Cooperstown, New York. Of the three whose names grace these party rooms, only one is still connected with the team. This is not exactly the sort of relationship you would expect with a franchise that seems to place so much value on tradition.

Frank Robinson came to the Orioles after the 1965 season, after ten brilliant seasons with the Cincinnati Reds, including Most Valuable Player honors in 1961, when he batted .323 with 208 hits, 39 home runs, 136 RBI, 117 runs scored, and 18 stolen bases. But the Reds figured they got the best they would get out of him, and traded him after the 1965 season, even though he had batted .296 with 33 home runs and 113 RBI. Frank Robinson was dealt to Baltimore for pitcher Milt Pappas, a decision that turned around the fortunes of the Orioles franchise. The deal came right at the same time that the New York Yankees, the Orioles' American League rivals, were about to go into a tailspin. Robinson led the Orioles to their first World Championship in 1966, batting .316 with 49 home runs and 122 RBI. He won the Triple Crown, the American League Most Valuable Player (the only player to win the MVP in both leagues), and the World Series MVP as well.

Frank Robinson went on to play five more seasons for the Orioles, establishing himself as one of the most popular players in the history of the franchise. He was traded to Los Angeles after the 1971 season, and his Orioles number was retired right after that. This made him the first player in the history of the Baltimore franchise to have his number retired. He played for California in 1972 and part of 1973 before being traded to the Cleveland Indians, where he made history in 1975 when he became a player manager, the game's first black manager. Frank Robinson retired in 1976 with 586 career home runs, 2,943 hits, 1,812 RBI, and a .294 batting average. An Orioles coach in 1979 and 1980 and from 1985 to 1987, he took over as manager of the Orioles from 1988 until 1991, when he moved to the front office as an assistant general manager.

Robinson was not the only assistant general manager. Doug Melvin was also an assistant general manager, and both men worked under GM Roland Hemond. Melvin left after the 1994 season to take a job as general manager with the Texas Rangers. Frank Robinson stayed on, hoping to take over the top job when Hemond retired. But he had a falling out with owner Peter Angelos and was frozen out of the process when Angelos fired Hemond after the 1995 season. Former Toronto general manager Pat Gillick was hired instead, and though Frank Robinson wanted to stay on as assistant general manager, the Orioles opted to hire Montreal general manager Kevin Malone. This choice left Robinson out in the cold. He resigned shortly afterward and is now a special assistant to the commissioner's office and is also in charge of the Arizona Fall League.

Brooks Robinson was known as "Mr. Oriole" during his twenty-three years with the team. He was also known as the "Human Vacuum Cleaner" because he swept up everything that came his way down third base. Many consider him the best third baseman to ever play the game. He shares the record for the most Gold Gloves, sixteen, with pitcher Jim Kaat, and he played in eighteen All-Star Games. Brooks Robinson retired after the 1977 season with 268 home runs and a 1,357 RBI. He was elected to the Hall of Fame in his first year of eligibility in 1983.

After retiring, Brooks Robinson went into broadcasting, doing Orioles games until the end of the 1993 season. He is rarely seen around Camden Yards these days, splitting his time living in Southern California and the Baltimore suburbs.

Jim Palmer, on the other hand, continues to be a dominating presence on the Orioles scene. The pitcher won 268 games during his nineteen-year career, all with Baltimore. He won three Cy Young Awards in a four-year span (1973, 1975, and 1976), and his 2.86 earned run average (ERA) is fourth on the all-time list among pitchers with 3,000 or more career innings pitched. Palmer won twenty games in a season eight times in his career and was elected to the Hall of Fame on the first ballot in 1990. The next season, at the age of forty-five, he tried and failed in a come-back attempt.

Palmer has remained a national sports figure, working as an analyst for network baseball telecasts and appearing as a pitchman for The Money Store, replacing Phil Rizzuto. Palmer has also been the analyst for Orioles games for the past six seasons and, unlike the other two Orioles who have achieved party-room status, is still an influential force within the organization. Palmer was a confidant of former Orioles manager Davey Johnson, a teammate of Palmer's, and has also advised Angelos on baseball matters.

The tour leaves the luxury-box level and goes downstairs, heading to the picnic area behind the two bullpens in left center field. One of the last features noted on the tour is the center field wall, a replica of Wrigley Field, with the ivy growing up the wall. At the end of the 1998 season, the ivy, which had been planted before the ballpark opened, nearly reached the top of the wall. The seeds of baseball past have also firmly taken root at Camden Yards as well, and, like Wrigley Field, it has an allure that draws people to it.

CHAPTER FOUR

Ancestors and Offspring

C amden Yards has spawned a series of offspring ballparks in major league baseball; it is sort of like the father of the ballpark version of the baby boom. Four ballparks have been built since Camden Yards opened in 1992, five more are on their way, and still others are in the planning stages. To look at what Camden Yards—or the Camden Yards plan, as baseball officials call it— has created, we must first examine where it came from, the fields of dreams that inspired the vision of Camden Yards and the other new ballparks.

Ebbets Field. Forbes Field. Crosley Field. Shibe Park. Old Comiskey. Fenway Park. Tiger Stadium. Wrigley Field. These cathedrals offered the blueprints for the concept of Camden Yards and its followers. There have been other models as well, but the roots of much of what you find in today's traditional, old-fashioned ballparks—the quirkiness, the intimacy—grew in places like Ebbets Field, Forbes Field, and the others mentioned above.

Perhaps no other ballpark ever built has captured the imagination of baseball fans the way Ebbets Field has, but only after it was gone. Much of that had to do with the team that played there, one of the most storied and beloved of all time, the Brooklyn Dodgers. But the ballpark itself had the charm and intimacy that gave the Dodgers a stage worthy of performing on.

Ebbets Field was the epitome of the urban ballpark. It was the heart of the borough of Brooklyn. People who grew up in Brooklyn say that three events caused the demise of that borough: the shutting down of *The Brooklyn Eagle* newspaper, the closing of the Brooklyn Navy Yards, and the Dodgers' departure to Los Angeles after the 1957 season. The ballpark would be gone three years later, torn down to make way for high-rise apartments.

Ebbets Field was located in the Flatbush section of Brooklyn, on a block surrounded by Bedford Avenue, Montgomery Street, McKeever Place, and Sullivan Place. Named after the man who built it, Dodgers owner Charles Ebbets, it opened in 1913, with a capacity of 25,000. In those days, ballparks tinkered with their form much more than has been done in recent times, and several changes took place at Ebbets Field. It opened as a pitcher's park and was transformed in the 1940s into a hitter's park, with the fences moved in. More seats were added to bring up the capacity to about 32,000.

When the ballpark opened, its dimensions were: left field, 419 feet; center field, 450 feet; right field, 301 feet. Its dimensions when it closed were: left field, 348 feet; center field, 393 feet; right field, 297 feet. The distinctive features of the ballpark included the main entrance, an 80-foot circle enclosed in Italian marble, with a floor tiled in the style of baseball stitches and a chandelier with twelve baseball-bat arms holding baseball-shaped globes; an Abe Stark sign in right field, in which the clothing-store owner advertised a free suit to any batter who hit the 3-foot by 30-foot sign; the field-level scoreboard and the Schaefer Beer sign above it, in which the "h" would light up if a hit was scored and the "e" would light up for an error—a feature that would be used at Camden Yards.

Several historical firsts occurred at Ebbets Field. One was the first televised game, on August 26, 1938, the first game of a doubleheader between the Dodgers and the Cincinnati Reds, with Red Barber behind the microphone. But the most important event—one of the single most important events in sports in the twentieth century—took place on Tuesday, April 15, 1947, when Jackie Robinson took the field for the Dodgers. He was the first African American to break the color barrier in baseball. All that history crumbled when the ballpark was razed in 1960.

Forbes Field in Pittsburgh had a special place in the development of the Camden Yards plan because it was where Larry Lucchino, the driving force behind the Baltimore ballpark, grew up watching baseball. Forbes Field was a park located in a park, Schenley Park. Built by owner Barney Dreyfuss in 1909, it was named after British general John Forbes, who captured Fort Duquesnse from the French during the French and Indian War and renamed it Fort Pitt.

Forbes Field was home to the Pirates from the year it opened until 1970, when they moved to Three Rivers Stadium, as well as to the legendary Negro League baseball team, the Homestead Grays, from 1939 to 1948. When Forbes Field opened, its dimensions were: left field, 360 feet; center field, 435 feet; right field, 376 feet. When the ballpark closed, its dimensions were: left field, 365 feet; center field, 435 feet; right field, 300 feet. Ivy covered the brick wall in left field and left center field, and a 14-foot Longines clock was mounted on top of the left-field scoreboard. Home plate is still there, almost in its exact same location. It is encased in glass on the first-floor walkway of the University of Pittsburgh's Forbes Quadrangle. Also, a plaque in a sidewalk there marks the place where Bill Mazeroski's 1960 World Series home run went out of the ballpark.

Cincinnati's Crosley Field opened in 1912 and was home to the Reds until 1970, when they moved to Riverfront Stadium, another of the cookie-cutter, multi-purpose stadiums. The park was named after Reds owner Powell Crosley. Located in

Cincinnati's west side, at the intersection of Findlay Street and Western Avenue, Crosley Field opened with a capacity of 25,000 and closed with a capacity of 29,603. Its double-decker grandstand curved around home plate and down the first and third base lines. When the ballpark opened, its dimensions were: left field, 360 feet; center field, 420 feet; right field, 360 feet. When Crosley Field closed, its dimensions were: left field, 328 feet; center field, 387 feet; right field, 366 feet. There was an incline in front of the fence all around the outfield; this was particularly noticeable in left field and left center field. On top of the Superior Towel and Linen Service laundry building beyond the left-field wall was a Spiedler Suit sign, and as with the Abe Stark billboard in Ebbets Field, if a batter hit the sign, he would win a suit. On May 14, 1935, Crosley Field was the site of the first major league baseball night game.

A reconstructed version of Crosley Field was built at the Blue Ash Sports Center about fifteen miles away from Cincinnati in 1989. The left-center-field scoreboard remains as it was when the last pitch was thrown on June 24, 1970. The reconstructed park includes 270 restored original Crosley Field seats.

Shibe Park opened in 1909 as the home of the Philadelphia Athletics, which it remained until the team left for Kansas City after the 1954 season. It was also the home of the Phillies from 1938 to 1970. Like the Pirates and the Reds, the Phillies then moved into a multi-purpose, cookie-cutter ballpark, Veterans Stadium. That year—1970—was probably the game's darkest year in terms of ballparks. Shibe Park, located in north Philadelphia, surrounded by Lehigh Avenue, North 20th Street, Somerset Street, and North 21st Street, was named after Ben Shibe, one of the owners of the Athletics. Its dimensions on opening day were: left field, 360 feet; center field, 515 feet; right field, 360 feet. When Shibe Park closed, its dimensions were: left field, 334 feet; center field, 410 feet; right field, 329 feet. In right field, a corrugated iron fence resulted in the ball taking some quirky bounces off the wall. The old Yankee Stadium scoreboard was installed in 1956 in front of the right-center-field wall, and a clock was added. Balls that hit the 75-foot-high clock were home runs. The park had a 20-inch-high pitcher's mound, the highest in baseball.

Comiskey Park—the first one—opened in 1910 and closed after the 1990 season. It was located on the south side of Chicago, surrounded by West 35th Street, Wentworth Avenue, 34th Place, and South Shields Avenue. It was home for the White Sox all that time, as well as the Negro American League's Chicago American Giants from 1941 to 1950. The ballpark had a capacity of 28,800 when it opened, and was expanded over the years to a capacity of 43,951 when it closed. When it opened, its dimensions were anything but quirky: 362 feet down the lines and 420 feet in center field. When old Comiskey Park closed, it was 347 feet down the lines and 409 feet to center field. The ballpark was named after White Sox owner Charles Comiskey, but it took on the ultimate ballpark personality under the ownership of Bill Veeck, who truly understood the concept of making a ballpark. Veeck put a picnic area in left field and put in a screen so the people there could still watch the game. He also installed the exploding scoreboard in 1960.

The ballpark suffered the most ignominious of deaths, however. It was torn down to be replaced by a new Comiskey directly across the street, a ballpark that fell far short of its predecessor. Where old Comiskey once stood is now a parking lot for the new ballpark. None of these model parks, in fact, is still standing. Of the next three baseball parks—Wrigley Field, Fenway Park, and Tiger Stadium—one is already scheduled to be replaced, another is under consideration, and the third is holding fast as a mecca for the game.

Wrigley Field is the standard bearer for anyone's field of dreams. The Chicago ballpark showed no signs of age when it took center stage again in the fall of 1998, when the Cubs reached the National League playoffs after the wild-card position came down to a one-game playoff between the Cubs and the San

Francisco Giants. This ballpark remains the most popular venue among baseball fans, and despite the success and atmosphere of Camden Yards, there is no denying that Wrigley Field is the original blueprint for ballparks.

Wrigley Field opened in 1914 at the corner of Clark and Addison streets as North Side Ball Park; it was then called a variety of names—Weeghman Park, Whales Park, and Cubs Park—before it became Wrigley Field in 1926. It opened with a capacity of 14,000 and currently can hold up to 38,765. When it first opened, its dimensions were: left field, 345 feet; center field, 440 feet; right field, 356 feet. Its dimensions now are: left field, 355 feet; center field, 400 feet; right field, 353 feet. Wrigley Park is the only remaining Federal League ballpark, as it was home for the Chicago Whales.

Wrigley Field was the last ballpark to install lights, holding out until 1988. Lights were scheduled to be installed in the 1940s, but Wrigley donated them to the war effort. It remained a day-game-only park until pressure from Cubs management forced the issue, overriding preservationists' protests by putting the future of the park in doubt unless lights were installed. The first night game was supposed to be August 8, 1988, but the game was postponed after three innings due to rain. So the official first major league night game at Wrigley Field took place the following night, August 9. An agreement with the city limits the number of night games to eighteen per season. That is because Wrigley Field is truly the ultimate urban ballpark—built in a neighborhood, rather than a downtown business district. One of the charms of Wrigley is the sight of people watching the games from the apartment building rooftops beyond the park.

A 27-foot-high, 75-foot-wide scoreboard was installed in left field in 1937. Even today, the score-by-innings and the pitcher's numbers are changed by hand. One of the long-standing traditions at Wrigley is to fly a flag bearing a "W" or an "L" on top of the scoreboard after a game—a white flag with a blue "W" for a win, and a blue flag with a white "L" for a loss.

Wrigley Field underwent extensive renovations in the 1980s to help modernize it. In 1989, sixty-seven luxury boxes were added. These were a key component to the future of the ballpark, since luxury-box revenue has become the mother's milk of today's baseball franchises. Those changes have helped the ballpark avoid any talk of the wrecking ball, along with the deep pockets and public-relations sensitivity of its owners, the Tribune Corporation. Wrigley Field looks as if it may be around for a long time to come.

This is not the case with Wrigley Field's American League counterpart, Boston's Fenway Park. In Boston, there has been talk of replacing the legendary home of the Red Sox with a new downtown ballpark. The Red Sox insist they need a new 40,000-seat facility to come up with the revenue to compete with cash-cow franchises like Baltimore and Cleveland. The Red Sox have hopes of building the new park along Brookline Avenue. There is talk of preserving Fenway even if the Red Sox leave, though, possibly as a museum. So far, however, all the discussion about a new ballpark has been nothing but that—talk.

Fenway Park opened in 1912 with a game between the Red Sox and the New York Highlanders (now the Yankees). The Boston Braves also played at Fenway in their World Championship season of 1914 while Braves Field was under construction. Owner John Taylor named the ballpark Fenway because it was in the Fenway section of Boston. Taylor also had changed the name of the team from the Pilgrims to the Red Sox in 1907.

When the park first opened, its dimensions were: left field, 324 feet; center field, 488 feet; right field, 313 feet. Today, Fenway Park's dimensions are: left field, 315 feet; deep center, 420 feet; right field, 302 feet. The park's capacity on opening day was 35,000 and is currently 33,871. Several fires changed the look of Fenway. On May 8, 1926, the bleachers along the left-field foul line burned down and were not replaced, giving fielders a chance to run down foul balls behind the third-base grandstand. Eight years later, on January 5, 1934, a four-alarm fire destroyed the construction underway by owner Tom Yawkey.

Fenway Park's most distinctive feature is the "Green Monster," a 37-foot, green-painted wall in left field. Before 1947, there were advertisements on the wall, but now it is all green. Once built of railroad ties and tin, in 1976 it was changed to a plastic surface. The screen on top of the fence, about 23 feet high, is the only such device in the field of play in baseball. It was installed to enable groundskeepers to retrieve batting-practice home-run balls. The classic picture of Fenway Park is a blend of old and new—the ancient Green Monster with the modern Citgo neon sign in the background.

Economics may now do what fire couldn't—destroy Fenway. Numerous renovations have taken place over the past fifteen years, including private suites built on top of the left-field and right-field stands. But team owners believe no more changes could be made at Fenway that would help them produce the revenue they want from privates boxes and other sources. When the talk of a new ballpark gets closer to reality, it is likely that there will be a strong preservationist movement against leaving Fenway. Nevertheless, that movement may not be enough to save Fenway. It wasn't enough to save Tiger Stadium, which will be torn down when the Detroit Tigers move to their new 40,000-seat ballpark for the start of the 2000 season.

Tiger Stadium opened in 1896 as Bennett Park, with home plate where right field is now, for a minor league baseball game. When the Tigers moved there in 1912, it was renamed Navin Field, then Briggs Stadium from 1938 to 1960, and has been called Tiger Stadium ever since. It was also home to several Negro League teams, the Detroit Stars and the Detroit Wolves. Its capacity was 23,000 when it opened and is now at 52,416. When it was first used for major league baseball, its dimensions were: left field, 345 feet; center field, 467 feet; right field, 370 feet . The stadium's current configuration is: left field, 340 feet; center field, 440 feet; right field, 325 feet. The ballpark has the only double-decker bleachers in the majors, and the right-field second deck overhangs the lower deck by 10 feet.

The Tigers franchise went into a downward spiral in the early 1990s and, without a winning team, suffered at the box office and on the field, drawing barely 1 millions fans. Those losses, combined with the pressures of new ballparks going up all around them, giving their competition financial resources the Tigers did not have, gave new owner Mike Ilitch the ammunition he needed to push for a new ballpark as part of his downtown revitalization project. He ran into tremendous opposition from a group known as Tiger Stadium Fan Club, which included architects that came up with their own plan to preserve the stadium while modernizing it at the same time—a seemingly viable plan. But the success of new ballparks like Camden Yards and Jacobs Field, combined with the terrible economics of downtown Detroit and the calls for any effort to inject new life into the heart of the city, made it difficult to fight against the new ballpark. The project also had the considerable political weight and finances of the city's power structure, including Mayor Dennis Archer. So a new old ballpark—built with brick and featuring many replicated traits of old parks—will be constructed, along with 108 suites (originally plans called for 80 suites). HOK, the designers of Camden Yards, Jacobs Field, and Coors Field, are the architects for the new Detroit ballpark, an estimated $245 million open-air facility.

Club president John McHale says the Tigers' survival depended on the new ballpark. "Moving on to a new ballpark was vital to the life of our franchise," McHale said. "It was like oxygen. Unless our owner or some other owner decided that he just wanted to subsidize this endlessly to the tune of $20 million or $30 million a year, there was no other way to go. Where we are now, we have five so-called suites at the top of the ballpark that we lease out on a game-by-game basis. We can literally fill the ballpark up, do as well as we ever could here, and still be in the bottom half of revenue among the thirty major league baseball clubs, and we know what the facts of life are for those clubs that are in the bottom half of revenue. It's not a great picture."

Still, it is difficult to believe that in these times, despite all of the emphasis on recreating the baseball palaces of the past, one that is still standing will be abandoned and then torn down. Even McHale acknowledged the loss to come. "As difficult as this place is to operate in, there is nobody that doesn't come here and understand the magic that this place has, and it's true in places like Fenway and Yankee Stadium as well," he said. "There is a real sense of communing with the gods of baseball in a building like this."

The stadiums that were constructed after these historic ballparks were deemed obsolete had none of that sense of baseball atmosphere. In the late 1960s and early 1970s, the momentum on ballpark construction had swung from football to baseball, in this sense: in the old parks, football teams had to figure out a way to play in baseball-only parks. But with the rise of the National Football League in the 1960s, the new facilities were built so that they could better handle both sports—thereby serving neither one in the best interests of the fans or the games. Three Rivers, Riverfront, Veterans Stadium—all were sterile places where fans were far removed from the action and felt none of the sense of tradition of baseball passed on from generation to generation.

Next came the domes, starting with the Houston Astrodome in 1965, followed by the Kingdome in Seattle in 1977 and the Hubert H. Humphrey Metrodome in Minneapolis in 1982. Out of this generation of ballparks, Kansas City's Royals Stadium in 1972 stands out as the only baseball-only ballpark built during that time.

Then two stadiums came along that have their own place in tracing the path of ballpark development, for different reasons. SkyDome in Toronto is the home of the Blue Jays, and new Comiskey Park in Chicago is the home of the White Sox.

SkyDome opened in 1989, and it was a mechanical, if not architectural, marvel. It was the first stadium with a retractable roof, allowing baseball to be played in the open air as well as protected from severe weather conditions. The roof featured a series of three movable panels and one stationary panel. When the roof opens, panels two and three slide on parallel rails while panel one slides on a circular rail tucking underneath two and three. The roof operates on a system of steel tracks and fifty-four drive mechanisms called "bogies," and it is powered by a series of motors that generate more than 750 horsepower. The roof is 339,343 square feet and weighs 11,000 tons. It takes approximately twenty minutes to open or close.

Other than the roof, SkyDome offered nothing particularly unique. It is a comfortable ballpark with high-tech amenities: the largest video screen in North America, restaurants, and a hotel looking out onto the field. It was later considered Toronto's biggest white elephant, at an estimated cost of more than $500 million for the entire complex. This was nearly three times the amount of original estimates. SkyDome's place in ballpark development, though, comes from the working concept of a retractable roof. Ten years would pass before another one was built—Bank One Ballpark in Phoenix—but others will follow in Milwaukee and Seattle, and more may be on the way.

Comiskey Park—the new one—has its place in ballpark history for one reason and one only: it stands out in the new wave of ballpark development, an aberration that has resulted in scorn and none of the warm feelings that Camden Yards and others have created. The new Comiskey has none of the distinctive features of the traditional, old-fashioned ballparks that have energized the game. It now sits empty most nights on the south side of Chicago, the ultimate contrast to the glorious baseball palace it competes with on the north side, Wrigley Field.

New Comiskey looks and feels more like a ballpark of the 1960s rather than having the retro look of the 1990s. No one is following the Comiskey Park blueprint. What is remarkable about new Comiskey are these two facts: it was designed by HOK, the same architects who designed Camden Yards, and it started construction just one month before Camden Yards did and finished a year before the Baltimore ballpark was done. "New Comiskey, it's genealogy is about equal to Camden Yards, but it is so much different a building," said Tigers president McHale. "Camden Yards is so much more attractive and better for the game."

Orioles vice chairman Joe Foss was blunt when asked about comparing the two ballparks built so close to the same time. "For one thing, it's not in the loop of Chicago," Foss said. "The facility is very unexciting architecturally. It's cold and it's stark. The upper deck is at such a pitch to make people feel uncomfortable about just sitting up there, let alone walking to and from their seats. They have been unable to fill out their club-level and suite-level seats in a city with Fortune 500 companies. Why? Because the park is nothing special." New Comiskey does have the exploding scoreboard transported from old Comiskey Park. But it doesn't belong.

When they were planning Jacobs Field, another HOK facility, the inspiration was Camden Yards, but the design was made with Cleveland in mind. Although Cuyahoga County voters turned down a property tax increase in 1984 for a proposed domed stadium, in May 1990 they approved an alcohol and cigarette tax to help fund the Gateway Sports and Entertainment Complex, which includes Jacobs Field and Gund Arena, the new home of the Cleveland Cavaliers. The ballpark opened at the start of the 1994 season, and its impact on the city and the Cleveland Indians franchise was remarkable. The Indians were historically one of the most pathetic franchises in the American League, and the city had a reputation to match that, often referred to as "the Mistake by the Lake." Jacobs Field had much to do with turning the city into a economic force and changing its image to a place where people wanted to come.

The new ballpark also coincided with the rise of the team's fortunes, from a cellar dweller to a division winner, thanks to the blueprint by owner Richard Jacobs and general manager John Hart, who developed a strong crop of young players in their minor league system and then signed these future stars, including Kenny Lofton, Jim Thome, and Manny Ramirez to long-term contracts. This set the stage for a winning team to take the field when Jacobs Field opened. The Indians were 76–86 in 1993, their last year at cavernous Cleveland Stadium. The following year, their first at Jacobs Field, they posted a 66–47 record in the strike-shortened season—their first winning record since 1986 and only their seventh in twenty years—and have not had a losing season since.

"The two most important areas are image and economics," said Indians vice president Bob DiBiasio. "From an image standpoint, it put a whole new, fresh, state-of-the-art, modernistic, first-class feel to what this organization wanted to accomplish when it walked away from Cleveland Stadium. That, first and foremost, in one stroke gave us a whole new appeal, both internally and externally. When you talk about image, most people think it is how you are perceived from the outside, but they forget it is how you are perceived from the inside as well. The ballpark changed everything, the whole face of how we do business, how we are perceived, how we feel about ourselves. That was a major positive impact on our business approach.

"Then economically it has provided for us the foundation to compete in major league baseball with the big boys," DiBiasio continued. "This facility has provided the wherewithal for us to compete for the star players." It most certainly has. The Indians have had 292 straight sellouts in the 43,368-seat ballpark, with a waiting list for season tickets and for the 125 luxury boxes. According to Cleveland city officials, the team, with the 1997 All-Star Game and the post-season games at Jacobs Field, had an economic impact of $142 million.

The $170 million ballpark itself is located in downtown Cleveland surrounded by Ontario, Carnegie, and East 9th streets. It is an urban ballpark that blends in with the city skyline, which is the view out past center field. The exposed steel design matches many of the city's bridges, and the vertical light towers match the smokestacks of the city's industrial personality. The field is 18 feet below sea level and, like the old ballparks, is asymmetrical: 325

feet down the left-field line, 370 feet in left center, 410 in the far-thest part in center field, 405 feet in dead center, and again 325 feet down the right-field line. Like Camden Yards' Eutaw Street, Jacobs Field has a plaza beyond the left-field wall where fans gather—and scatter when a home run lands there. The ballpark has borrowed a page from Fenway Park, with a 19-foot-high ver-sion of the Green Monster in left field, which also has the out-of-town scoreboard. Above the wall are the bleachers. Above them is what the Indians say is the largest free-standing scoreboard in the United States, measuring 120 feet high by 220 feet wide.

Those are the numbers and features that make up Jacobs Field. How Cleveland feels about itself these days as a result of the ball-park cannot be measured. "The image of this facility and the team being good, what it has done for our city and how people perceive Cleveland these days, is a whole lot different from how it used to be perceived," DiBiasio said. "That is priceless."

None of this would have likely happened without Jacobs Field. "Without this ballpark there would be no major league baseball in Cleveland," DiBiasio said. "Baseball commissioner Fay Vincent held a press conference on the field at Cleveland Stadium and said pretty much that, if the referendum for the project did not pass, the fortunes of major league baseball in Cleveland are not on a solid ground as people would think. It was very tenuous. The oddity of all this is that if you had asked someone at that time which major league franchise would not be here in this town and which one would be and playing for a world championship, most people would have said the Indians will be out of town and the Browns will be playing in the Super Bowl. It just happened the exact opposite."

The irony of it is that the Browns moved to Baltimore because of the stadium deal offered there—all part of the Camden Yards blueprint that helped guide the development of Jacobs Field. "Camden Yards had a strong influence on us," DiBiasio said.

That same season, another new ballpark opened, this one lit-erally taking the idea of a ballpark, rather than a stadium, and using it for the name of the facility—The Ballpark in Arlington, home of the Texas Rangers. The Ballpark in Arlington is part of the same family that was born out of the success of Camden Yards. But although the concept may have been Camden Yards–driven, the ballpark is different in many ways from its brethren. First of all, there is the location. Unlike Camden Yards and Jacobs Field, The Ballpark in Arlington is not in an urban setting, neither in downtown Dallas or Fort Worth, the twin cities of the team's fan base. It is located in the suburban community of Arlington, next to an amusement park—hardly the sort of appealing center-field backdrop that makes the view from Camden Yards and Jacobs Field so scenic. Then again, there is no view in center field at The Ballpark in Arlington. Since there is nothing to look at, the ballpark is enclosed all the way around. Also, the ballpark, a $189 million project (which includes offices, an amphitheater, lakes, youth parks, restaurants, and other facilities besides the ballpark, which cost about $89 million of that figure) is not an HOK-designed facility. The architects were David M. Schwarz Architectural Services of Washington.

The 49,178-seat building is located just across from the old Arlington Stadium site. Like the others of the Camden Yards prototype, it is asymmetrical—possibly too much so, a forced attempt to be quirky, one of the criticisms of the new ballpark when compared to Camden Yards and Jacobs Field. The ballpark is 332 feet down the left-field line, increasing to 390 feet in the left-field power alley. Straightaway center is 400 feet, and right-center field is 407 feet. Continuing along the outfield, a 381-foot power alley changes to 377 feet at the right corner of the Rangers bullpen. The distance then drops off significantly to 325 feet down the right-field line.

The right-field seats are nearly a carbon copy of those in Tiger Stadium, with a double-decker home-run porch. This doesn't blend in well, though, with the Wrigley Field bleachers in center field and the manual Green Monster scoreboard from Fenway Park in left field. All of the new ballparks have borrowed from the old ones, but the transition from one feature to another just does-n't seem to work well at The Ballpark in Arlington. Given its sub-urban environment, it may just be the park's location that makes it difficult to conjure up images of Ebbets Field or even Fenway Park. The Ballpark in Arlington also has some distinctive features that fit the Texas image: a double-arched exterior with brick façade, a Southwest look with longhorn figures burnished into the brick, and the Texas granite that covers the bottom of the façade.

Although the park is in a difficult location, in a community where baseball has always played second fiddle to football, it has served its purpose well, providing a destination that draws people to it for something more than just a baseball game. It has a "Legends of the Game" baseball museum behind the right-field home-run porch, plus other amenities, and with 120 luxury boxes, the park provides the franchise with a steady stream of income to enable the team to compete and sign star ballplayers. It may not be Camden Yards, but it brings the Rangers Camden Yards results.

Perhaps the closest offspring of Camden Yards has been Coors Field, the Denver home of the Colorado Rockies, designed by HOK. Ballpark design consultant Philip Bess called Coors Field "The Ballpark in Arlington with good taste and urban context." Coors Field opened on April 26, 1995, the season that began late because of the baseball strike, and has been sold out on a regular basis ever since. Located on the corner of 20th and Blake streets, the ballpark served to revitalize this lower downtown section of Denver known as "LoDo." More than twenty-five restaurants have opened since 1993, and sixty-one liquor licenses have been granted within seven blocks of Coors Field between 1991 and 1997. People are moving to the district as well, with housing units in the surrounding area rising from 270 when the park opened to nearly 1,100, with more in the works.

"Coors Field shifted the whole downtown area of Denver to the lower downtown," said Rockies owner Jerry McMorris. "We have had an impact of more than $50 million a year in the lower downtown area. Coors Field has become the number one venue in the Rocky Mountain area, where people get together and have a great time."

The $215 million red-brick ballpark blends in with both the gritty city and the view of the Rocky Mountains from the first base and right-field side of the ballpark. The building materials used included a red-brick façade that matches the look of the old warehouses in the lower downtown district and natural sandstone from a Colorado quarry. "We wanted an open-air, grass ballpark that would fit into lower downtown Denver in a 1920s period," McMorris said. "We made the ballpark look old, but with all the latest technology and modern conveniences. It was also important that the ballpark have a great view of the mountains."

The ballpark has the required manual scoreboard and left-field bleachers to replicate the old ballpark era, and modern conveniences such as a waterfall feature added before the start of the 1997 season to recreate a Colorado landscape. When the Rockies take the field, hit a home run, or win a game, seven water jets explode into the air for thirty seconds from a retaining pond at the bottom of the waterfall. The home runs come often.

One of the quirks of the ballpark is that with its intimate design and dimensions, it has become a home-run haven, with a record total of 222 home runs hit there in 81 games in 1997. The home runs will sometimes land in a place in center field known as "The Rockpile," a section designed to keep baseball affordable. Here admission costs $4, but $1 for children age twelve and under and for senior citizens fifty-five and older.

Coors Field was financed by an increase in the six-county metropolitan area of 0.1 percent in the sales tax. The park followed the tremendous success of the expansion Rockies franchise at Mile High Stadium, where they drew 4.4 million fans in their first season in 1993 and 3.3 million fans in just thirty-two home dates in the strike-shortened season of 1994, averaging 57,000 fans a game in those two seasons at Mile High. Those attendance figures resulted in numerous revisions in the plans for Coors Field, from a capacity of 41,000 in the initial plans to 43,500, then 45,500, and finally 50,381, with fifty-eight luxury boxes. Its dimensions are 347 feet down the left-field line, 415 feet in straightaway center, and 350 feet down the right-field line. The playing field is 21 feet below street level. The twentieth-row seats in the upper deck are purple, representing a mile above sea level.

Ironically, the man who is overseeing the replacement of Tiger Stadium in Detroit—the real thing, an old-style ballpark—with a new ballpark there, John McHale, was the chairman of the Stadium District in Denver and helped push forward Coors Field, resisting pressure from some of the city's business leaders to put the ballpark at another location.

McMorris also acknowledges the decisions about site and design on Coors Field are beholden to the success of Camden Yards. "It was the model we were looking at," he said. "If it had not been successful, I think it [Coors Field] would be different."

Two years later, another new baseball park opened, this one a whole different animal, with its only predecessor a disaster—Turner Field, the new home of the Atlanta Braves. After Fulton County Stadium closed following the 1996 season, the Braves moved across the street to a ballpark that was given to them, but they did not have the same input in design and construction that other teams with 1990s ballparks did. Turner Field was Olympic Stadium for the 1996 Olympic games, the place where Michael Johnson made history. The Atlanta Olympic Committee then turned over the $250 million stadium to the Atlanta-Fulton County Stadium Authority and its tenant, the Braves. This presented a challenge that teams like the Orioles and Indians did not face in the development of their ballparks. The last time an Olympic stadium was used for a baseball field was Montreal's Olympic Stadium after the 1976 games, and that facility has nearly driven the Expos out of Montreal.

But Braves general manager Stan Kasten and later Janet Marie Smith, who helped oversee the construction of Camden Yards for the Orioles and was now vice president of development in Atlanta, worked to try to make sure that, as much as possible, the retrofitting of Olympic Stadium into a ballpark would closely follow the Camden Yards blueprint for success. "The stadium has the luxury of being designed as a baseball park while it was on the drawing board," Smith said. "So some of the things that might have made us all cringe at the idea that we might have another Olympic stadium like the one in Montreal were averted by Stan Kasten's firm hand at the table. Stan had the audacity, it might have been seen at the time, to say on the one hand don't look a gift horse in the mouth, but on the other hand if the teeth are not good, I don't want it. The city and the Olympic committee worked with the Braves to make certain that when it was being designed that things would be compromised for the Olympics for the sake of making it a great baseball park."

The exterior of the 50,528-seat ballpark follows the Camden Yards pattern: the old-fashioned look, with steel trusses and a masonry façade featuring red shades of brick on a stone base with arches at each opening. The look from the inside, though, does not quite measure up to Camden Yards, Jacobs Field, or Coors Field. The park is only slightly asymmetrical. The dimensions are 335 feet down left field, 401 feet in straightaway center, and 330 feet down the right-field line. There is no downtown skyline view because Turner Field is not located in the heart of Atlanta's downtown, a drawback to the location. So it was up to the Braves to come up with characteristics to add to the park to make it unique, to give it the attraction as a destination. "The biggest challenge was trying to give the place some personality, some character," Smith said. "While it is unfortunate that though it is downtown, it doesn't have the same kind of urban pressures that give Camden Yards and Coors Field character. From a design perspective, what we had to do is think about how to pepper the ballpark with uses and with fun things on the inside that would extend one's knowledge, pleasure, and interest in being at the park and being part of the game. That was harder than at Camden Yards, where all of that came very naturally and easily because of the site we were on."

One way they did that was creating an entertainment center at the entry plaza on the north side of the ballpark beyond the center field fence. It includes such features as the Braves Museum and Hall of Fame, Monument Grove, a Kids Zone play section, and an area known as "Scouts Alley," an exhibit that features life-size visuals of popular Braves players and their actual original scouting reports, as well as skills games and interactive activities. The plaza also features a video wall displaying every major league game in progress.

Atlanta fans may demand even more from their ballpark. They failed to sell out several of their 1998 playoff games at Turner Field, with just 42,000 showing up for one game.

Monument Grove includes a statue of Hank Aaron, but the one monument that many Atlanta fans wanted for Aaron—his name on the ballpark—went instead to Braves owner Ted Turner, who gave the credit to Time-Warner chairman Gerald Levin. "I wouldn't have done it myself," Turner said. "And I wasn't going to do it. I really didn't know what to do. I was more than happy to call it Olympic Stadium. I didn't want to sell the name. I was kind of blown away when Gerry Levin announced the name. I feel greatly honored."

There were no such sentiments in Phoenix when the expansion Arizona Diamondbacks and their owner, Jerry Colangelo, sold the rights for the name to their new ballpark to Bank One, which opened at the start of the 1998 season. With $75 million in cost overruns, raising the cost of the ballpark to $350 million, with primary funding from a sales tax increase, no revenue sources could be wasted on sentiment. Then again, it costs a lot of money to build a retractable-roof ballpark with a swimming pool inside.

Bank One is no Camden Yards, nor was it meant to be. There is no rich tradition of major league baseball in Phoenix, no gritty urban area to feed off of, though the park does have a nice feature from the old ballparks of the dirt pathway between home plate and the pitcher's mound. Ellerbe Becket, Inc., the Kansas City architectural firm and HOK rival, instead opted to try to emphasize a Phoenix-style look, using construction materials similar to those found around the warehouse district. But what makes Bank One unique is its state-of-the-art, ballpark-technology roof, leading the way for a string of new ballparks to come with retractable domes. The Bank One sliding roof is similar to that of a collapsible bill cup. Each piece slides over another smaller piece when the cup retracts, taking just five minutes to open or close. This is a dramatic improvement over SkyDome in Toronto, although there have been complaints that the roof leaked.

The ballpark's dimensions are 330 feet down the left-field line, 407 feet to center field, 413 feet at the deepest part of the ballpark, and 334 feet down right field. Bank One has a capacity of 49,779, with sixty-nine private luxury suites. It has its share of restaurants and other amenities, which are now required to draw people into today's ballparks. But the unique attraction is the pool pavilion, a swimming pool located in the lower-level seating in right field, rented on a per-game basis for groups up to thirty people.

Although not in the Camden Yards image, Bank One may set new standards for financial, if not architectural, success. According to *The Sports Business Journal*, the Diamondbacks' revenues are projected to rise to $134 million by 2003, when profits are expected to reach $22.2 million, even after the $11.2 million annual debt service is paid.

The Diamondbacks' fellow expansion team, the Tampa Bay Devil Rays, also played in a domed stadium in their inaugural 1998 season. But, unfortunately for the Devil Rays, they played in a facility that was ready to open in 1990, and unlike SkyDome, it wasn't the retractable kind.

The $138 million Florida Suncoast Dome opened in March 1990—with no baseball team. Government officials had built the ballpark with the hopes of attracting a major league franchise, but it wound up being the biggest white elephant in sports.

Baseball franchises used St. Petersburg as a threat to get their own stadium projects or other financing deals until finally, in March 1995, owner Vince Naomoli was awarded an American League expansion franchise. Baseball owners made this backdoor deal to avoid protracted lawsuits as a result of major league baseball blocking the sale of the San Francisco Giants to a Tampa Bay group in 1992.

The ballpark was used for monster car shows, Arena football, track meets, figure-skating competitions—anything to keep it from sitting there empty, reminding everyone every day of the ballpark they did not have. The name was changed to the ThunderDome in 1993 when the National Hockey League's expansion franchise, the Tampa Bay Lightning, began playing there. It was renamed Tropicana Field when the Devil Rays made a deal with Tropicana Dole Beverages in 1996 for the naming rights.

Tropicana Field was an appropriate name for this facility, because another $85 million was spent trying to turn this lemon into lemonade. They made the most of it, trying to bring some flavor of the traditional, old-style formula with its eight-story rotunda entrance, which was designed from the blueprints used in the rotunda at Ebbets Field. The park's field is asymmetrical— 315 feet down the left-field line, 415 feet in left center field, 407 feet in straightaway center, 409 feet in right center field, and 322 feet down the right-field line. The ballpark also has tried to blend in some Florida features, with tile walkways depicting the sun, sea, and beach, and an upper-deck area in left field known as "The Beach," an effort to build their own Florida version of the Wrigley Field bleacher bums. Tropicana Field has all the bells and whistles of a destination spot: specialty restaurants, interactive games, even computer screens in seats behind the home-plate area that allow fans to access the telecast or statistics.

But the ballpark is still a relic, a domed stadium whose time has come and gone. Even with all the window dressing, it doesn't compete with the Camden Yards wave of ballpark design. The

Devil Rays drew just 2.5 million fans in their first season, compared to 3.6 million by their Arizona counterparts. If you factor in the novelty of the team's first year, it adds up to very little interest in making the trip to Tropicana Field. Devil Rays owners are taking steps to draw more people in 1999. For example, they have dropped some of their ticket prices—not exactly the sort of results that these new ballparks are supposed to bring about.

Another refurbished ballpark that made its debut in 1998 was Edison International Field of Dreams, formerly known as Anaheim Stadium, the home of the Anaheim Angels. The team's new owners, Disney Corporation, spent $117 million on renovations to the thirty-two-year-old facility, using HOK to come up with a design to modernize the park and give it a more intimate feel. The owners tore down some of the outfield seating, creating a window out onto the mountains in the distance and reducing the capacity from 65,000 to 45,050. With the Disney touch ever present, the company added interactive video games and the requisite restaurants, including the Diamond Club, which has tables in a patio area just eighteen rows behind home plate. With a display of large bats and caps 42 feet high decorating the home-plate entrance to the park, and with the rock formation and water fountains beyond the left-center outfield wall, the park looks like something out of a Disney theme park. Edison International Field of Dreams is asymmetrical—330 feet down the left-field line, 396 feet down the left-field power alley, 370 feet down the right-field alley, and 408 feet out to center field.

The ballpark brought in fans, with attendance rising from 1.7 million to 2.5 million in 1998, as the Angels competed down to the wire for a playoff position. Edison drew rave reviews when it opened, and one *Orange County Register* columnist called it "Camden Yards West," although that is not quite accurate. Edison Field does not conjure up images of baseball past. But it does make the high costs of going to the ballpark an experience beyond that of the game—the other part of the Camden Yards equation.

The ballpark craze kicked off by the Camden Yards success will explode when the new ballparks in Seattle, Milwaukee, San Francisco, Detroit, and Houston open. Three of them—Milwaukee, Seattle, and Houston—will have retractable domes.

The San Francisco Giants, who have played in the flawed former Candlestick Park (now called 3Com Park since 1960) will be moving into the new 42,000-seat Pacific Bell ballpark. When they were the New York Giants, the team played in one of the great old parks, the Polo Grounds. The new ballpark in San Francisco is being designed by HOK, and its location along the waterfront in the China Basin has exciting potential. Former owner Bob Lurie endured many failed efforts to get government funding for a new ballpark for the Giants, two times in San Francisco and two more in Santa Clara and San Jose. He threatened to move the team many times. But the Giants, under owner Peter McGowan, came up with a private financing plan that consisted of selling personal seat licenses, securing long-term sponsorship deals, and agreeing to take on the remaining debt for the $306 million ballpark.

Giants vice president Larry Barr has no qualms in saying what they hope to build in San Francisco: another Camden Yards, but with a San Francisco personality. "We wanted an intimate downtown ballpark that we called Camden Yards meets Wrigley Field," he said. "It will have a heavy San Francisco flavor to it. Behind the right-field fence next to the water there will be portholes where fans can look in and watch a game free, like the old Knothole Gang. We expect kids in inner tubes and rafts with baseball gloves in the water catching home runs. But the old-fashioned style that HOK's Joe Spear and Larry Lucchino and everyone else who did such a great job with Camden Yards is the plan adopted by us."

Commissioner Bud Selig owned the Milwaukee Brewers until he turned over control of the team last year to his daughter shortly after being named permanent commissioner. But before he left, he engineered the drive for a new $250 million retractable-dome ballpark for the Brewers called Miller Park. Unlike San Francisco, Selig relied heavily on public funding, as he fought a bitter battle with government officials to get $160 million through an increase of one-tenth of the sales tax in five Milwaukee-area counties.

Like every baseball owner facing a stadium funding fight, Selig maintained that the future of the franchise in Milwaukee rested on the fate of the new ballpark. He still believes this. "Without a new ballpark, we couldn't survive there," Selig said. "You need a ballpark to produce the revenue streams you need to be competitive. The battle for Miller Park was for the survival of the team here."

That talk hit home. Milwaukee had lost the Braves after the 1965 season when the franchise moved to Atlanta. Selig's tireless efforts enabled the city to secure another franchise when his ownership group was awarded the ill-fated Seattle Pilots in bankruptcy court. They began playing in County Stadium in 1970, which is right next to the location for the new 43,000-seat ballpark, which, with seventy private luxury suites, will bring the Selig family that revenue stream they could never have at County Stadium. The new park will call on baseball tradition with some of its design, but its location, outside downtown Milwaukee, means it will be missing the urban-center factor of the successful formula. "Every city is different," Selig said. "We are about six minutes from downtown."

The Seattle Mariners' new ballpark—Safeco Field, also a retractable dome, but not totally sealing the ballpark from the temperatures—will be downtown. This $417 million complex will include a parking garage and 45,000 seats. Safeco Field will very much follow the urban-ballpark plan of Camden Yards, with red brick and green steel, an asymmetrical field—331 feet down the left-field line, 407 feet to center field, and 324 feet in right field—and all of the necessary attractions.

The interesting part about how the Seattle ballpark came to be is that the Mariners literally played their way into a new park.

Voters had turned down a proposed sales tax increase in 1995, and owners said the team was going to be put up for sale to out-of-town buyers. But the Mariners put on a late-season rally and made the playoffs as the wild-card team, creating a wave of momentum that resulted in state legislators bypassing the defeated referendum and coming up with their own financing plan for the ballpark.

The park will have a tremendous effect on baseball in Seattle. The Mariners have lost more than $80 million over the last six years playing in the Kingdome, possibly the worst baseball facility in the American League. That dreary, soulless place built in 1972 had to be shut down in July 1994 for the rest of the strike-shortened season when four ceiling tiles fell before a game against, ironically, the Camden Yards tenants, the Baltimore Orioles.

In Houston, the Astros' situation was a little different than that of the Mariners. Their owner, Drayton McLane, frustrated in his efforts to increase attendance and get a commitment for a new ballpark from government officials, had sold the team in the fall of 1995 to a group of Northern Virginia businessmen. They wanted to move the team to the Washington area, which has not had major league baseball since the Washington Senators left after the 1971 season for Arlington, Texas. But baseball did not want to abandon the Houston market and killed the deal. Houston officials responded by agreeing to build a $265 million retractable-roof ballpark in downtown Houston, with $180 million in public funds and the rest from the Astros and other sources.

The 42,000-seat ballpark will be about 7 miles away from the Astrodome, next to Union Station, a 1911 railroad station; it will be called The Ballpark at Union Station. Another HOK-designed facility, it will accentuate the urban Texas atmosphere of Texas Avenue, one of the city's most historic streets, and will offer a view of the Houston skyline when it opens next season. The ballpark's dimensions will be 315 feet down left field, 435 to center field, and 326 down the right-field line. The park will have a left-field scoreboard wall measuring 21 feet high, and natural grass, not artificial turf.

While the Astros will leave the Astrodome behind, it is worth noting the significance of the ballpark that was touted as one of the "Wonders of the World" when it first opened on April, 9, 1965. After all, it was the world's first all-weather, multi-purpose, domed stadium. It was the pioneer of the domed-stadium and artificial-turf movements. Although these two developments would fly in the face of the intimacy and character that baseball thrives on, they are still significant developments in the evolution of the ballpark.

The Pittsburgh Pirates will have their own version of Camden Yards when their HOK-designed, 38,000-seat ballpark on the Allegheny River opens in the spring of 2001. This $230 million facility will be paid for with sales and hotel taxes, ticket surcharges, state funding, and private investments. Unlike Three Rivers Stadium, the sterile cookie-cutter home of the Pirates since 1970, whose enclosed situation gives fans no sense of where they are, the new ballpark, next to the Sixth Street Bridge, will offer a view of the city's downtown skyline and will strive to bring back the memories of Forbes Field.

Like Seattle, voters in Pittsburgh and the surrounding communities turned down a proposed sales tax increase to pay for the Pirates ballpark and a new stadium for the Pittsburgh Steelers. As in Seattle, government officials came up with a new financing plan, bypassed voters the second time, and approved the funding for both facilities.

The Camden Yards influence doesn't stop at these projects, though. Most of the remaining major league franchises that haven't built a new ballpark in the past ten years or have one in the pipeline are making noises about building their own version of Camden Yards. For example, in Montreal, the future of the Expos hangs in the balance of their efforts to get a new 37,000-seat, retractable-dome, downtown ballpark built there. The team, with an $11 million payroll last season, still lost $20 million, drawing a little more than 11,000 fans per game at Olympic Stadium, the lowest figures in major league baseball. The team's fund-raising efforts for the proposed $250 million (Canadian) ballpark failed; they were able to bring in just $40 million of the $100 million in private financing they sought through the sale of personal seat licenses, and got no commitment for $150 million in government financing they sought. The club was nearly put up for sale to out-of-town buyers in October, but some of the club's owners made an agreement with major league baseball to delay any sale until they could come up with a plan for new local investors for the team and a new ballpark plan. In June, Montreal officials came to Camden Yards for a first-hand tour to see how successful the Baltimore ballpark has been.

In San Diego, Padres president Larry Lucchino, the driving force behind Camden Yards, is leading a drive for another new ballpark. This 41,000-seat, HOK-designed, $270 million park is part of a $410 million downtown redevelopment project near San Diego Bay.

In Cincinnati, the Reds have a deal for a $235 million, 45,000-seat ballpark along the river in the Queen City. But it won't be Riverfront Stadium. It will follow the Camden Yards plan, including an HOK design, on a site on the west side of the Suspension Bridge downtown. The Reds have hopes of opening the ballpark by spring of 2002.

The Minnesota Twins were nearly sold last year to Don Beaver, who wanted to move the team to the Triad area of North Carolina. Twins owner Carl Pohlad said they could not continue to operate at the Metrodome without a new ballpark, but those pleas fell on the deaf ears of Minnesota politicians. They called Pohlad's bluff and dared him to try to move the team. Pohlad backed down, signing a two-year lease and agreeing to try to find a local buyer for the team. But it appears inevitable that even though the Metrodome is hardly an old facility—it opened in 1982—the Twins will need a new ballpark to survive in

Minnesota and compete against all the other franchises with their own versions of Camden Yards.

The future of another franchise, the Florida Marlins, also hinges on whether or not they can get government financial backing for a retractable-dome downtown ballpark in Miami. So far the existence of the expansion Marlins, who have played in Pro Player Stadium, a football facility, since they first took the field in 1993, has been chaotic. Owner Wayne Huizenga went on an $89 million spending spree to bring in free agents like Bobby Bonilla and Moises Alou to buy a World Championship in 1997. But because of poor attendance and failure to get support for a new ballpark, Huizenga dismantled the team in 1998, trading all of the big-name players and reducing the payroll to less than $10 million. He sold the club to John Henry, a minority investor in the New York Yankees, who is sending the same message: the fate of the franchise depends on a new ballpark.

The pressure for new ballparks has even raised the prospect of new ballparks to replace two of the legendary places in the game—Dodger Stadium and Yankee Stadium. Dodger Stadium, built by the late Walter O' Malley shortly after he moved the franchise from Brooklyn, has been the envy of other baseball franchises ever since it opened in 1962. In the era of multi-purpose, cavernous facilities that followed, the 56,000-seat Dodger Stadium stood out as a pristine, baseball-only facility, owned and operated by the Dodgers, with a view of the San Gabriel Mountains past the outfield. But a shockwave went through baseball in March 1998, when Peter O' Malley sold the team for $311 million to Rupert Murdoch's Fox Group. Shortly after that, Fox officials examined how to renovate Dodger Stadium to create more luxury boxes and other revenue and found that it may cost nearly as much as building a new ballpark.

Back in New York, the Camden Yards impact is being felt by both the Yankees and the New York Mets. The Mets are hoping to build a $500 million, 45,000-seat, retractable-dome ballpark next to Shea Stadium in Queens in the image of Ebbets Field. No one is outraged about leaving thirty-five-year-old Shea Stadium behind.

There have been howls from owner George Steinbrenner's threats to move the Yankees to New Jersey unless a new ballpark is built for his team on the west side of Manhattan, a plan supported by New York mayor Rudy Giuliani. Steinbrenner has turned down suggestions to renovate the 76-year-old legendary ballpark. All of this controversy can be laid at the foot of the success of Camden Yards. Steinbrenner wants his own Camden Yards, and in October, Bronx Borough President Fernando Ferrer offered a $500 million plan that would refurbish historic Yankee Stadium, turning it into—yes—Camden Yards.

"Yankee Stadium is the most historic baseball venue in America," Ferrer said. "The Yankees belong here. You want Camden Yards? You've got it right here."

CHAPTER FIVE

Lucchino's Vision

Larry Lucchino dreamed about a lot of things when he was a ten-year-old kid sitting in the stands at Forbes Field, watching his Pittsburgh Pirates. He dreamed of playing second base like Bill Mazeroski. He dreamed of hitting a ball like Roberto Clemente. He didn't dream of building another Forbes Field.

But Lucchino did just that. He built a modern-day version of Forbes Field, Ebbets Field, Wrigley Park, and other baseball palaces when he forged the vision for Camden Yards, and he had as much impact on the game as most Hall of Fame players. The planning and development of Camden Yards formed a watershed in the history of the game. In Baltimore, Maryland, baseball discovered a way to breathe new life into the national pastime and pump new blood into a hemorrhaging business. If Camden Yards has been the stage for baseball, Larry Lucchino helped create the theater.

Numerous individuals contributed to the success of Camden Yards: Edward Bennett Williams pushed the need for a new ballpark, Governor William Donald Schaefer battled for the Camden

Yards location, Maryland Stadium Authority chairman Herb Belgrad campaigned to keep the B&O Warehouse, and Orioles vice president of planning and development Janet Marie Smith did research on ballparks of days past and how those touches could be implemented at Camden Yards.

But one person was the consistent, driving force behind the ballpark project, and that was Lucchino. "Larry has never gotten the credit that he earned and deserved," said Belgrad, who was the chairman of the Maryland Stadium Authority during the Camden Yards process. "It was Larry who initiated the whole idea of the design of the stadium, even though he wasn't an architect. And it was Larry who pushed hard through to achieve a lot of what we achieved.

"It was Larry who initially used the term 'traditional, old-fashioned ballpark," Belgrad continued. "He had it in the very first memorandum of understanding. It was Larry who was in on every negotiating session that I ever participated in. It was Larry who led the fights for steel versus concrete. He's not an architect, and I don't think he tried to take any credit architecturally. Joe Spear [of HOK] deserves an awful lot of credit, and I don't think he has gotten as much credit as he is entitled to. But Larry was the moving force. There were different people involved throughout this—different owners, different negotiators—but Larry was the constant."

Who deserved the credit was a touchy issue when Camden Yards opened in 1992. Orioles owner Eli Jacobs took a lot of the credit, and vice president Janet Marie Smith received a huge amount of credit. But years later Smith said Lucchino deserved much of the credit for the vision of the ballpark. "Larry's inspiration and continual push to do this old-fashioned, traditional ballpark with modern amenities was one of the most significant things that made Camden Yards what it is," said Smith, who now works for the Atlanta Braves as the vice president of development. "He had this idea, and he had it in a sound bite, so that by the end of the project it might as well have been tattooed on our heads."

Lucchino nearly drilled his idea into the heads of everyone with the Orioles who was involved in the ballpark project. "We fined people who used the S [stadium] word," Lucchino said. "It so caught on that the next ballpark that was built after ours— Texas—they liked the term so much that they used it in the name of their facility," Lucchino noted, referring to The Ballpark in Arlington. "There is a real difference between a ballpark and a stadium," he continued. "Ballparks are smaller, more intimate, and not necessarily built of concrete. You don't play football or soccer in them. Stadiums are larger, generally concrete, built for football or soccer, combination-purpose stadiums. We truly would fine people $5 if they used the S word."

The seed may have been planted back in his Forbes Field days in Pittsburgh, though Lucchino's visions in those days were that of an athlete. He was an All-City basketball player and a second baseman on the city championship baseball team at Taylor Allderdice High School. He would go on to play basketball at Princeton University, playing on two Ivy League championship teams coached by Butch Van Breda Koff; Lucchino's senior-year team went 25–3, the school's best record until the 1997–1998 season. As a sophomore, Lucchino was a teammate of former U.S. Senator and New York Knicks great Bill Bradley in the year Princeton went to the final four.

Lucchino's future, though, was in law. His brother Frank became a prominent Pittsburgh attorney and controller for Allegheny County, and Lucchino, after graduating with honors from Princeton in 1967, went on to Yale Law School, where he earned his law degree in 1972.

Just a month later, five burglars broke into the Democratic National Headquarters offices at the Watergate office complex in Washington, DC. It was just a short story in *The Washington Post* the next day, but it would wind up being an influential moment in Lucchino's life. The Watergate break-in and cover-up would ultimately become one of the biggest stories of the twentieth century, sending some of the highest-ranking government officials to jail and forcing President Richard Nixon to resign. Shortly after graduating from law school, Lucchino went to work for the Senate Watergate impeachment committee. He never got to complete his work, however, because Nixon resigned on August 9, 1974.

Lucchino had another Watergate connection. The legal advisor for *The Washington Post* through its Watergate coverage was Edward Bennett Williams, perhaps the most famous trial lawyer of the twentieth century. When Lucchino was out of work after Nixon left office, he wanted to go work for Williams and his firm. "It was a litigation firm, and that was something I was interested in, and it was a firm that had a different kind of client base— newspapers, sports figures, and the like. They did criminal work, and it seemed like an interesting firm to work for."

That is an understatement. Williams represented some of the most powerful and colorful people in the country, and would be on most lists for the most important and interesting people of the twentieth century. He represented such historic figures as Jimmy Hoffa, Joe McCarthy, Robert Vesco, and George Steinbrenner. Williams was a key advisor for *The Washington Post* during its battles with the Nixon administration over the Pentagon Papers and Watergate, and was also asked by both Gerald Ford and Ronald Reagan to run the CIA. He was gregarious and colorful, but he was also volatile, demanded excellence, and was fiercely loyal.

Those latter qualities could be used to describe Lucchino, which is no surprise. You don't work for a man like Edward Bennett Williams for fourteen years and not be strongly influenced by him. You also don't work as closely as Lucchino did with Williams all that time and not have something in common. "I learned a lot from him about management, politics, religion, law, life, humor, etc., etc.," Lucchino said. "He dwarfed most of us who worked around him and with him, and yet he was such a great guy to work for because he was such a good guy. You could argue with him and then at the end of the day go out and have a drink with him."

Williams was also in the forefront in the sports world as owner of the Washington Redskins. Lucchino shared his passion for sports, and this connection would bring the two men together. "Williams came into my office the first day I was there," Lucchino said. "We talked for about two hours, about everything under the sun, especially sports. It was clear he was a great sportsman. He knew that I had played college basketball, and I started talking about Pittsburgh sports, and he knew the Rooneys [the family that owned the Pittsburgh Steelers]. I remember thinking, my first day, the senior partner comes in and we sit around talking about baseball and football. It's a hell of a place. Little did I realize how rigorous and demanding the job would be."

Lucchino's sports background appealed to Williams, and the legendary trial lawyer began looking to Lucchino more and more to do work for the Redskins. First Lucchino began handling legal issues concerning the team, and was eventually named general counsel to the team. He later began getting administrative assignments from Williams, such as negotiating radio contracts and other issues.

Even though Lucchino had worked on the Senate Watergate Committee, working for the Redskins was probably one of the most glamorous jobs in Washington, DC. The franchise had been a perennial loser until Williams convinced Vince Lombardi to leave Green Bay and come to Washington. Lombardi would coach for only one season, 1969, succumbing to cancer the following year. But he energized the franchise with a winning season in his only year and set the tone for a change in direction for the team. This was picked up two years later by George Allen, who built the "Over the Hill Gang" that transformed the Redskins from a franchise with a core loyal following to the city's obsession.

For someone who grew up as a sports fanatic, being an integral part of this high-profile franchise should have been the culmination of a career for Lucchino. But it was just the beginning. Williams purchased the Orioles team from Jerry Hoffberger on August 2, 1979, for $12 million. The purchase was controversial because Orioles fans feared that Williams, a Washington fixture, had intended to move the team to the District, which had not had major league baseball since the Washington Senators left for Arlington, Texas, after the 1971 season. "I'm positive that Edward Bennett Williams was going to move the team to Washington," said former Maryland governor William Donald Schaefer. "There was no question about it. He had made up his mind." But Orioles fans began turning out in record numbers at Memorial Stadium, and Williams began to fall in love with Baltimore. If he could get a new ballpark, he would keep the club in Baltimore.

To help run the franchise, Williams turned to Lucchino, who had handled some of the acquisition of the team for him. Lucchino recalls the conversation with Williams. "He said, 'You know a lot of this stuff. Many of the issues will be the same, so why don't you handle both?' So I became general counsel of both the Redskins and the Orioles in 1979, and I did both jobs until 1985, when he sold his interests in the Redskins," Lucchino said. "It all happened fortuitously. It was not planned. I wanted to go to an interesting law firm that had a great reputation."

In 1985, Lucchino was on the board of directors of both the Redskins and the Orioles, but was becoming much more involved in the Orioles operations. "I was doing contract negotiations, player negotiations, radio and television stuff, moving from the legal world to the business world." Even though the Orioles would not move to Washington, DC, one of Williams and Lucchino's objectives was to market the team regionally, pushing sales in the Washington area. This proved to be a successful strategy. Today the Orioles claim that of the 3.6 million fans they draw to Camden Yards, 25 percent come from the Washington, DC, area.

Lucchino soon faced his greatest challenge. Williams started looking into a new ballpark for the Orioles the day after he bought the team in 1979. Several days after the purchase of the team went through, Lucchino was on vacation in Martha's Vineyard. There, he got a call to come back to help look for a site for a new ballpark. It would become Lucchino's quest.

Williams was battling cancer during his years as the Orioles owner, and it would slowly take its toll on him. In a cruel, ironic coincidence, Lucchino also developed cancer, non-Hodgkins lymphoma, one of the deadliest forms, in 1986. He underwent five weeks of experimental therapy at the Dana Farber Clinic in Boston, where Williams was also receiving chemotherapy treatments. "I was diagnosed on the same day that a fortieth birthday party was to be held for me," Lucchino said. "Williams and one of my friends, Jay Emmett, donated a satellite dish to the clinic in Boston provided it could pick up Orioles games. What happened was that I became more determined to get my life back to where it was. I didn't say I wanted to stop and smell the roses and write poetry on the beach. I wanted to get back to being a hard-working, somewhat-driven guy."

Lucchino recovered and went on to become the moving force behind the Orioles' search for a new ballpark. He came up with the concept of the "old-fashioned traditional ballpark with modern amenities," and he pushed and pushed for that concept. "We had to write it up early on as to what we were looking for, and that was the phrase that came to mind," Lucchino said. "I was involved as an officer with the team and the lead negotiator for the deal, but I was still trained as a lawyer, so I had to find a way to write these things out. That was the phrase we used. If we used it once, we must have used it 2 million times. It was a concept that we had cut out of the baseball experience of those of us who had represented the Orioles. There were two things that came to my mind at first—it had to be irregular, and it had to be intimate."

Lucchino put together his own architecture and design firm, but he lost that battle and had to go along with the decision by an appointed committee to go with HOK rather than the Orioles' choice. "We did not get the architect that we wanted," Lucchino said. "I was in favor of another architectural team that had an urban planner, a design architect, a sports architect, and a graphic design specialist from three different firms. But the state was paying for the ballpark, and the committee was stacked, so we had to go along with it."

That began a sometimes explosive process between Lucchino, the stadium authority, and HOK to make Lucchino's vision a reality. He and HOK clashed on design. The architects, according to Lucchino, first came to him with a plan like new Comiskey Park, which angered Lucchino. He battled with the Maryland Stadium Authority over costs because the state was feeling the political pressure of using public funds—even if they were lottery funds—for a ballpark. The image of building a costly Taj Mahal could have cost a lot of politicians their jobs at the ballot box.

Like most people with a passion and vision, Lucchino is not always the easiest person to deal with, particularly when he is not getting his way. "Larry's fuse is very short," said former stadium authority chairman Herb Belgrad. "There were some pretty explosive sessions. But we agreed that we wouldn't let it be personal. So the two of us would go out to dinner at least once every few weeks. That relationship has continued to this day because both of us recognized that the project was bigger than the people who were involved in it."

Lucchino's temper is a common cause for debate among those who have worked for him in Baltimore and San Diego. His critics say privately that he can sometimes be cruel and is difficult to work for. Even his supporters say that Lucchino is demanding and does not have much patience for those who don't meet his goals and standards. The chairman of San Diego's redevelopment agency, Peter Q. Davis, told *The San Diego Union* in July 1998 about a finance meeting during which Lucchino jumped up in a flare of temper when someone didn't choose his words as well as he could have. But Davis also said he enjoyed debating with Lucchino, because the debate never gets personal.

Lucchino's supporters say that he encourages creativity among those who work for him and will back new ideas. He is also, they say, fiercely loyal and expects that loyalty in return. It is worth pointing out that though Lucchino clashed with HOK, he hired the firm as the architects for the proposed San Diego Padres downtown ballpark.

Lucchino's role with the Orioles continued to grow. With Williams near death, Lucchino was appointed president of the team in May 1988, and then became the club's chief executive when Williams passed away on August 13, 1988. There was some panic among the Orioles management that the team, now up for sale by the Williams estate, would wind up being bought by some out-of-town interests who would try to move the team. Although Lucchino was able to help find a buyer who would keep the team in Baltimore, he was no Edward Bennett Williams.

Eli Jacobs purchased the team on June 30, 1989, for $70 million. Sargent Shriver—the same Sargent Shriver who founded and directed the Peace Corps for his brother-in-law, the late President John F. Kennedy—had been part of the Williams group and would be part of the new ownership group. So would Lucchino, who would get 9 percent of the club.

Jacobs, though, was the majority owner, and he was the exact opposite of Williams, who was an outgoing man with a dynamic personality. Jacobs, who made his money on leveraged buyouts, was a loner with a cold manner. But he had the money to buy a team and wanted to own one. So he bought the Orioles. He did his best to keep a low profile, at least from the public. He was a Washington insider, a defense buff, for lack of a better description, and he liked to rub elbows with some of the government's top power brokers, who were often his guests in his private box at Orioles games.

By this time, the ballpark project was well on its way, but Jacobs, who also considered himself an architectural buff, told the story in Peter Richmond's book *Ballpark* that he was the design force behind the ballpark. He claimed he was the one who dictated changes to make Camden Yards the successful ballpark it became. Jacobs's time with the club was brief, though; he was forced into bankruptcy in 1993, and the club was put up for sale in a bankruptcy auction to pay off creditors.

Lucchino had been the one constant from the time Williams bought the team in 1979, throughout the entire Camden Yards process, and he hoped to stay with the team now. Cincinnati businessman William DeWitt approached Lucchino about forming a group to purchase the Orioles. "At one point he thought about buying the Orioles back in 1989, and that's when I originally met him," Lucchino said. "Then he came back again and had an interest in buying the team from Eli's bankruptcy estate. Had he been successful, I was to stay on as president and chief executive officer."

Lucchino and DeWitt thought they had a deal in place to buy the team for $141 million. But then Peter Angelos, the Baltimore attorney who made his fortune litigating asbestos cases, decided he wanted to put together a group of local investors to make sure the team was owned by local interests. "I was disappointed we were not successful in structuring a deal for the sale from the Jacobs estate," Lucchino said. "We had to sell our interests, Sarge and I did, because we were minority owners, and the team had to be sold off as a whole, which it was. We didn't have the option of staying. We had to leave and come back with a new group." This was the DeWitt group.

The Orioles wound up for sale in a bankruptcy auction in a New York courtroom on August 2, 1993. DeWitt made a deal with Angelos to join forces against the other bidder, art dealer Jeff Loria, who shocked everyone by going toe-to-toe with Angelos in the courtroom until Angelos went as high as $173 million in the winning bid for the franchise—at the time a record amount for a sports franchise. Lucchino said he helped put that deal together, but by doing that he would be bringing about the end of his time with the Orioles. It became clear early on that Angelos, as the majority owner in a group that included author Tom Clancy, sports announcer Jim McKay, and film director Barry Levinson, was going to run the Orioles the way he wanted to and not be turning the reigns over to Lucchino to continue to do business as he had for so many years.

"Angelos decided he wanted to be chairman and chief executive officer of the team, but he offered me a position to stay on as vice chairman," Lucchino said. "We spent a couple of weeks sorting out what our respective roles would be, and it became clear to me that he was going to be the pilot of the ship and did not need me to play the role that I had played for the last few years. So I thanked him for his offer and simply declined the position."

Angelos closed his deal to buy the team on October 4, 1993. By the end of the month, Lucchino ended his fourteen-year relationship with the Orioles. For the first time in nearly twenty years, Lucchino wasn't part of the Baltimore-Washington sports scene. "I was disappointed with the way things turned out," Lucchino said. "I felt deeply connected to Baltimore and deeply invested in the ballpark and the franchise. I would have liked to have stayed on. It was a labor of love for me. I thought the upside for the Orioles was quite high, given the success of Camden Yards, and I would have loved to stay there."

Several months later, it appeared that Lucchino might again become part of the Baltimore sports scene. He had talks with Angelos about working together on acquiring an NFL franchise for Baltimore. But those talks didn't go anywhere, and Angelos eventually failed to get a football team for Baltimore. Instead, Art Modell brought football to Baltimore by moving his Cleveland Browns.

Lucchino was out of the Baltimore-Washington sports picture, but he had many options. He remained in sports; he had been so involved in so many facets of it, it would be difficult to step away from the sports industry now. Lucchino has the distinction of having a World Series ring (Orioles 1983), Super Bowl ring (Redskins 1983), and a Final Four watch (Princeton 1965). Baseball insiders knew of Lucchino's influential role in seeing the Camden Yards project through, from its inception to its opening. The success of the ballpark had raised his profile and reputation so much that there had been actually talk of Lucchino as a candidate for commissioner of baseball after Fay Vincent was forced out.

One of those baseball people seeking out Lucchino's services was one of baseball's newest owners, Wayne Huizenga, whose deep pockets brought South Florida an expansion franchise during the 1991 sweepstakes. This club joined the Colorado Rockies as baseball's newest teams, beating out a group from Washington in the process. Huizenga had big plans. He was a hard-nosed businessman who made his fortune in a tough business, waste disposal, building Waste Management, Inc., into the world's largest waste collection and disposal company. He also owned Blockbuster Entertainment Corporation, Joe Robbie Stadium (now called Pro Player Stadium), and the Miami Dolphins. He wanted to build an entire sports and entertainment theme park complex known as Blockbuster Park, although it was also called "Wayne's World" in the media.

"I had gotten to know Wayne Huizenga from baseball meetings, and he asked me to work as a consultant on Blockbuster Park," Lucchino said. "He knew my role at Camden Yards and was impressed with what we did there. I went down there and spent several months planning a baseball facility for South Florida."

That wasn't the only iron Lucchino had in the fire, though. He wasn't interested in making a living helping other people run franchises or build ballparks. He had seen too much success in Baltimore to stop now at the age of forty-seven. Lucchino wanted to own another baseball team, and the dream of a lifetime seemed to be presenting itself: his hometown team, the Pittsburgh Pirates, was for sale.

The Pirates' glory years were the 1970s, starting with Roberto Clemente and the 1971 World Series win over the Orioles, and ending in 1979 with Willie Stargell and the World Series win, also over the Orioles, when Williams and Lucchino were just taking over. But the Pirates fell on hard times in the 1980s, and when the Galbreath family put the franchise on the block in 1985, there was no line of prospective local buyers. It appeared the franchise was in danger of being moved out of town.

Pittsburgh Mayor Richard Caliguiri and lawyer Carl Barger came through by patching together a hodgepodge group of local corporations, Carnegie Mellon University, and individual investors to keep the team in Pittsburgh. The Pirates then rebuilt the franchise through a remarkable farm system that produced such stars as Barry Bonds, and Bobby Bonilla. Under manager Jim Leyland, the Pirates won the National League East from 1990 to 1992 but were beaten three straight times in the League Championship Series. After 1992, the team could not afford to keep free agents like Bonds and Bonilla, and the franchise, unable to compete with richer competitors, began to disintegrate, finishing 75–83 in 1993 and 53–61 in the strike-shortened season of 1994. The team was put up for sale again in 1995.

Lucchino had a chance to come home. He had strong family roots in Pittsburgh—his parents still resided there—and the idea of owning the Pirates stirred a lot of emotions inside. "That was my hometown," Lucchino said. In fact, Lucchino's investment group was called "Hometown Partners."

Those investors included DeWitt again and high-profile names such as Dolphins quarterback Dan Marino, who grew up in Pittsburgh, and political columnist George Will. Some others expressed interest, but by the end of 1994, the Pirates' owners had narrowed their choices down to two buyers—Lucchino's group and cable-television magnate John Rigas.

While Lucchino was doing this—advising Huizenga on Blockbuster Park and trying to buy the Pittsburgh Pirates—he received a call from Charlie Noell, an investment banker at Alex

Brown in Baltimore, and a Texas multi-millionaire named John Moores, who made his fortune in computer software. Moores was moving to San Diego, and when he heard the Padres were for sale, he told Noell, his banker, that he wanted to buy the franchise. Noell told him if he wanted to buy a team, he first should talk to Lucchino, who was taken aback by the call. "It came completely out of the blue," Lucchino said.

Within the baseball community, Lucchino was afforded great respect for what he had done at Camden Yards. He was advising Huizenga on Blockbuster Park, trying to buy the Pirates, and getting calls on buying the Padres. He was also scheduled to speak in Milwaukee to the Wisconsin Stadium Authority because Milwaukee Brewers owner Bud Selig was hoping to use Lucchino's influence to help him convince Wisconsin state officials to fund his own Camden Yards–like project for the Brewers. Moores and his financial advisors wanted to meet with Lucchino right away, "but I told them I couldn't that day because I had to give this presentation in Wisconsin," Lucchino said.

Eager to make the Padres deal and to meet Lucchino, Moores flew out that night to Milwaukee and met Lucchino after he spoke to the stadium authority. Accompanying Moores was his son, an investment banker, a lawyer, and another business partner. Moores is one of the most unassuming millionaires in America today, and he and Lucchino clicked right away. "We hit it off immediately," Lucchino said. "We were going to the hotel restaurant to eat, and they stopped Moores, who is worth $500 million and told him he wasn't dressed well enough to go into the restaurant. He was wearing a T-shirt and jeans. I said, 'Boy did you make a mistake. You let the wrong guys in and kept the wrong guy out.' So we went into the coffee shop instead. It's about 8 P.M. and nobody is there except us, and he asked me to work with him on his efforts to acquire the Padres. I said I'd be happy to do that, but I'm trying to buy the Pirates, and I want to pursue that. That's my first choice. But if you guys need some help with the baseball issues and the acquisition issues, I'll be happy to work with you."

Lucchino began working with Moores as an advisor, helping him negotiate a deal to buy the Padres. But all along, Moores was planning to try to convince Lucchino to join in on the Padres purchase. "In the fall, he said to me, 'We can have this team, but I'm not going to agree to buy this team unless you join the partnership and run the team for me.' I told him that I wanted to do the Pirates. I'm all set to go back there. We have a group in place and all that," Lucchino said.

But the situation in Pittsburgh was far from a sure thing. The Pirates ownership was dragging its heels, and there was no guarantee that Lucchino's group would come out on top. Later, however, Rigas fell by the wayside in the process and another buyer, Kevin McClatchy, eventually put together a group to buy the franchise in February 1996. So it's likely Lucchino's group could have ended up as the owner of the Pirates.

"What it came down to was a bird in the hand," Lucchino said. "It was a very touchy situation in Pittsburgh because we were one of two there, but we could be one of one in San Diego." He went back to Pittsburgh to talk it over with his family. The presence of Moores made it difficult to turn away from the San Diego opportunity. "Here's a wonderful guy. I don't know him very well but our working relationship has been very comfortable, and he can get the Padres deal if I will join him and invest with him and run the team," Lucchino said. "Or I can stay in Pittsburgh as one of the final two and go *mano à mano* with Rigas."

Lucchino chose Moores and San Diego, and has no regrets. "It was one of the best decisions I've ever made," he said. "John Moores is as good a partner as there could be in any business. This has been a great professional challenge, and San Diego is a wonderful place to live. I'm very happy there."

Many of Lucchino's friends and associates doubted that

Lucchino, an intense competitor and diehard easterner, could possibly be happy in laid-back San Diego. "When I got on the plane to move out here in January 1995, a couple of my friends went with me to make sure I was not going to get on the plane in the front and get off on the back and not really go," he said. "I did come to San Diego feeling like I was being transplanted from my roots. But San Diego is an incredible, appealing, attractive, comfortable place to be, and the professional challenge could not have been greater."

Lucchino has made the West Coast adjustment more smoothly than his friends believed he would. He has a beach house in La Jolla and sometimes rides his BMW R-1100 motorcycle. When he arrived in San Diego, he had a familiar neighbor at the stadium, Bobby Beathard, the San Diego Chargers general manager, who was friends with Lucchino dating back to the days when Beathard was the Redskins general manager and Lucchino was the team's general counsel. In fact, Williams and Lucchino interviewed Beathard for his Redskins job. Despite the friendship between the two, the Padres and Chargers have feuded often over different issues involving the use of the stadium.

Lucchino was right about the depth of the professional challenge facing him. The Padres were about at the lowest a franchise could be before Moores and Lucchino took over. They were owned by a group headed by Hollywood television producer Tom Werner. Remember the infamous moment when Roseanne Barr (Werner produced the show *Roseanne*) tried to sing the national anthem before a Padres game, was booed for her effort, and then grabbed her crotch and spit on the ground? That was illustrative of the Padres franchise under Werner, who quickly found he was in over his head with the rising finances of the game. He conducted the infamous San Diego fire sale, trading players such as Fred McGriff and Gary Sheffield for minor league prospects. Werner's regime drew just 1.3 million fans in 1993, the franchise's lowest total in a non-strike year since 1980. Combine that with all the animosity toward baseball as a result of the bitter baseball strike, and Moores and Lucchino had their work cut out for them in San Diego.

"The first thing we did when we got here was to put the word 'new' in front of every place we saw the San Diego Padres," Lucchino said. "It was the 'new' Padres." They did a lot more. Moores and Lucchino shared a commitment for customer service, and they put that commitment on paper in the form of three promises to San Diego fans:

"To put a team on the field worthy of the fans' support."
"To provide new entertainment experiences at the ballpark and to market the club to a new broad region."
"To be active participants in the community."

They met all those commitments, starting just one week after they bought the team on December 21, 1994, when they made the biggest trade in baseball in thirty-seven years, dealing outfielders Derek Bell and Phil Plantier, infielders Ricky Guitierrez and Craig Shipley, and pitchers Doug Brocall and Pedro Martinez (not the future NL Cy Young winner) to the Houston Astros for infielders Ken Caminiti, Andujar Cedeno, and Roberto Petagine, outfielder Steve Finley, pitcher Brian Williams, and a player to be named later. Finley and Caminiti became All-Star players and helped the Padres win the NL West in 1996 and again in 1998. Moores and Lucchino made the best of a ballpark that is not conducive to baseball. They gave Qualcomm Park (formerly Jack Murphy Stadium) a San Diego look with palm trees in the outfield, just beyond the fence. They added a new scoreboard and JumboTron screen. They created a "Kids Corner," a section catering to children, and they established good will ambassadors throughout the ballpark known as the "Pad Squad."

Lucchino also spearheaded an effort to market the team regionally, which meant heading south of the border some 20 miles—into Mexico. Lucchino flew to Washington to meet with immigration officials to come up with a plan to ease border crossings for organized bus trips to Padres games. They also played a three-game series against the New York Mets in Monterey from August 16 through August 18, 1996.

As far as community service, Moores and Lucchino enlisted the help of Padres players to establish the Padres Scholars, one of a number of community-service programs they implemented. They donate college scholarships for twenty-five middle school students each year. Now they are overseeing plans to create the same sort of success that Lucchino did at Camden Yards with a new ballpark in downtown San Diego.

"I think there is the same potential to stabilize the franchise that there was in Baltimore," Lucchino said. "One of the things I am most proud of with the Orioles and with Camden Yards is not just the architecture and the field and the atmosphere of the place, as much as I like all those things, but it succeeded in stabilizing a franchise that had some degree of instability for several years. I'd like to do the same thing here in San Diego."

PART TWO

The Drama

CHAPTER SIX

All-Star Ballpark

C amden Yards was hardly a secret by July 13, 1993. It had basked in the glow of rave reviews since it opening day in 1992. But in the mid-season of its second year of existence, the Camden Yards that everyone had written about and talked about was truly going to take center stage for the first time in the sports world by hosting the 64th Annual All-Star Game.

Like the ballpark itself, this year's game would prove to be a memorable one, for some obvious moments and for some not so obvious events. The impact of Camden Yards spilled over into the game because this was the year that the game became a week-long festivity. This was also the year that FanFest, the selling of baseball through interactive games, memorabilia, and other activities, broke through and became a huge success. It drew more than 110,000 fans and wiped out the record set the preceding year in San Diego.

With the ballpark as the centerpiece, the game evolved in Baltimore into a week-long celebration of baseball. "That All-Star Game was a chance to show off the city to the world, and we made the most of it," said former governor William Donald Schaefer. "That was the first time a city turned it into an entire week of events," Schaefer said. "When you have an event, make it a big one."

Besides FanFest, there were street festivals, concerts, symposiums, kids' carnivals, and a variety of other activities. These attractions, the All-Star Workout the day before the game, and the game itself generated an estimated $30 million in direct spending for the city, according to the Baltimore Area Convention and Visitors Association.

The seed for this All-Star Game in Baltimore was planted long before Camden Yards became a reality. The Orioles filed an application with Major League Baseball to host the game in 1986, but timed it so they would host the game when the ballpark was opened, at least by the second season. The last time Baltimore played host to the game was 1958. So by the time 1993 came around, the thirty-five-year stretch was the longest time any team had gone in between hosting the game.

The time was right. Even during the glory years of the Orioles in the late 1960s and early 1970s, the team didn't draw very well, and club officials were worried that they wouldn't be able to sell out the game. Also, the city back then was more like the dismal place Randy Newman sang about in the song "Baltimore" than the showplace community, with its Inner Harbor attractions, that the city had become by the time Camden Yards opened.

Baltimore was buzzing with the excitement of the sports world coming to town when the Orioles took the field in the final game of the first half of the season, the finale of a four-game series against the mighty Chicago White Sox. Fans who attended that Sunday home game got an early preview of the next day's Home Run Derby, as the "Big Hurt," Frank Thomas, blasted two home runs in an 11–5 Chicago win. The loss left the Orioles within one and a half games of first place in the American League East, behind their rivals, the defending World Champion Toronto Blue Jays. That rivalry was born out of the last weekend of the 1989 season, when the Orioles and Blue Jays battled for the division title in Toronto. The competition reached new heights as a result of this All-Star Game, turning ugly in the process and capturing the attention of the national media.

Baltimore had two All-Star representatives: Cal Ripken, voted in as the starting shortstop for the tenth straight season, and Mike Mussina, selected for his second straight All-Star team. Mussina proved to be the central figure in a melodrama that made this All-Star Game a memorable one, worthy of the Camden Yards stage, though not for the reasons baseball people would like.

Orioles fans were already upset with Toronto manager Cito Gaston, the AL skipper, because he went out of his way to take care of his own players. Three Blue Jays—first baseman John Olerud, second baseman Roberto Alomar, and left fielder Joe Carter—were voted onto the squad by the fans. Gaston raised some eyebrows by then picking four more of his players—pitchers Duane Ward and Pat Hentgen, designated hitter Paul Molitor, and center fielder Devon White.

That meant 25 percent of the American League team consisted of Toronto players, but Gaston scoffed at the criticism he was receiving for his selections. "I brought six world champions and one Hall of Famer," Gaston said. "I don't have to apologize to anybody," he noted, adding, "anyway, I'm used to being criticized. It happens all the time up in Toronto." Gaston, though, would soon face criticism that he couldn't have dreamed of when he gained the privilege of being the league's All-Star team manager.

American League president Dr. Bobby Brown defended the selections. "The manager, each year, has the final selection," he said. "All I try to do is make sure he doesn't forget to think about everybody. I just try to remind him of all the players I think should be considered." It was too bad Dr. Brown wasn't sitting next to Gaston in the dugout during the game. He could have reminded the manager of one player who should have been considered. The selection would have saved Gaston a lot of grief but would have denied the sports world great theater.

That saga, however, would not unfold until the end of the game. Until then, the star of the show was Camden Yards. The accolades mounted from the greats of the game in the National League who were getting their first look at the ballpark on the workout day before the game.

"This is the prettiest ballpark I've ever seen," said Jay Bell of the Pittsburgh Pirates. "You just look at this park, and it makes you feel good. It makes you want to go out there and play. It's exciting what a new stadium brings to the city. I can't picture a more beautiful place."

John Burkett of the San Francisco Giants said, "I've heard so much about it that my expectations were high, and it's great that it has lived up to those expectations. I saw it on television, but it's so much better in person. It's a new park that's designed to be old, but look new. What else could you want?"

Ryne Sandberg of the Chicago Cubs commented, "We see so many round, concrete stadiums, it's great to play in a ballpark with a lot of character like Wrigley Field. This is high-tech, yet it's got such an old-time feel to it. It's got a lot of good, fun things about it."

"It's beautiful, it's really beautiful," said Robby Thompson of the San Francisco Giants. "You're not supposed to think of a ballpark as being beautiful, but this is. When I was driving through town, I started looking for it and I almost missed it, it blends in so well with the rest of the downtown. Some ballparks stick out like a sore thumb, but not this place."

Perhaps Pittsburgh Pirates outfielder Andy Van Slyke had the most intelligent and prophetic insight into Camden Yards: "This is the future of baseball, and this should be the future. A stadium like this is an amazing example of what can happen when a city does something right."

But leave it to Barry Bonds, the talented but sometimes clueless San Francisco outfielder, to utter the quote of all quotes: "The warehouse? What is the warehouse?"

By the time these All-Star festivities were over, everyone, including Bonds, would know about the B&O Warehouse. The longest building on the East Coast, sitting on the other side of Eutaw Street over the right-field scoreboard, had become the white whale for home-run hitters, particularly left-handed ones. Sam Horn, the large and colorful Baltimore slugger, had professed time and time again in the first year the park opened that he would be the first one to hit the warehouse. Sam never did, and by 1993 he was gone, on his way to Japan, where he professed he would become a "Yenyionaire."

The warehouse became the showcase for the Home Run Derby, which had become the most anticipated event of the work-out the day before the All-Star Game. The 1993 lineup was impressive: Juan Gonzalez, Ken Griffey, Cecil Fielder, Albert Belle, Barry Bonds, Bobby Bonilla, David Justice, and Mike Piazza. On a sun-filled afternoon, a sold-out crowd of 47,981— the largest crowd to date at Camden Yards—showed up for what amounts to batting practice. The public reaction was illustrative of the attraction of Camden Yards, which made the workout day an unprecedented special event.

Gonzalez had the longest blast of the Home Run Derby, smashing one shot 473 feet, hitting the bunting on the lower railing off the upper deck in right field. This was the longest ball ever measured in the ballpark. That came as no surprise, since the big Texas slugger had already hit the longest ball at Camden Yards during a game, a 450-foot homer off Mike Mussina on July 26, 1992.

But the home run that made headlines was delivered by Ken Griffey, who at 5:26 P.M. on July 13, 1993, got a piece of Moby Dick. The ball traveled 445 feet and hit a piece of plexiglass about eight feet up on the warehouse. Before the contest, Griffey had told reporters that he might be able to hit the warehouse "if I was standing on second base using a fungo bat." Now he tried to downplay the accomplishment. After all, to him, it was a batting-practice home run. "It just means it will be written about for a while," he said. "When somebody does it in a game, then it will mean something."

No one has ever done it in a game, and they still talk about the day Ken Griffey hit the warehouse. This hit overshadowed the outcome of the Home Run Derby, which the American League won 21–12. But Griffey's home run was not nearly the longest of the contest. Besides the mammoth shot by Gonzalez, who won the competition, both Cecil Fielder and Barry Bonds hit longer shots. Griffey's shot, however, added to the lore of what was becoming the "Home of the Game" during this All-Star festival.

Griffey's hit wasn't all the fans were talking about that day. The Upper Deck Heroes of Baseball old-timers game had a special treat: The last old-timers game in Baltimore featured Mr. Oriole, Hall of Famer Brooks Robinson. Moreover, Robinson went out in style, starting two double plays at third base and driving in two runs.

A younger old-timer also created a spectacular moment, but not during the game. Reggie Jackson, who would be inducted into the Hall of Fame three weeks later, captured the spotlight after the Celebrity Home Run Challenge by grabbing a bat while the fans chanted "Reggie, Reggie." He took some hacks until he blasted one over the right-field scoreboard and out onto Eutaw Street. It was a great Reggie moment, and a great Camden Yards moment.

Before Reggie put on his show, though, all eyes in the ballpark were on the featured guest in the Celebrity Home Run Challenge, Michael Jordan. In a contest that included Tom Selleck, Bill Murray, and Patrick Ewing, Jordan won and, although no one knew it at the time, gave everyone a glimpse into his future. Several months later, the NBA great would announce his retirement from basketball, and soon after take on the challenge of minor league baseball.

Looking back, it's remarkable how the events surrounding Jordan that day would be a prelude of things to come. Jordan, a former high-school baseball player, came to the park early that

The first steel for Camden Yards is set by then governor William Donald Schaefer on August 16, 1990. Schaefer held to the position that the new ballpark should be in the city, not the suburbs. (Courtesy of the Maryland State Archives, William Donald Schaefer Photograph Collection, MSA SC 4326-10. Photograph by Richard Tomlinson, Governor's Press Office.)

Herb Belgrad, chair of the Maryland Stadium Authority, joins Governor
Schaefer and Orioles president Larry Lucchino at Camden Yards. All three
had worked closely on the project. Belgrad helped push the idea of separate
facilities: a baseball-only ballpark and a football stadium. (Courtesy of the
Maryland State Archives, William Donald Schaefer Photograph Collection,
MSA SC 4326-37. Photograph by Richard Tomlinson, Governor's Press Office.)

Oriole Park at Camden Yards in the process of being completed. The ballpark opened on April 6, 1992, after years of discussion, debate, and perseverance. (Allsport)

Camden Yards, with Baltimore's skyline as a backdrop. This well-attended theater provides the stage for baseball's drama. (Allsport)

A back view of the ballpark in its park-like, yet urban, setting. The design connection to Baltimore's architectural history is evident. (Allsport)

Former Orioles president Larry Lucchino, now president of the Padres, provided the driving vision of Camden Yards as a traditional, old-fashioned ballpark. He grew up watching the Pittsburgh Pirates at Forbes Field. (San Diego Padres)

Baltimore and Ohio Railroad.

The historic Camden Station (c. 1870) of the Baltimore & Ohio Railroad, witness to Lincoln's funeral train when it transported the assassinated President home to Illinois. Babe Ruth left from Camden Station to join the Red Sox as a major league player. (Courtesy of the Maryland State Archives, M.E. Warren Collection, MSA SC 1890-4648)

Babe Ruth, second from right, helps tend bar in one of his father's Baltimore taverns. One of them, Ruth's Cafe, stood in what is now center field at Camden Yards. George senior is on the right. (Babe Ruth Birthplace and Museum, Baltimore)

While home to the Brooklyn Dodgers, Ebbets Field epitomized the urban ballpark. Camden Yards is one of its descendants. Jackie Robinson took the field at Ebbets. Red Barber was usually behind the microphone. (*The Sporting News*)

Fans gather for a game at Wrigley Field, home of the Chicago Cubs. Wrigley opened in 1914. It was the last ballpark to install lights, holding out until 1988. (Allsport)

Peter Angelos, center, and William DeWitt, center right, emerge victorious from their 1993 bid for the Orioles at Federal Bankruptcy Court in New York. Their winning offer was $173 million. (AP/Wide World Photos)

Rick Sutcliffe keeps his concentration in a pitch against the Angels in Anaheim in 1992. Sutcliffe, one of the most liked and respected players in the clubhouse, won twenty-six games for the Orioles in two seasons. (AP/Wide World Photos)

Mike Mussina in action against the New York Yankees at Yankee Stadium. Baltimore fans still talk about Mussina's warm-up for the 1993 All-Star Game at Camden Yards, in which he didn't get to pitch. (AP/Wide World Photos)

Cal Ripken acknowledges the fans' cheers for his record-breaking Streak. In 1995, Ripken tied and then broke Lou Gehrig's record of 2,130 consecutive games. The Streak finally ended in 1998 with game 2,632. (Allsport)

Bobby Bonilla hits a sixth-inning double against the Oakland A's at Camden Yards, lifting the Orioles to a 3–1 win in this 1996 game. A fan favorite, Bonilla had a falling out with manager Davey Johnson and signed with the Florida Marlins as a free agent after the 1996 season. (AP/Wide World Photos)

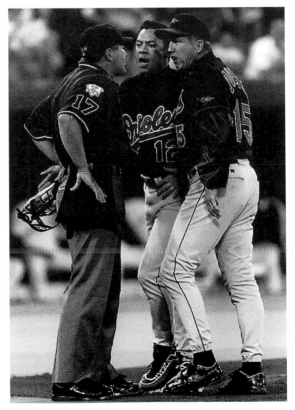

Second baseman Roberto Alomar and manager Davey Johnson argue with umpire John Hirschbeck in 1996. Alomar was ejected from the game against the Toronto Blue Jays. (AP/Wide World Photos)

Eric Davis at bat in the Championship Series against the Cleveland Indians, Jacobs Field. Davis was out of action in 1995 but returned in 1996 in a triumph of the human spirit. (Allsport)

Second baseman Roberto Alomar leaps above Yankees baserunner Darryl Strawberry in Game 5 of the AL Championship Series at Camden Yards. Alomar completed a double play by throwing out Yankees batter Paul O'Neill at first. (AP/Wide World Photos)

Tony Tarasco argues with umpire Richie Garcia over fan interference at the 1996 AL Championship Series while Roberto Alomar and Cal Ripken look on. Right-fielder Tarasco's catch was a given, until an eager young fan reached out from the stands. (Allsport)

Orioles manager Davey Johnson and home plate umpire Ted Barrett reason together over a first-inning decision at Camden Yards in 1997. When Barrett ejected batter B. J. Surhoff, Johnson argued for Surhoff and received the same fate. (AP/Wide World Photos)

Brady Anderson watches his grand-slam home run fly over the right field fence at Camden Yards. This was his fifteenth home run in 1997, his first grand-slam of the season, and it tied the score 4–4 with the Royals. Anderson set the club record for home runs in one season when he hit fifty home runs in 1996. (AP/Wide World Photos)

Scott Erickson pitches in his eleventh complete game of the 1998 season, beating the Angels 8–3. He gave up nine hits, three earned runs, and had four strikeouts. Erickson is one of the most successful trades in Oriole history. Acquired from the Minnesota Twins in July 1995, he went on to win fifty-four games for Baltimore. (AP/Wide World Photos)

First baseman Rafael Palmeiro makes a diving stop. His subsequent throw to
first base was fielded by pitcher Sidney Ponson, who made a diving tag to get
Detroit Tigers' Paul Bako for an out. One of the greatest home-run hitters in
Oriole history, slugging 182 home runs in five seasons, Palmeiro left after the
1998 season to sign with his old team, the Texas Rangers. (AP/Wide World
Photos)

day for extra batting practice against the pitching machine underneath the stands, getting tuned up to win the contest. Afterwards, Jackson, the designated celebrity batting coach, had some interesting words: "Michael has some big league skills." As it turned out, Jordan barely had enough Class AA skills.

The next day, the major leaguers took the field for real, and by the end of the 64th All-Star Game, all hell would break loose. Fans began milling about Camden Yards long before the doors opened for batting practice, waiting outside on Eutaw Street for the Orioles Baseball Store to open, standing in line at the U.S. Postal Service van to get the special Oriole Park at Camden Yards All-Star cancellation, and eating lunch at Boog's Barbecue.

There was more going on around this game today than baseball, though. Because of its close proximity to Washington, DC, this All-Star Game would have some political overtones as well. The day before, the Reverend Jesse Jackson led a march through the streets of West Baltimore, urging people to join him in a protest of major league baseball. Jackson was very critical of the lack of minorities in front-office jobs in the game and because there remained no minority ownership. Before the game, Jackson led about 300 marchers outside of Camden Yards, chanting slogans like "Cut us in or cut us out" and carrying placards calling on the memory of Jackie Robinson to protest baseball's minority hiring efforts. "Baseball has not adopted an affirmative action law," Jackson said. "Major league baseball has been an obstruction to the process of affirmative action. They have a poor won-loss record."

They still have a poor won-loss record, but what was ironic about the march was that the Orioles were one of the few teams to employ minorities in front-office positions. Former NFL running back Calvin Hill was vice president of administrative personnel, and Frank Robinson, baseball's first African American manager, was the Orioles' assistant general manger.

Not all of the politics were confined to the pickets outside the ballpark. Inside, about twenty-five members of Congress had gotten some free tickets from some murky source. The legislators found themselves having to defend their freebies. Scalped tickets were going for as much as $700, and many baseball fans had been frozen out of the game.

One of the more bizarre and frightening moments took place during the game. Because Vice President Al Gore was in the audience, Secret Service agents were stationed throughout the ballpark, and some armed agents were on the roof. Yet during the fourth inning of the game, an animal-rights activist climbed up to the top of the center-field scoreboard, where a Budweiser advertisement looms large, and unfurled a banner reading, "August Busch III. Free Willy? Corky! Shamu! Respect Gods Creatures." The banner was directed at the Busch family, owners of the St. Louis Cardinals and Sea World. This activist was later arrested by police, but the spectacle was an embarrassing security risk for the Secret Service, as this man was able to climb to such a high, and prime, location at the ballpark. He had a clear view of the luxury box that Gore was sitting in during the game.

But the controversy that grabbed the headlines for days following the game did not involve any politicians or picketers. After starting in the home-team bullpen, the furor took place on the field. The crowd was at a fever pitch by the time the players were about to be introduced, and they were particularly anxious to greet their hometown heroes, Cal Ripken and Mike Mussina. The fans let loose a remarkably loud and long ovation when Ripken was introduced. "The ovation was beyond anyone could comprehend," Ripken said after the game. "I haven't had the best first half, and I'm humbly thankful that I'm here at all. To have the fans react like that was special."

Ripken was right. He had a poor first half, and shortly after he was voted in, while batting .215 at the time, Ripken said he might have considered withdrawing from the game if it were not in Baltimore. But the fact that he was voted in with a .215 average—up to .224 by the time the game came around—was a testament to his popularity and the respect fans had for the way he approached the game. That popularity and respect would rise to levels rarely seen in the game two years later, when he would break Lou Gehrig's consecutive-game streak of 2,130.

Baltimore fans also roared when their other player, Mussina, was introduced. He was the pride of the franchise, emerging as one of the best young pitchers in the game, and he was a fan favorite at Camden Yards.

The largely hometown crowd, still angry about the domination of the Toronto players on the All-Star roster, booed most of the Blue Jay players and manager Cito Gaston. The crowd of 48,147 would soon replace those angry feelings with something far deeper.

James Earl Jones, who had been on hand for the Camden Yards opening day in 1992, made another appearance to recite "The Star-Spangled Banner" as part of the All-Star pre-game ceremonies. Geddy Lee, lead singer of the Canadian rock group Rush, sang the Canadian national anthem. The American League squad then took the field, and Mark Langston threw the first pitch to Marquis Grissom.

It started out to look like a National League rout. At one time, the NL dominated the game, winning eleven games in a row from 1972 through 1982. But the AL dominated in recent years, winning every game since 1987. After Grissom fouled out to Wade Boggs, however, the NL seemed determined to break the AL winning streak. Barry Bonds doubled down the right-field line, and Gary Sheffield gave the National League a 2–0 lead by blasting a 1–2 pitch into the left-field seats. John Kruk flied out to Kirby Puckett in left, and Langston struck out Barry Larkin to end the inning.

The AL bounced back to get on the board in the bottom of the second against Terry Mulholland. After leadoff batter John Olerud grounded out to second baseman Ryne Sandberg, Puckett homered to center on a 2–2 count. One inning later, the AL tied the score at 2–2.

The top of the third inning resulted in one of those legendary, albeit comical, All-Star moments that baseball fans remember. With the hard-throwing giant lefthander Randy Johnson on the mound for the AL, John Kruk, a lefthanded batter, was not looking forward to stepping in the box against Johnson, who is murder on lefthanded hitters. In fact, Kruk may have feared for his life when a wild fastball by Johnson sailed several feet over Kruk's head. He gingerly got back in the box, but he nearly ran to the dugout by the time the next Johnson pitch reached the plate, a comical scene.

"If he's going to hit me, it's going to have to be a moving target," Kruk said after the game. Johnson would later say that "it was a bit humid out there, and the ball just got away from me." Kruk came back and swung meekly for the third strike, getting out without a scratch.

The NL wouldn't get out without any damage. In the bottom of the fifth, with John Burkett pitching, Texas catcher Ivan Rodriguez hit a ground-rule double that bounced into the left-field stands. Roberto Alomar grounded to second, and Rodriguez moved to third on the play. Albert Belle, pinch-hitting for Paul Molitor, singled to right, scoring Rodriguez for a 3–2 AL lead, with Belle advancing to second on an error by David Justice.

Ken Griffey singled to right, scoring Belle, and Griffey moved to second on the throw home. Burkett struck out Joe Carter for the second out—the second out by a Toronto player in the inning—but then he hit Cecil Fielder with a pitch. Puckett continued his Most Valuable Player performance by doubling to left center field, scoring Griffey for a 5–2 AL lead. Steve Avery was brought in and got Ripken on a ground ball to third for the final out.

Jack McDowell had been on the mound in the top of the fifth, so he was now the pitcher of record for the AL. Another Gaston player, Jimmy Key, would come out to pitch the top of the sixth, the fourth AL pitcher used. Mussina, the hometown hero, sat in the bullpen, awaiting his call. The NL scored one run off Key to close the deficit to 5–3. Bonds doubled down the right-field line and moved to third on a single by Sheffield. Kruk struck out, but Bonds scored on a sacrifice fly by Larkin. Mark Grace grounded to first for the third out.

At this point, in the bottom of the sixth inning, the game was essentially over, and a contingent of Atlanta Braves players—shortstop Jeff Blauser and pitchers Steve Avery and in particular John Smoltz—brought about their league's demise. With two outs, Carlos Baerga reached safely on an error by Blauser. Avery then walked Belle and gave up a double to right by Devon White, scoring Baerga for a 6–3 AL lead. Belle moved to third on the play.

Smoltz then came in to relieve Avery, and in a wild, bizarre scene, he allowed Belle to score on a wild pitch for a 7–3 AL lead. Smoltz walked Juan Gonzalez, and with Fielder at the plate, Smoltz let loose another wild pitch. This enabled White to score and opened up the lead to 8–3. Fielder hit a fly ball to left, and the inning was over—but so was the game. All that was left for happy AL fans was to see the hometown pitcher take the mound. After all, Gaston would have to use Mussina sometime over the next three innings, right?

Not necessarily. Jeff Montgomery came in to pitch the top of the seventh. The AL opened up the game even more in the bottom of the seventh on a run-scoring double by Terry Steinbach. But yet in the top of the eighth Gaston brought in Rick Aguillera.

When the top of the ninth rolled around, there were rumbles throughout the ballpark and in the Orioles front-office luxury box. Why wasn't Gaston putting Mussina in the game, even if just for one ceremonial batter? After all, Gaston must realize how important it was to Mussina and the hometown fans to see him pitch. How many times does this chance come up? In Baltimore so far, once every thirty-five years.

Gaston was oblivious to it all, and to make it all the more insulting, he brought in his own closer, Duane Ward, to pitch the ninth. The fans booed as Ward came in, but then the scene took a wild turn. When Mussina got up to warm up during the inning, the television operators showed him on the JumboTron screen, to the delight of the fans. When they saw him, they roared and chanted loudly, "We want Mike! We want Mike!"

Gaston had not told Mussina to get up, though, and had no intention of using him in the ninth, even with a 9–3 lead. "I would have put Mussina into the game if it went extra innings," Gaston said, "but I didn't have any intention to have him finish the game."

Mussina later claimed he was simply getting in work for his next start, and was up on the advice of Orioles bullpen coach Elrod Hendricks to go ahead and do so. But anyone who knows Mussina knows that this Stanford graduate is far too smart to think that his warm-ups wouldn't incite the hometown fans. It was a rebellious act, at least in baseball protocol, by a young pitcher with an affinity for bucking authority. But Gaston seemed remarkably ignorant of the fact that this game is played for the fans, and he showed that sometimes the worst decisions in baseball are made by baseball insiders, isolated from the people who buy the tickets and essentially pay their salaries.

As the game ended, this was the scene: the AL had just won 9–3, yet the crowd in this AL ballpark was booing as loudly as could possibly be, certainly louder than anything ever heard yet at Camden Yards. They cheered as Mussina walked in from the bullpen, and he acknowledged their cheers by waving to them. It was a remarkable melodrama.

Lucchino, the club's president, said he was "outraged," and general manager Roland Hemond said he couldn't fathom how Gaston could not have enough sense to have put Mussina in "Why you can't get Mike Mussina in a 9–3 game is beyond me," Hemond said. "I don't care what the explanation is. If you say you have to save him for extra innings, you don't have faith in Duane Ward."

Mussina wasn't buying Gaston's explanation, either. "You can make that excuse if you want," he said. "But it was a 9–3 game." Mussina insisted that he was merely thinking about his next regular start. "When do you want me to throw?" he asked. "I did what I had to do to pitch for the next start. I can't get up in the fifth. It's not wise because I can't get up in the fifth and get up again in the ninth or tenth."

Mussina also said that, based on Gaston's pre-game pitchers meeting, he knew he wasn't going to pitch in the game, but Baltimore manager Johnny Oates said he was under the impression in a conversation with Gaston that Mussina would pitch. "At the start of the game, I assumed Mussina would pitch," Oates said. "I may have misinterpreted what he said."

Mussina said he didn't think warming up would be a problem. "I didn't stir the fans up," he said. "I was just warming up. Whoever kept putting me on the screen was stirring it up." It was stirred up, all right. The next day, the Mussina controversy dominated the headlines of All-Star coverage in newspapers all across the country. The talk shows in Baltimore were flooded with callers and hosts alike screaming bloody murder over Gaston's snub of Mussina. "Cito Gaston insulted the city of Baltimore," said sports talk-show host Jeff Rimer. He was joined by Orioles announcer Jon Miller. "After all the efforts the people of this city put forth this week, to have Cito Gaston do something like this was like he was thumbing his nose at the city of Baltimore," Miller said. "It was a showcase week and event, and it ended on a down note."

The controversy would go on for several weeks, and it was taking an ugly turn. Sides were clearly being taken according to race, with African American baseball officials and players lining up behind Gaston, and white players and others, for the most part, backing Mussina. "I'd like to think that it's not a racial thing," said Davey Lopes, an African American and the Orioles' first-base coach. "I don't know what it is. But the fact is that when a minority makes a decision, it seems like too much attention is paid to it."

While Lucchino and Hemond vented against Gaston, Frank Robinson, the Orioles assistant general manager and the first

African American manager in the history of baseball, said he was unhappy with the post-game booing and attacks on Gaston by Baltimore fans. "I'm disappointed in the fan reaction," Robinson said. "I don't think it's right. I'd like to have seen Mussina get in. But there was no reason for that. It's an All-Star Game, an exhibition."

That, according to Mussina's supporters, was exactly the point. "It was terrible," said Orioles pitcher Ben McDonald. "I can't see how the guy couldn't get Mike in, even if it was just to pitch to one batter. This is his hometown crowd."

But Lopes said Gaston was "a man of character. From what I know about Cito, he wasn't about to change his plans to appease the fans. Here we are, second-guessing the manager in an All-Star Game. It's ridiculous." Lopes added that some thought Mussina should not have been in the game. And so it went—whites siding with Mussina, and African Americans backing Gaston.

Orioles pitcher Jamie Moyer commented, "Mike will probably be at the All-Star Game every year the rest of his career, but when is it going to be in Baltimore again? How many opportunities do you have to play in your own city?" Baltimore second baseman Harold Reynolds said, "You can't overlook the issue of who is the boss of the show and that's the manager. As a player you have to respect that."

The fans felt that Gaston didn't show them the respect they deserved, and Citophobia gripped the city. Fans showed up to the ballpark in droves wearing "Cito Sucks" T-shirts and carrying signs with such remarks as "Will Rogers never met Cito Gaston."

It got to the point where Gaston said he feared for his safety as well as that of his players when the Blue Jays would return to Baltimore. "There are a lot of weird people in this world," he said. "I don't want to see any of my players getting hurt." When asked if he would take any extra security measures when his team returned to Camden Yards for the final three games of the season, Gaston joked, "Maybe I'll have a shotgun strapped to my leg.

We'll just have to wait and see. If we do, I don't want anybody to know about it."

Gaston may have been the target of the wrath of Baltimore fans, but his former players jumped to defend him. "He's a good man," said Dave Winfield, who played on the 1992 World Champion Blue Jays squad for Gaston. "I was happy to play for him and win with him." David Cone, who was also on the 1992 team, said Gaston was a "player's manager. When I first got there he made me feel right at home." Cone continued, "He took me out to dinner and made things easier for me. And on the field, he gave me a chance to pitch in some pretty big games."

Gaston had a mediocre ten-year playing career during the 1970s, and was a coach on Toronto manager Jimy Williams's staff when he was named interim manager when Williams was fired on May 15, 1989. At the end of that season, Gaston was given the job on a permanent basis, and would eventually lead the Blue Jays to two world championships.

But even in Toronto, fans and the media often criticized Gaston for some of his baseball decisions, even though he was the winningest manager in franchise history. The 1992 championship win was fortunate, according to Gaston. "If we hadn't won last year, everyone was thinking I was going to get fired," he said. "I didn't much appreciate that." He made it clear that he also didn't appreciate Mussina's warm-up stunt, saying the young pitcher had "no class. When you're a baseball player, you know what it means when someone says you're not pitching unless the game goes into extra innings. I don't blame the kid for getting up in the bullpen, but when he was asked about it, he should have said why."

Mussina didn't blindly follow the rules, though. He was a high-school scholar-athlete, excelling in football. He still owns records at Montoursville, Pennsylvania, High School with 119 career receptions, 1,734 receiving yards, 18 field goals, and 84 extra points, and Penn State offered him a football scholarship as a place kicker. As a basketball player, Mussina averaged 24 points a game his senior year. In baseball, he was the Pennsylvania High School Player of the Year in 1986 and 1987, and had a career record of 24–4 with an 0.87 ERA.

Mussina remains very close to his hometown, living in Montoursville during the off season and helping coach the high-school receivers, defensive backs, and kickers. He was devastated when, in July 1996, a group of high-school students from Montoursville were among those killed in the TWA800 explosion.

The Orioles wanted Mussina right out of high school, drafting him in the eleventh round in 1987, but he chose to accept a scholarship to Stanford University, where he compiled a career record of 25–12, tied for sixth in career wins in school history. He also graduated early with an economics degree, and was Baltimore's first-round draft choice in 1990.

Mussina started his professional career with the Orioles Class A team in Hagerstown, but he wasn't there long. After putting together a record of 3–0 with a 1.49 ERA in seven starts, he finished the 1990 season with Class AAA Rochester. The following season, he had nineteen starts with Rochester, posting a 10–4 mark with a 2.87 ERA. In the midst of a 67–95 losing record, the Orioles called up Mussina on July 31. He was their best starter in the final two months of the year, going 4–5 with a 2.88 ERA.

In 1992, Mussina emerged as one of the game's best young pitchers, with a record of 18–5 and a 2.54 ERA. He has since gone on to become one of the winningest percentage pitchers in the history of the game, fourth among twentieth-century pitchers with ninety or more career wins.

With the talent, however, has come the temperament, and Mussina has never easily accepted authority. After all, this is a pitcher who once ordered his pitching coach, Pat Dobson, off the mound when he came out to talk to Mussina during one game in 1996. But after the 1993 All-Star Game, Mussina found that his rebellious nature had him knee-deep in controversy.

The flap continued until two weeks later, when the Orioles were coming to Toronto for a two-game series. Before going to Toronto, Mussina said that he would seek out Gaston to apologize to him. "I want to apologize, " he explained. "I know I obviously caused him some problems. I heard they were advertising his fax number on the radio. I'm going to try to talk to him. If nothing else, to apologize for whatever trouble I've caused him." Mussina made it clear, though, that any problems his warm-up caused were unintentional.

Mussina was probably sincere. Though most believe he was motivated to force Gaston's hand and show him up when he got up to warm up in the bullpen that night in Camden Yards, even he could not have anticipated the furor it created, and likely did not intend for it to go this far. "If it would have been in Pittsburgh or Texas, I don't think anybody would have thought anything about it," Mussina said. "But because it was at our place, the fans got caught up in it and the media got caught up in it, and it really got out of hand, pitting me against Cito."

But when the Orioles arrived in Toronto, the papers were filled with stories still fueling the controversy, and urging their fans to come out in force to boo Mussina and the Orioles. "I don't know what I'm going to do," he said. "I don't want to make it worse. I just want to clear it up."

It would finally end. Mussina apologized by telephone, rather than face-to-face, calling Gaston from Johnny Oates's office in SkyDome about three hours before the game. "I talked to him, and as far as I'm concerned, it's settled," Mussina said. "Everything was worked out, and the case is closed."

Mussina called their conversation friendly. "He explained where he was coming from, and I explained my side," he said. "What it came down to was that I didn't make any kind of statement to the media after the game that I knew I wasn't going to pitch unless it was extra innings." He made other statements, though, after the game that indicated that even if that was the game plan, Mussina believed with the score 9–3, he should have been given a token appearance, if nothing else.

Gaston agreed the matter was closed. "I'm not mad at the kid," he said. "We went into the game with a plan, and it helped us win the game." There would still be leftover Citophobia in Baltimore when the Blue Jays came to Baltimore at the end of the season for the final series. But with the Orioles out of the race by the end of August, it had lost much of its steam. The furor, however, served as a larger-than-life melodrama, a fitting tale for the legend of Camden Yards.

CHAPTER SEVEN

The Streak

Joe Foss and John Angelos hurried through the terminal at the Baltimore-Washington International Airport. They were two men in a hurry to make sure they met a very important person as he came off the plane—Joe DiMaggio, the ultimate in baseball royalty.

They were running late, and the last thing you want to do is be late for DiMaggio, a very particular man. They wanted to make sure that everything went particularly right for this particular man, who was coming to Baltimore for a very particular event: Cal Ripken's long-anticipated, record-setting 2,131st consecutive game, which would break Lou Gehrig's long-standing mark of 2,130 straight games. The event was shaping up to have huge implications. Baseball had reached an historic low after the worst strike in sports history resulted in the cancellation of the 1994 playoffs and World Series.

But to truly put the stamp of tradition and class on the celebration to come at Camden Yards—a fitting place for such drama—on this night of September 6, 1995, Joe DiMaggio would have to be there. He was a teammate of Gehrig's and would be the link between the two iron men. Even without that connection, it would be important to have DiMaggio on hand. He was one of the legendary figures of the twentieth century, immortalized in song by Paul Simon by the line "Where have you gone, Joe DiMaggio?" He had married and then was divorced by the biggest sex symbol in the history of Hollywood, Marilyn Monroe. He was considered one of the greatest and most graceful players in the game at a time when baseball was truly the national pastime. He was the leader of those great New York Yankee teams. Other players had better numbers, but the image of Joe DiMaggio is one of baseball excellence and consummate style.

Privately, DiMaggio was considered a reclusive, eccentric man, distrustful of all but a few close confidants. He refused to let people into his life to get a look at anything other than the pristine DiMaggio image he had cultivated and guarded for so many years. A man like this doesn't like to be kept waiting. So John Angelos, the son of Baltimore Orioles owner Peter Angelos, ran ahead of Joe Foss, vice chairman of the Orioles, to make sure someone greeted DiMaggio as he got off the plane.

The eighty-one-year-old DiMaggio was just coming out when John Angelos reached the gate. He greeted DiMaggio, who was alone, and got an airport cart to take him through the terminal to pick up his luggage at the baggage claim on the lower level. As they waited for DiMaggio's bags to come out, a man in his sixties approached DiMaggio for his autograph. "I stood back and watched this scene," Foss said. "I knew DiMaggio had this reputation as being difficult to approach, and I wanted to see what happened. The guy approached DiMaggio with great reverence, and DiMaggio treated him beautifully," Foss said. "It was a baseball, and DiMaggio said he would be happy to sign it."

People were starting to notice DiMaggio, and others began asking him for autographs as well. "He was polite and signed them all," Foss said. "Then the same man who had gotten the ball signed came back asking for another autograph. Well, this guy had crossed the line. DiMaggio stared at him, and the look could have bored a hole through his head. 'Didn't I just sign one for you?' DiMaggio asked the guy, and the guy backed off."

DiMaggio, Foss, and Angelos got into a stretch limousine heading for Harborcourt Hotel, about a block from Camden Yards, where the Orioles owned a suite that DiMaggio would stay in. Foss told him that there was going to be a VIP reception before the game at the B&O Warehouse, and he was welcome to come if he wanted to. "I told him we didn't expect him to come, but if he wanted to he was more than welcome," Foss said. "We were thrilled just to have him at the game. I told him he could join us in our private suite to watch the game, and if he didn't mind joining us on the field after the game, he would be introduced as Gehrig's teammate. All he would have to do is wave and not say anything."

DiMaggio asked some questions about the party, and told Foss he would like to go. Then he surprised the Orioles vice chairman before leaving the limo. "I'd like to say a couple of words if I could after the game, if that's all right." DiMaggio told Foss. "It was like I died and went to heaven," Foss said. "We never expected him to say anything. We were just grateful that he came."

DiMaggio, though, had seen enough in baseball over the years to know when something special was about to happen. On September 6, 1995, something special would happen that would immortalize Cal Ripken and make Camden Yards the center of the baseball universe.

The Streak, as it came to be known, was the salvation of baseball. After the controversial strike and its aftermath, fans were turned off by the business of the game and were reluctant to return. But in Ripken's Streak, fans found something worthy of their adoration and attention: a working-man's record in a game full of millionaires.

It was like no other record. All it required was for Ripken to show up and play every day. But in this age of selfish, pampered athletes, the idea that a player would never ask for a day off, and would always be in the lineup when you paid your money to see a game, struck a chord amidst all the bad feelings. It took some attention away from the bitter taste in the mouths of baseball fans everywhere.

In a way, Cal Ripken was a 1990s version of Babe Ruth—not talent-wise, but symbolically. On the heels of the 1919 Black Sox Scandal, when the game was at a similar low point with the public, Ruth came along and saved baseball with his exploits. While Ripken has put up Hall of Fame numbers, no one would say he is Babe Ruth on the field. But his march toward Lou Gehrig's record served the same purpose as Ruth's exploits.

Another factor that made The Streak far bigger than a baseball record is that it also became an issue during the baseball strike. In fact, Orioles owner Peter Angelos's refusal to use replacement players was based, at least publicly, in large part on not jeopardizing the Ripken Streak. This led to city and state legislation barring the use of replacement players at Camden Yards. The whole state of Maryland had mobilized behind the Ripken Streak.

The widespread support and reverence for what Ripken was about to accomplish had gone so far that at least one player, Houston Astros pitcher Todd Jones, went on record as saying that some of the members of the Major League Players Association had privately agreed that it would be all right for Ripken to cross the picket line if it meant preserving The Streak. This was a remarkable admission, and one that Ripken didn't want any part of. He steadfastly refused to even consider being an approved "scab."

Angelos had other reasons to buck his fellow owners—for example, he was closely tied with labor unions in Baltimore—but he stood to pay a big price if the owners went ahead with their replacement-player plan. He could be fined $250,000 for each game that was played in which he didn't field a team. If it had come to that, Angelos might have sued baseball in what would have been a bloody legal mess.

American League president Gene Budig was faced not only with the prospect of tangling with Angelos, but also an ultimate no-win situation: deciding what the status of Ripken's streak would be if there was replacement baseball without the Orioles participation. Fortunately for Budig, he didn't have to make that decision. Federal judge Sonia Sotomayor ended the strike on March 31 when she granted an injunction sought by the National Labor Relations Board against major league owners on an unfair labor practice charge resulting from the bitter labor dispute.

The injunction led to the players calling an end to their strike, the owners reluctantly agreed to take the players back under the terms of the old labor agreement, and replacement baseball ended before it ever began. That decision came hours before Budig would have had to announce his decision on Ripken. Though Budig has never said point-blank how he would have come down, there is little doubt that he would have ruled to somehow preserve The Streak. "On numerous occasions I assured everyone that the league would make every effort to protect The Streak," Budig said. "It was important that Cal Ripken be given the opportunity to keep his record going. I always thought it was in the best interests of major league baseball. He clearly deserved the right to challenge the record."

Angelos was convinced that Budig would have sided in Ripken's favor. "I don't think they had any intention to obstruct The Streak or prevent him from accomplishing his goal," Angelos said. "I believe the league would have declared those games forfeits, subject to the court action we surely would have taken against that, but therefore Cal would not have missed those games, and The Streak could have been preserved."

All of this only served to make Ripken uncomfortable. "I think it's commendable that he [Angelos] acted on his beliefs, and even though The Streak became part of that, I would still like to believe that my particular situation wasn't the motivating reason why he took the stand that he took."

It even got to the point where the 1995 schedule, without accommodations for whenever the strike would be settled, had the record-breaking event taking place on August 18 in Oakland. Everyone in baseball agreed that the historic game that breaks Lou Gehrig's record should take place at Camden Yards—not only Ripken's home ballpark, but now baseball's crown jewel, a stage equal to the drama that would unfold.

Everyone, that is, except Sandy Alderson, Oakland's general manager. During the winter, Alderson said there was no way the A's would trade the home date with the Orioles. "I'm going to watch that game from our box in Oakland," Alderson said. "We may have a seat for Angelos somewhere in the ballpark."

Angelos was already hated by much of the baseball establishment for his refusal to go along with their replacement-player scenario, but Alderson had more personal reasons to make life difficult for Angelos. Several months earlier, the Orioles owner had tried to talk to Oakland manager Tony LaRussa about taking the Baltimore job—even before Angelos had officially fired Johnny Oates. LaRussa had a window in which he could consider other offers, but Alderson was still angry that Angelos made a run at LaRussa—an unsuccessful run, with Angelos eventually hiring Phil Regan for the job—and wasn't about to make a deal with Angelos easily.

Eventually, the powers that be in baseball would have prevailed on Alderson to make the change for the good of the game. It turned out to be a moot point, however, when the 1995 season didn't begin until the strike was settled. With the new 144-game shortened schedule, the record-breaking game would be played on September 6 at Camden Yards.

But there was little room for acts of God that could play havoc with a baseball schedule at anytime—such as rainouts. The next day, September 7, was an off day, so that provided some cushion. But after that the Orioles were scheduled to go to Cleveland for a three-game series, and Indians general manager John Hart indicated that they were not able to trade a three-game series at

Jacobs Field in September when the Indians were marching toward their first post-season appearance since the 1954 World Series.

All of these political and social ramifications swirling around The Streak only made the record grow larger. Still, it hardly needed any added significance; it would be a historic accomplishment that could stand on its own in baseball history without all the baggage now attached to it. Furthermore, the last thing Ripken wanted was to put more weight on the accomplishment. Before the record-setting 1995 season, Ripken had done his best to downplay The Streak, at times even refusing to discuss it. After all, he had claimed all along that he doesn't play for The Streak, that he plays because he feels an obligation to be in the lineup every day. He learned this work ethic from his father, Cal Ripken, Sr., a lifelong baseball man who had been with the Orioles organization for thirty-six years, first as a minor league manager, then in a brief, unsuccessful tenure as Orioles manager, and finally as third-base coach. When he was fired after the 1992 season, the move caused a bitter rift between the Orioles front office at the time—team president Larry Lucchino and general manager Roland Hemond—and Ripken.

Ripken has grown defensive about The Streak over his career. Inevitably, when he was slumping—and for a "streak" hitter, the slumps come—he would be criticized for not sitting down and taking a rest. Invariably, however, he would play himself out of the slump. So he was cool at best to the idea of talking very much about The Streak, and now he was about to find himself in the center of a nuclear media spotlight.

Ripken had a glimpse of it when he hit game number 2,000 in Minnesota on August 1, 1994, and had to deal with a press conference for the milestone. He wasn't particularly comfortable about it, and he adopted his usual position of downplaying The Streak. "It is just a by-product of my desire to play," Ripken said.

The so-called "by-product" began on May 30, 1982, when manager Earl Weaver started Ripken at third base against

Toronto at Memorial Stadium. He would go on not only to play every game since, but for six seasons never even missed an inning, playing in a record 8,243 consecutive innings over a period of 904 games, until September 14, 1987. The manager that day took Ripken out in the bottom of the eighth inning and inserted Ron Washington in an 18–3 win over Toronto. The manager that day? Cal Ripken, Sr.

The inning streak ended, but The Streak continued, and even on that day when his father sat him down, it would have been a reach to think that it would continue on for so long. After all, ballplayers get hurt. Everyone gets sick. Surely something would come up to stop someone from playing every single game for fourteen seasons. Nothing, though, stopped Ripken, though he came close on several occasions to sitting out. Those moments themselves are milestones in the Ripken legend.

On April 10, 1985 (Game 444), Ripken sprained his left knee during a pickoff play in the third inning of a game against the Texas Rangers. He did not leave the game. He sat out the club's next game, an exhibition game against the U.S. Naval Academy, but was in the lineup the following night against the Toronto Blue Jays.

On September 11, 1992 (Game 1,713), Ripken ran out a double against the Milwaukee Brewers and suffered a twisted right ankle. He didn't come out of the game, but the Orioles called up Manny Alexander from Class AAA Rochester as a precaution. Ripken not only didn't miss a game, but he didn't even miss an inning for the next week.

On June 6, 1993 (Game 1,790), the most serious potential Streak ender occurred. A huge brawl broke out in a game at Camden Yards between the Orioles and the Seattle Mariners, and Ripken twisted his right knee in the fight. He stayed in the game, but his knee swelled up, and the next day he told his wife and manager Johnny Oates that he might not be able to play. He tested the knee in pre-game workouts and felt strong enough to play at game time. "It was the closest I've come to not playing," Ripken said.

Now Ripken was getting closer to the moment that all of baseball was waiting for, and the reluctance he had shown throughout his career about calling attention to The Streak would no longer do. He could no longer fight it. His wife, Kelly, told him as much before he went into the shortened spring training; she suggested that he should enjoy it and embrace the attention that awaited him, not fight it.

Ripken took that advice and met reporters for the first time that historic season the day after he arrived at spring training in Sarasota. With a standing-room only crowd on hand, Ripken came into the press conference and said, "I am announcing that I am retiring and going to play professional basketball this season." He was only joking, of course. But writers immediately told Ripken that he would have an easier time of things in the NBA. After all, the record there at the time for consecutive games played was 906 by Randy Smith of the old Buffalo Braves.

Everyone got a big chuckle out of Ripken's remark, but it was an indication of how he wanted to approach the tidal wave of media that awaited him this coming season: to enjoy the spotlight, rather than battle it. To do so would require planning. Orioles public relations director John Maroon, just on the job for a few days, came up with a system for Ripken to handle the crush of press during the season and still maintain some order in his life.

"We agreed to meet with reporters on the road the first day of every road trip," Maroon said. "He fought that tooth and nail at first. He thought it was presumptuous to assume that people would want to talk to him in every city. I said, 'Trust me, they'll want to.' We tried it, and he realized it would work, because once you deal with the madhouse the first day, then he would get a couple of days off." That was how it went. City after city, when the Orioles went on the road, Ripken would handle the horde of reporters the first day, meeting either in the dugout or in interview rooms to answer questions like these:

MINNESOTA REPORTER: "You're known as someone who's great with fans. How important is it for you to be that way this year and reach out for you and Major League Baseball?"

RIPKEN: "The way I look at it is that I'm just so happy that baseball is back. I'm just happy to be out on the field playing. . . . I'm going to handle myself the same way I've always handled myself over the years, making myself available by shaking hands sometimes or signing autographs [he engaged in a number of two-hour signing sessions that year after games at Camden Yards] or just by talking to people. You know that's a special part of the game. Spring training was always a special time because it was a more relaxed atmosphere, with smaller stadiums and people closer to you. Sometimes the big league game with the big stadiums and crowds and the seriousness of the championship season, sometimes the fan-player interaction is pushed to a distance. But I try to do everything I can to keep that close."

BOSTON REPORTER: "Could you tell us about your work ethic? Who had been influential in your life?"

RIPKEN: "My approach to the game has probably been influenced by my father. Essentially, in a team game like baseball, your teammates rely on you to be in the lineup every day. From the very beginning, my Dad preached that it was important to be there, in the lineup, on a daily basis. Maybe I've exaggerated the point a little bit, but I still think it is important to go out there and play in a baseball season for 162 games. . . . you can help your team win in the first inning by turning a double play or guessing right on a hit and run, and the coverage was right, and you avoid a bad beginning. It's always been preached to me to be out there and in the lineup every day. My father is the one that turned me in that direction."

NEW YORK REPORTER: "What about the comparisons between you and Lou Gehrig?"

RIPKEN: "The only comparison that can be made is that we share a desire to play, a desire to be out there and the fact that we have this consecutive-game streak. There can be no comparison saying who was the better hitter because it is obvious that Gehrig was one of the greatest players to ever play the game. I can't compare my career to that. We just share a desire to want to go out and play, maybe a work ethic and a love of the game, too."

OAKLAND REPORTER: "How have you been able to keep your body together and avoid injuries?"

RIPKEN: "I think there's a lot of luck involved in staying away from injuries. We all have a different threshold of pain in some regard, and we all have different ability to go out there and focus on a daily basis. I feel very fortunate to have stayed away from serious injuries or even sickness that would keep you out of the lineup. The other thing was that I've had the ability to establish my career early, to focus on my job and not have to be in a platoon situation. I could go out there and prepare for each and every day."

In city after city, Ripken went through the same ritual—until the Orioles arrived in Seattle in late August, the last road trip before he was coming home for the historic home stand. That was when the season-long celebration turned ugly. Someone identifying himself as Lou Gehrig, Jr.,—although Gehrig had no children—called the Kingdome and threatened to shoot Ripken if he played in the August 23 game against the Mariners. This was not the first death threat Ripken had received during the year, so a security agent had been assigned to travel with Ripken the month before.

Nothing came of this new threat, and Ripken, who played all nine innings of the game, was not even told about it until after the game. His teammates learned about it from reporters the next day when the Orioles moved on to Anaheim to play the Angels. "You have to just deal with it," Ripken said. "It's something that you have to think about and take certain precautions," he noted, adding, "in the very best world, I'd like to think that I'm just a baseball player. I want to come out and play baseball and be like everybody else. But when something like this happens, you have to think about things in a little bit different way."

Ripken's outlook was typical of the man. "I'm not going to let it affect the way I'm playing," Ripken said. "I'm not going to let it inhibit the way I live my life."

The Orioles left Anaheim without any more incidents and headed home to start the nine-game home stand that would immortalize Ripken. The Orioles also headed home with a dismal 54–60 record in what had been a disappointing season. Manager Phil Regan, hand-picked by Angelos's special hiring committee, turned out to be a disaster. He lost the respect of the players early on by clashing right from the start of spring training with Ripken and other veterans. The relationship never got better, but Regan had Ripken to thank for not being fired during the season.

Baltimore had climbed back to around the .500 mark by the end of July and was showing signs of competing for a playoff spot when the roof caved in on August 1. Reliever Doug Jones blew a 10–6 lead over the Toronto Blue Jays, losing 12–10. Jones and Regan were booed so loudly that night that Angelos wanted to fire Regan right on the spot, but general manager Roland Hemond and assistant general manager Frank Robinson talked him out of it.

Less than two weeks later, the Orioles were swept in five straight games in Boston. After the final game of that series, when the team finished with a record of 46–53, Angelos considered firing Regan again. However, he determined that the attention to such a move, coming within four weeks of the Ripken record-breaking game, might detract from the attention that was about to come to the franchise because of The Streak. So Angelos figured he would ride out the season with Regan, who was fired in October. None of that seemed to matter much when the home stand leading up to the record-breaking game began, a two-week period that would forever etch Camden Yards in the hearts and minds of baseball fans everywhere.

At one time, Ripken probably believed he would be playing this game—if he got this far—at Memorial Stadium, where Ripken used to roam as a child, soaking up the major league atmosphere all around him when his father was an Orioles coach. This stadium was also where Ripken broke in as a rookie and played every game from May 30, 1982, until the Orioles left after the 1991 season—1,573 consecutive games.

Would Ripken rather have broken the record back at Memorial Stadium? In his fourth season at Camden Yards, did he feel at home? "When we left Memorial Stadium, I was really torn between what I represented as old Orioles history and what I really loved about baseball, and how I associated that with Memorial Stadium," Ripken said. "As a player, you know that you are playing in the same place that someone like Brooks Robinson played in, the same place where all those World Series games were played. It just made you feel like Memorial Stadium was a special place.

"I was worried that when we went to Camden Yards, we would lose that feeling," Ripken continued. "I wasn't sure how it would be. But the strangest thing happened. When we started playing in Camden Yards, it felt like a place where baseball had been played for years. It felt like home." The home of the game— the perfect setting for what was to unfold over the next nine days.

The challenge for Ripken was simply to do what he had been doing since 1982: play. The Orioles management had a far greater challenge: coming up with a way to commemorate The Streak that was equal to the accomplishment.

"We figured we had to do something leading up to it, so we had some brainstorming sessions," said Maroon. "It was an unusual event. Even Cal said, 'How do you celebrate this? I go out and play a game. I don't have to hit a home run. I don't have to get a hit. I don't have to do anything. How do you celebrate it?'"

What the Orioles came up with out of those sessions was this: the rule declaring an official game would be put up on the JumboTron after the top of the fifth inning. John Tesh music would be cued up, and on the B&O Warehouse past the right-field scoreboard, beyond Eutaw Street, the numbers commemorating the countdown to 2,131—the new record—would be displayed in four unfurled banners, one for each number.

The first night the Orioles performed the ceremony was August 29, during the first game of the home stand, against the Oakland Athletics, a game the Orioles lost 3–1. As Ripken took the field in the bottom of the fifth inning, the ceremony began. The official game rule was posted on the JumboTron in center field. The music came up, and the 10-foot orange and black banners unfurled from the warehouse: 2,123.

Nothing. A few cheers, mild applause, but it barely caused a ripple among the 41,512 people that night at Camden Yards. "No one really got it," Maroon said. "We knew that might be the case at first, but it still made us nervous. We played the music, put the rule up there and dropped the numbers, and there was a smattering of applause. We got a little nervous, and we talked about it, and said, 'Oh my God, what if people hate it?' We gave it a couple of days. We figured maybe people didn't understand what was going on because we didn't publicize it. We just did it." Ripken wasn't comfortable with anything that would call attention to himself, particularly during an inning that might interfere with the flow of the game. So it was awkward for him on the field when this ceremony took place the first couple of games.

But something special was evolving at Camden Yards. Fans were embracing the whole thing, and by game 2,126, the fifth-inning commemoration had become a remarkably emotional event that caught everyone by surprise, particularly Ripken. He found himself having to keep his emotions in check as fans stood and cheered longer with each game as the numbers dropped and the inspirational music filled the ballpark.

The ceremony affected everyone in the ballpark, opposing players included. "I get goose bumps during that ceremony," said Seattle's Rich Amaral, when the Mariners came to Camden Yards for games 2,126 through 2,128. "It's amazing what he has done. We all have so much respect for him and what he is doing. I feel lucky to have been here these past few days to see this."

The entire Seattle team showed its respect for Ripken by standing on the steps of the dugout and applauding along with the 46,269 fans at Camden Yards that Sunday afternoon. Ripken was deeply touched by the display. "It's a tremendous honor, especially when it comes from your peers, the people you play against," Ripken said after the game. "I've been lost out there when that happens. The ovations get louder and louder, and longer and longer. You start to think back on your career and how you've been received by fans, and you get a little teary eyed. There's a lot of power in that moment."

The power was enough to ignore the play of the Orioles, who lost the game 9–6 for their eighth loss in their past ten games. Baltimore won just one of seven games on this home stand, while all this hoopla was going on. There were some frayed nerves and, as the day got closer, more concern than ever that something might happen to Ripken—illness or a baseball injury—to stop him from breaking the record.

In game 2,129 against the California Angels, one moment caused general manager Roland Hemond some anxiety. He was sitting next to Frank Robinson in the private box when Troy Percival came in to pitch for the Angels against Ripken. "I'm not a pessimist, but I was concerned," Hemond recalled. "He can throw 100 miles an hour. I said to Frank, 'Wouldn't it be awful if he hit him with a pitch.' Then I said, 'Hey, Frank, forget I told you that.'

"Well, lo and behold, the next pitch Cal went down like a sack of potatoes," Hemond continued. "He avoided getting hit, but it was real close. It would have been catastrophic. Each of the next two days I was checking the clubhouses early in the afternoon, checking to see if Cal arrived yet to make sure he got there safely. Maybe we should have sent for a chauffeur. I was nervous."

Finally, September 5 came, and losing just didn't fit in with what fate had in store for Cal Ripken and Camden Yards. His Baltimore teammates seemed determined not to let this historic game—Ripken's 2,130th, tying Gehrig—be a losing effort. They put on a remarkable display in the second inning, with four solo home runs. Chris Hoiles led off with a homer to left. After Harold Baines flied to right, Jeff Manto followed with a shot that cleared the center-field wall. Mark Smith then hit one to left, and Brady Anderson followed with another shot to center, sending the Orioles on their way to an 8–0 win over the California Angels. Scott Erickson did his part by shutting down the Angels, who were free-falling out of first place in the American League West.

"Emotions were running so high, it meant a lot to all of us on the team to come away with a win," said Hoiles. "First of all, the way things have been going for us, we were desperate for a win. To have a game like that on Cal's day makes it so much more special."

The sellout crowd—tickets were being scalped for this game and the following one for as much as $1,000—went hysterical when another Oriole blasted a home run. Like something from a Hollywood movie, Ripken blasted a sixth-inning drive over the left-field wall. In fact, after the game, Ripken himself said it was worthy of the Silver Screen. "I'm not in the business of screen-writing, but if I were, this would have been a pretty good one," he said.

The only damper on the home-run story is that Ripken would not get the baseball. A 32-year-old carpenter from Sykesville caught the ball and wound up selling it for $41,000. "It would have been nice to have the ball," Ripken said. "It's one ball that when you look at it, it means something. But I have the memory of rounding the bases after hitting the home run, and I don't need a ball to remind me of that." Little did Ripken know that he would get a chance at another ball, perhaps even bigger in stature and significance, the next night.

The big moment, though—the historic one, the one everyone paid to see, the one that made this night like something out of a movie—came after the top of the fifth inning. As Ripken returned to the dugout after Greg Myers flied out to center fielder Brady Anderson, the fans were already standing and roaring. His teammates were standing on the steps of the dugout, waiting to greet him. The "Day One" music began to play. The rule describing an official game was put up on the JumboTron. And at 9:19 P.M., the numbers 2,130 descended on the B&O Warehouse. Cal Ripken had achieved what had seemed impossible for decades in baseball. He had tied Lou Gehrig's consecutive-game record.

The noise rolled through Camden Yards like a tidal wave of sound as everyone—all 46,804 people fortunate enough to be there that night, along with the California Angels—stood and cheered, going on for nearly ten minutes. The scoreboard flashed images of both Ripken and Gehrig. Ripken's Baltimore teammates shook hands with him, and some hugged him. He came out of the dugout for what would be the first of three curtain calls. It looked as if Camden Yards was exploding, with thousands of flashes from cameras going off—a glittering scene. What still cameras might have missed, video cameras captured, including those by the Baltimore players themselves. Rookie Curtis Goodwin, who was holding his minicam, recorded a moment he will pass on someday to his children and grandchildren.

With each curtain call, Ripken mouthed the words "Thank you" to the crowd over and over, tapping his chest to show that he was touched by the outpouring of emotion. He looked to his wife, Kelly, who was sitting in the front row near the dugout along with his brother, Fred, sister, Ellen, and mother, Vi, who had played catch with Ripken when he was a young boy and Cal, Sr., was on the road. Then Ripken looked up to a private box to acknowledge the man who instilled in him the desire and drive to reach this point, his father. It was the first time Cal, Sr., had been at an Orioles home game since the team fired him as the third-base coach after the 1992 season.

After each curtain call, Ripken went back to the dugout, expecting it to end and play to resume. After the second curtain call, home-plate umpire Al Clark told Manto to get back into the batter's box. But the crowd was having none of that, with the noise still at a level that forced the celebration to continue. "No way was I going to start hitting then," Manto said. Clark saw it was futile, and waved his arms as the crowd chanted Ripken's name over and over again. "There was no way that an umpire is going to steal from a positive moment for the game like that," Clark said later. "That was not just for Cal Ripken, but for all of baseball."

Ripken eventually sat down in the dugout next to his best friend, Brady Anderson, and shook his head in disbelief. "I understand why this day is amazing and why tomorrow is amazing," Anderson said after the game. "But when you play with Cal every day, it seems normal. But I know Cal has been moved by all of this."

No one on the team knew Ripken better than Anderson, who came to the Orioles as a minor league prospect in a trade with the Boston Red Sox for pitcher Mike Boddicker in 1988. Anderson had come into his own as a star player in 1992, when he set leadoff hitting records with twenty-one home runs, eighty runs batted in, and fifty-three stolen bases. When Anderson first came to the Orioles and got to know Ripken, the shortstop asked him what he thought The Streak meant. "I told him it would mean that he would be remembered as one of the greatest players in history," Anderson said. "He said he hadn't thought of it that way."

Before the game, as they always did, Ripken and Anderson were stretching out in right field. Anderson looked up at the warehouse, where the numbers were furled up, waiting to drop later on to mark Ripken's place in history alongside Lou Gehrig. "I was looking up at the numbers and asked him if he was getting nervous," Anderson said. "He said, 'Yeah.' I think the week will mean more to him in the future, and it will be a relief when it's over."

The attention meant a lot to him that night, though, and the Orioles' post-game festivities were both reverent and light, with the emphasis on light. Team management got some criticism for some of the post-game moments, with rock stars and soap-opera stars, and talk-show host David Letterman's top ten reasons for Ripken to take a day off. They were as follows:

10. Not only about to break Lou Gehrig's record, but claims to have had daily conversations with him.
9. His infield chatter consists of, "Man I'm tired, man I'm tired."
8. Also about to break "consecutive days without showering record."
7. Recently removed appendix during seventh-inning stretch.
6. Built his own Wonder Bra using two batting helmets.
5. For the last 350 games, has been throwing like a girl.
4. Actually enjoys the stadium nachos.
3. Now getting mail delivered to second base.
2. He is starting to think that old dude who sells pretzels is kind of hot.
1. Five words: Jock full of stadium mustard.

The Orioles were criticized for cheapening the event with some of these program selections, but this would be a two-night celebration, and the following night would prove to be more than reverential enough. Some big moments took place this night, though, too, mixing in with the foolishness. Earl Weaver, Ripken's first manager and the one who had the foresight to eventually move him to shortstop, threw out the first pitch. Hank Aaron, baseball's all-time home-run king, presented Ripken with his Atlanta Braves jersey. One of the all-time heroes of sports in

Baltimore, the Colts Hall of Fame quarterback Johnny Unitas, presented Ripken with a blue jersey with number 19 on it.

But the most touching moment of the celebration night was when little-known pitcher Jim Gott came out of the dugout and presented Ripken with the ball from Ripken's first game of The Streak, which was on May 30, 1982. The game was also Gott's first major league victory when he was playing for the Toronto Blue Jays. Ripken was moved by the gesture and even tried to convince Gott to keep the ball. "That was hard," Ripken said. "I didn't want to accept it. The thing about baseball is that everybody carves their own moments. I told him, 'This is yours. I'm honored that you gave it to me. I might be more honored if you kept it.'"

After the game, Ripken met with an army of international reporters who came to Camden Yards that night to record the historic event. He said he felt some relief now that 2,130 had come and gone. "There seems to be a little easing of the pressure," he said. "It hasn't been great pressure, like a home-run record or a hitting streak. It's an event, and we're moving through that event, so it's getting a little easier."

Ripken didn't leave Camden Yards until shortly after 2 A.M. He left realizing that the moment everyone had anticipated—far more than he—was nearly at hand. "Now I knew it was inevitable," he said. "The next day would be the record, and I was anticipating it now. It finally felt like there was a finish line, although there really isn't one, or even a starting line, in my mind."

Ripken didn't sleep much that night, which turned out to be unfortunate. After all, he had a big event the morning of September 6, which was his daughter Rachel's first day of school. Ripken was determined to take her. "I didn't get much sleep, and then we wound up sleeping late," he said. " I kept pushing the alarm again and again and falling back asleep. When we finally got up, we were rushing around to get her to school." Ripken noted that a lot of people apparently showed up at his daughter's school, wanting to see him that morning. "But since we were late, by the time we got there and dropped her off, no one was around waiting."

Ripken tried his best to take it easy that day and keep things normal. But he knew nothing would be normal that day when he arrived at the ballpark at about 4:30 P.M. to find Secret Service agents all over the place, getting security in order for a group of very interested fans—President Clinton, Vice President Gore, and their families. No one in the clubhouse was trying to say much about the coming moment early that afternoon, but in the silence of Ripken getting his ankle taped by Orioles trainer and longtime friend Richie Bancells, something special was happening.

Mike Mussina sat in front of his locker, preparing mentally for one of the biggest games of his brilliant career. He waited for this moment for much of the season. "After the All-Star Game, I counted back five days [the turn for a pitcher in a rotation] and realized that I was scheduled to pitch on September 6," Mussina said.

Despite Ripken's best efforts, the atmosphere around the clubhouse was far from normal. Bobby Bonilla, Curtis Goodwin, and others were walking around with video cameras, taping everyone in sight, and Ripken as much as they could. "It was totally different," Ripken said.

Talk about different. Soon, President Clinton, Vice President Gore, and their families came into the Orioles clubhouse to meet Ripken. Now, it was not unusual for political figures to show up at Camden Yards. Since it is so close to Washington, DC, members of Congress or cabinet officials can often be spotted at the ballpark. In fact, that day, Maryland Democratic Senator Barbara Mikulski asked Senate majority leader Bob Dole if the evening session of the Senate could be postponed so Capitol Hill ticket holders could go to the game. "I'm so excited, it feels like New Year's Eve," she said. Earlier in the day, a proclamation was read on the House floor in honor of Ripken.

But this was different, bringing the most powerful man and his right-hand man into the clubhouse to meet Ripken, who tried to remain cool and collected while meeting Clinton, Gore, and company about forty-five minutes before game time. "This is the closest thing to an out-of-body experience," Ripken told the President. "It is like someone else is in your shoes."

"He began perspiring like he was having a heart attack," Maroon said of Ripken. "He was signing stuff for Clinton and Gore and their families, and the sweat was dropping off his forearms. He seemed like a nervous wreck, and he is normally so cool under pressure. It was like he was finally realizing what was going on."

Clinton joked with Ripken, telling him not to get writers cramp from signing all the memorabilia he was giving them. Ripken went out of his way to pay attention to the children, including Gore's son, Albert III, who was seriously injured in a car accident after the Orioles' opening day game in 1989 at Memorial Stadium. Orioles players brought their own children to the clubhouse to meet Clinton, taping the moment with their own minicams. Later, sitting in on the ESPN telecast, Clinton said Ripken's streak was a symbol of all the hard workers throughout America. "I think these stands here are full of people who do their jobs and are not recognized," Clinton said. "These people make the country go. Cal Ripken has made heroes of them all."

In the manager's office, Phil Regan was filling out six copies of a lineup card for the historic game. Earlier in the day, there was a slight panic at Camden Yards when someone realized that there was only one American League lineup card for the game. Extras were eventually found, and Regan filled out the cards. Because it was such a special occasion that everyone wanted to be part of, Regan wrote in the names of the four starting pitchers who would not be on the mound that night. Normally, those names are not put on a lineup card. Ripken, Regan, Angels manager Marcel Lachemann, the National Baseball Hall of Fame, the American League, and the Babe Ruth Museum would all get an official copy of the lineup card for game 2,131.

While Regan was filling out the lineup card, the hundreds of media in attendance were all struggling to come up with a way to put The Streak in perspective, as well as come up with a proper way to report on the night. Perhaps second baseman Bret Barberie put it best while sitting in front of his locker, near Ripken. "You know what this record is about?" he asked. "It's all about guts. It takes guts to do what he has done."

That night, Cal Ripken set a new standard for guts and reached a new level of glory. He took the field for his pre-game warm-ups with his teammates shortly after 5 P.M. He took batting practice and then signed some autographs by the Orioles dugout. After the lineups were announced, Bruce Hornsby and Branford Marsalis presented a brilliant, soft-jazz version of the National Anthem—a version befitting the evening and the ballpark. Then Ripken went to the mound to join his two children, Rachel and Ryan, who were throwing out the first ceremonial pitch.

Ripken took his place at shortstop shortly after, to a standing ovation. At 7:44 P.M. on September 6, 1995, Mussina threw the first pitch of the night. Like Erickson the night before, Mussina was determined not to lose such an important game, not to let anything take away from the good feelings that filled up Camden Yards and all of baseball.

But it didn't appear at first that the script would go according to plan. After Tony Phillips led off with a pop fly to Jeff Huson in foul territory near third base, Jim Edmonds hit a fly ball to Bobby Bonilla in right field for the second out. But then Tim Salmon blasted an 0–2 pitch from Mussina over the center-field wall to give the Angels a 1–0 lead. Chili Davis struck out looking for the final out.

But the Orioles would bounce back in the bottom of the first. After Brady Anderson hit a foul pop to Salmon near the seats in right field and Manny Alexander struck out, Rafael Palmeiro sent a 3–1 Shawn Boskie pitch over the right-center-field wall for a solo homer, tying the game at 1–1. Bonilla ended the inning by striking out.

Mussina breezed through the second inning, getting J. T. Snow and Garret Anderson on fly balls and striking out Rex Hudler. Fans rose from their seats in the bottom of the second and cheered long and hard as Ripken came out of the dugout to lead off the inning. He acknowledged the reaction and stepped in against Boskie. He popped out to the catcher, but two innings later Ripken rocked the ballpark with dramatic flair for the second straight night, with all of America watching.

The score remained tied until the bottom of the fourth, when Bonilla led off the inning with a home run over the center-field wall. Ripken came up to hit, receiving another standing ovation, and this time the fans stayed on their feet. As if his heroics in game 2,130 were not big enough, Ripken would top that in game 2,131. With the count 3–0, Boskie hung a ball out over the plate that Ripken drove into the left-field seats for a home run. This sent 46,272 fans into a frenzy and turned Camden Yards into the best theater in sports. But the game would only get better.

Unlike the night before, when the fan who caught the ball refused to return it to Ripken, opting instead to sell it later, this time the ball was caught by an Orioles fan who would later give it back to Ripken. Bryan Johnson of Pasadena, Maryland, managed to catch the ball after it bounced in the stands, even though his right hand was in a cast. As he was led from the stands by security, Johnson received an offer on the spot for $5,000, but turned it down. "This is Cal's moment," said Johnson, who met Ripken after the game and received some autographed items in return for the ball.

Mussina did his best to get to the moment at hand as quickly as possible by getting Hudler to hit a fly ball to Mark Smith in left field, Jorge Fabregas to hit a ground ball to second, and Damion Easley to pop out to second for the third out of the top of the fifth. As Ripken and his teammates ran off the field and into the dugout, fans stood and cheered, looking toward the B&O Warehouse for the ceremony that had touched so many people on this home stand.

The music began playing. The official game rule was posted on the center-field scoreboard. Then the numbers on the warehouse dropped—2,131.

This was the moment when Camden Yards truly became the "Home of the Game." With fireworks exploding and the crowd standing and roaring, the game of baseball—lost in the bitterness of the strike that had turned the game inside out—was coming back to the field. This was a celebration of baseball, in all its glory and tradition.

Ripken came out of the dugout, sending the crowd into an even greater fever pitch of applause and emotion. He waved, then looked up to the private box where his parents, Cal, Sr., and Vi, were, and waved his arms towards them. He walked over to the seats near the field where his wife, Kelly, and children were. He took off his game jersey and gave it to Kelly, Rachel, and Ryan. "I wanted to give it to someone who would get something out of it, and I couldn't think of anyone better than my kids," he said. Under his jersey, Ripken had been wearing a black T-shirt with the following: 2,130+Hugs and Kisses for Daddy.

Ripken picked up Ryan and kissed Rachel. Then he reached over and shook his brother Billy's hand. Billy Ripken had played with Cal from 1987 through 1992 for the Orioles; he was let go when their father was fired. Billy spent the next two seasons with Texas, but wound up playing the 1995 season with the Cleveland Indians Class AAA team in Buffalo. There was some question about whether or not Billy could make the game in Baltimore, but there he was, to share this historic moment with his brother.

Ripken waved to the crowd and kept tapping his chest to let the fans know that he was touched by their reaction. Boskie started to warm up to try to get the game going, but the fans would have none of it. They were simply too loud and too distracting for any baseball to be played. They had to dispose of a lot of baggage that baseball had saddled them with, and they didn't want this moment to end so quickly.

Ripken went into the dugout. Then he had to come out. He went in again, and then came out for curtain call after curtain call. This was not like anything ever seen in baseball. Ripken couldn't believe it, shaking his head, smiling, not really sure what to do next.

Bobby Bonilla and Rafael Palmeiro decided it for Ripken. They pushed him out of the dugout and told him that the cheering wouldn't stop until he literally ran around the ballpark. And so he did, giving the night the memorable touch that may never be equaled again. Ripken ran by the stands toward right field, slapping and shaking hands of fans as he went by. He ran around the warning track in right field, waving to fans and then, when he got to the Orioles bullpen, he stopped and shook the hand of Elrod Hendricks, the longtime Orioles coach who used to watch Ripken run around Memorial Stadium when he was a little boy. He continued around the field and then stopped at the Angels dugout, where all the players had been lined up at the top of the steps, standing and clapping. He shook hands with them and got a hug from coach Rod Carew and former teammate Rene Gonzales. Ripken stopped again at the seats where his family was sitting, and eventually—twenty-two minutes and fifteen seconds after play had stopped—the game began again.

"It still has a dream-like feel for me," Ripken said recently, reflecting on that night. "There were some great moments in that mid-game celebration. There was a lot of great interaction between my Dad and myself in a quiet way, with him in the sky-box and me in the middle of the field. Having my wife and two kids right there, too, and Billy, that made it special. But the lap was like a series of one-on-one celebrations, and that was cool. And the ways the California Angels responded was great. Shaking each of their hands, that was a very powerful moment within the celebration for me."

Everyone had their own way of celebrating it. General manager Roland Hemond added his own personal touch. "My office window was located between the 3 and the 1, and my wife put a picture of our grandson and granddaughter up there in the window," he said. "So whenever it is shown, we can see the pictures of our grandchildren. No one else can, but we can."

The teams played the rest of the game, with Baltimore winning 4–2. But after Ripken's lap around the field, the whole ballpark rested and gathered their emotional strength for the post-game celebration, a program that would be fitting for the occasion.

Orioles broadcasters Jon Miller and Chuck Thompson introduced the Orioles lineup from the May 30, 1982, game, the first in The Streak for Ripken. Then Ripken came on the field with his arms around his parents. He received presents from teammates, including a pool table, and a landscaping stone with 2,131 etched on it. Joe DiMaggio told the crowd that wherever Lou Gehrig is, "I'm sure he's tipped his cap to you."

Brady Anderson, Ripken's best friend on the team, spoke of the inspiration that Ripken had been for his teammates and the meaning of breaking Gehrig's record. "For fourteen years, Cal Ripken has played for the Orioles with skill, determination, and dedication," Anderson said. "His inspiration has always been a love for the game, his teammates, and the devoted fans of Baltimore. The record which has been broken today speaks volumes about a man who never unduly focused on this achievement, but accomplished it through years of energy, incredible inner resources, and an unflagging passion for the sport. But fame is a double-edged sword, and his is no exception. Incredible pressure has been placed on Cal as it became increasingly apparent that this achievement could be realized. In breaking this record, he surpasses the playing streak of Lou Gehrig, an exceptional baseball player so universally loved and admired that sentimentalists might have hoped it would remain untouched in deference to the man himself. Gehrig's haunting farewell speech at Yankee Stadium, his brilliant career, and his quiet courage leave a legacy of heroic proportion which will grace the game of baseball forever.

"I know Cal is honored to be in the company of such a legend, just as we know that each man's accomplishments and contributions enhance, rather than diminish, the others," Anderson continued. "For what finer tribute can one player give to another than his uncompromising excellence? We are thrilled to play beside him today, and we wish to thank Cal—our teammate, friend, and mentor—for enabling us to share this wonderful moment in time. We acknowledge his extraordinary performance in breaking this record but we acknowledge as well his excellence throughout the fourteen seasons."

Then, shortly after midnight under the clear Camden Yards sky, Ripken stepped up to the microphone to tell everyone who poured their hearts out that night what was in his. "When the game numbers on the warehouse changed during the fifth innings over the past several weeks, the fans in this ballpark responded incredibly," he said. "I'm not sure that my reactions showed how I really felt. I just didn't know what to do."

As fans cheered nearly every sentence, Ripken went on. "Tonight, I want to make sure you know how I feel," he said. "As I grew up here, I not only had dreams of being a big league ballplayer, but also of being a Baltimore Oriole. As a boy and a fan, I know how passionate we felt about baseball and the Orioles here. And as a player, I have benefited from this passion. For all your support over the years, I want to thank you, the fans of Baltimore, from the bottom of my heart. This is the greatest place to play.

"This year has been unbelievable. I've been cheered in ballparks all over the country. People not only showed me their kindness, but more importantly, they demonstrated their love of the game of baseball. I give my thanks to baseball fans everywhere. I also could express my gratitude to a number of individuals who have played a role in my life and my career, but if I try to mention them all, I might unintentionally miss someone and take more time than I should.

"There are, however, four people I want to thank specially. Let me start by thanking my Dad. He inspired me with his commitment to the Oriole tradition and made me understand the importance of it. He not only taught me the fundamentals of the game of baseball, but also he taught me to play it the right way, and to play it the Oriole way. From the very beginning, my Dad let me know how important it was to be there for your team and to be counted on by your teammates. My Mom, what can I say about my Mom? She is an unbelievable person. She let my Dad lead the way on the field, but she was there in every other way, leading and shaping the lives of our family off the field. She's the glue who held our lives together while we grew up, and she's always been my inspiration.

"Dad and Mom laid the foundation for my baseball career and my life, and when I got to the big leagues, there was a man— Eddie Murray—who showed me how to play this game, day in and day out," Ripken said, with the crowd going wild at the mention of Murray, the one-time Orioles great who was traded after the 1988 season after a bitter battle with owner Edward Bennett Williams and the local media. Murray returned for one season in 1996 and then, after retiring, joined the Orioles as a coach in 1998. "I thank him for his example and for his friendship. I was lucky to have him as my teammate for the years we were together, and I congratulate him on the great achievement of 3,000 hits this year.

"As my major league career moved along, the most important person came into my life—my wife, Kelly. She has enriched it with her friendship and with her love. I thank you, Kelly, for the advice, support, and joy you have brought to me and for always being there. You, Rachel, and Ryan are my life. These people, and many others, have allowed me, day in and day out, to play the great American game of baseball.

"Tonight I stand here, overwhelmed, as my name is linked with the great and courageous Lou Gehrig," Ripken said. "I'm truly humbled to have our names spoken in the same breath. Some may think our strongest connection is because we both played many consecutive games. Yet I believe in my heart that our true link is a common motivation—a love of the game of baseball, a passion for our team, and a desire to compete on the very highest level. I know that if Lou Gehrig is looking down on tonight's activities, he isn't concerned about someone playing one more consecutive game than he did. Instead, he's viewing tonight as just another example of what is good and right about the great American game. Whether your name is Gehrig or Ripken, DiMaggio or Robinson, or that of some youngster who picks up his bat or puts on his glove, you are challenged by the game of baseball to do your best day in and day out. And that's all that I've ever tried to do. Thank you."

After the ceremonies ended, Ripken and the others left the field, and the fans went home feeling good about baseball for the first time in a long time. Ripken said he still has people to this day who come up to him and talk about that remarkable night. "Camden Yards only holds about 48,000 people, but it seemed like a lot more than 48,000 people told me they were there," he said.

The next day, a parade and ceremony were held in downtown Baltimore. And it would not stop there. The day after, in Cleveland, Ripken's 2,132nd game, Indians fans gave Ripken a standing ovation, and were treated to a surprise. Ripken and Murray delivered their lineup cards for their respective teams to the umpires at home plate. The two men shook hands and talked for several minutes. The standing ovations would go on in every ballpark on the road the rest of the season, just as they did as Ripken approached the record-breaking game. In the postseason, Ripken got another standing ovation, this time at Fulton County Stadium, when he threw out the first pitch for a 1995 World Series game.

While there was celebration of The Streak this year, it had been a controversial record before 1995, when people criticized Ripken for playing every day. In 1996, Ripken became the focal point of controversy when Orioles manager Davey Johnson moved him for six games to third base after fourteen years at shortstop in the middle of the season, replacing him with Manny Alexander, who turned out to be a disaster. Johnson himself was taken aback at the furor this decision created. During the off season, the Orioles' front office orchestrated a carefully planned changing of the guard, meeting with Ripken to discuss moving over to third, and bringing in someone Ripken could accept as a replacement, Mike Bordick, who came over from Oakland as a free agent and signed a three-year contract. This plan went as far as Bordick actually talking to Ripken on the telephone to make sure that he was all right with Bordick coming to Baltimore.

Ripken suffered from serious back problems in 1997 that nearly forced him to sit out. He received a barrage of criticism for continuing to play every day, but he came back to be the Orioles best player during the postseason. The criticism grew even worse in 1998. The same media that sang Ripken's praises in 1995—and profited from it—now ridiculed his record and called for his benching. *The Baltimore Sun*'s Sunday Perspective section on August 2 ran a lead article titled "Time to End The Streak," written by the associate dean of the College of Notre Dame of Maryland. "For the sake of a splendid organization with a rich tradition, for the sake of a team that needs to find its soul and its spirit, Cal Ripken should step aside for a few games and let the organization free itself of this psychological barrier," the article stated.

Eventually Ripken gave in and sat down. On September 20, 1998, when the country was caught up in the Mark McGwire–Sammy Sosa home-run race, word spread minutes before a Sunday night game against the New York Yankees that Ripken would not play. He went to manager Ray Miller shortly before the start of the game and told him, "It's time." Miller crossed Ripken's name off the lineup card and penciled in rookie Ryan Minor, who, when told he was playing that night, nervously asked Miller, "Does Cal know?"

The Streak ended at 2,632, on Ripken's terms, as well it should have been. He earned that right, and the rival Yankees paid tribute to Ripken by standing on the steps of the dugout and cheering, as did the packed house at Camden Yards, who called for Ripken to come out of the dugout. He did, waving to the crowd during an ovation that lasted several minutes before play began again.

After the game, Ripken met with reporters at a press conference with his wife, Kelly. He said he was "very proud, not necessarily of the number of The Streak but the fact that my teammates could always depend on me to be out there."

It made sense to end The Streak at this time. Ripken, who had a mediocre season, with fourteen home runs, sixty-four RBIs, and a .271 batting average, had not played in a meaningless September since 1993. There was no September in baseball in 1994 because of the strike, and 1995, the season of the Lou Gehrig record, there was no way Ripken was going to sit down. The next two Septembers the Orioles were involved in pennant races. In September 1998, with Baltimore laboring through a disappointing season, there was no good reason for Ripken to play every day.

The record—2,632 consecutive games—will likely never be broken. McGwire, who set the most revered record in baseball when he broke Roger Maris's record of sixty-one home runs in a season, with an astounding seventy home runs in 1998, said Ripken's record "is the one that blows all the others away."

The Streak may always be debated. But there is no debate about this: on September 6, 1995, the center of the baseball universe was Camden Yards, and Cal Ripken's 2,131st consecutive game was a supernova, lighting up an entire nation.

CHAPTER EIGHT

The Playoffs

Camden Yards was about to be christened for the 1996 postseason play. The Baltimore Orioles were about to play their first playoff game since 1983, when they defeated the Philadelphia Phillies to win the World Series. Now they were facing the powerful American League defending champion Cleveland Indians in the 1996 division series. The Orioles struggled for much of the year, squabbling and underachieving for much of the time, but they managed to turn it on the last two months of the season and squeezed into the playoffs as the second wild-card team in history. They clinched their spot on the next-to-last day of the season with a 3–? win over the Toronto Blue Jays at SkyDome.

But all eyes were on Camden Yards on this October 1 afternoon not to see the Orioles play the favored Indians. They were watching to see if the umpires would show up. Nothing big ever seems to happen at Camden Yards without drama surrounding it. Drama once again was engulfing the ballpark and the Orioles in a morality play that began north of the border several days before but had taken center stage at Camden Yards, capturing the attention of the entire nation and endangering the playoffs themselves. No one in baseball was sure if the major league umpires would take the field for the playoffs this day, all because of a brief incident that set off a firestorm of controversy.

The Orioles went into Toronto in the final weekend of the season battling the Seattle Mariners for the American League wild-card position. They beat the Blue Jays in the first game 4–1, behind the pitching of rookie Rocky Coppinger. They needed one more win to clinch a wild-card spot, and hoped to do it on Friday, September 27. But nearly at the very start of the game, in the top of the first inning, all hell broke loose.

Batting second, Roberto Alomar took a called third strike from home-plate umpire John Hirschbeck. On the replays, it looked like a ball, and Alomar wasn't pleased with the call. He was already in a bad mood because of the negative reception he had received from Toronto fans, after spending five years with the Blue Jays. So as Alomar walked back to the dugout, he was yelling at Hirschbeck, stopping once. Hirschbeck said he gave Alomar a warning. Both men, however, were yelling at each other, Alomar from the dugout and Hirschbeck from behind home plate. Hirschbeck then threw Alomar out of the game, waving his hand. Hirschbeck said later that he warned Alomar to stop, "twice at the plate, once going way, and once in the dugout."

Davey Johnson and Alomar ran out of the dugout, with Alomar screaming at Hirschbeck. Johnson tried to keep them apart and carry on the argument, but Hirschbeck and Alomar went at it until Alomar spit in Hirschbeck's face. Johnson steered Alomar back to the dugout, but the second baseman was still yelling at Hirschbeck, and the umpire continued to scream back. This was bad enough, but there would be more, much more.

After the game, the umpiring crew was livid at Alomar. They were going to send a videotape of the incident to the American League office, and Hirschbeck said that he had never been spit on before as an umpire. "He spit all over my face," Hirschbeck said.

This alone would create a furor. But what happened after the game, and the next day, lit the fuse on this explosive situation.

Alomar gave a remarkable post-game interview, surrounded by reporters in front of his locker, in which with each word, he dug himself a deeper hole. "He missed that call by a whole lot," Alomar said. "A professional umpire should do a better job than that in such a big game. Then he called me bad names. There was no reason for that. He should admit he made a mistake, too." When someone asked Alomar if he regretted spitting in Hirschbeck's face, the second baseman said, "No, I don't regret it at all. I don't regret nothing."

Then Alomar said the words that sent this whole controversy into orbit and that would take the issue out of everyone's control. Alomar, who had been kicked out of a game by Hirschbeck back in July, said the umpire's personality had changed after the death of his son John, who had succumbed at the age of eight to a rare disease called adrenoleukodystrophy (ALD). "I think he had problems with his family after his son died," Alomar said. "I know that's something real tough for a person. He just changed personality-wise. He got more bitter."

Reporters were shocked that Alomar would bring up such a subject in the context of being thrown out of a baseball game. Whether he meant it to be or not, the comment was cruel and tasteless. Hirschbeck had not only lost one son; he had another one with the same disease.

Remarkably, during all of this, no one in this veteran clubhouse—with players like Cal Ripken, Eddie Murray, and Rafael Palmeiro—went to Alomar's aid to protect him. Finally, Bobby Bonilla, who had been tagged as a troublemaker by Davey Johnson, stepped in and pulled Alomar out of the crowd of reporters. By then, though, it was too late.

No one knew for sure the extent of the explosion that would come the next day. The Toronto papers were full of stories about Alomar's spitting, and ESPN, the sports network, began running the clip of the incident over and over again. The Orioles determined they had enough of a crisis on their hands and that, to soften some of the criticism, Alomar would have to apologize for spitting on Hirschbeck. They prepared a statement of apology for Alomar, which he was going to read to reporters from the visitors' dugout at SkyDome. But about ninety minutes before the game, reporters went into the umpire's dressing room to get comments from Hirschbeck about what Alomar had said the night before. It was the first time writers had a chance to tell Hirschbeck what Alomar had said, and there was an obligation to give him the opportunity to respond.

When Hirschbeck heard about Alomar's comments about the death of his son, the umpire responded with a fit of rage. "He brings up my son? I'm going to kill him," Hirschbeck said. He appeared near tears, and umpire Jim McKean asked reporters to leave the room. Several seconds later Hirschbeck bolted from the dressing room and told reporters, "You want a story? I'll give you a story. Where is he?" Hirschbeck headed for the visitors' clubhouse, where Alomar and several other Orioles were sitting around their lockers. With fellow umpire Jim Joyce coming behind him, Hirschbeck burst into the clubhouse and tried to attack Alomar, screaming, "I'll kill him." He was held back by Joyce and eventually gotten out of the room. The controversy had reached a new level. Nothing would ever be the same for Alomar again.

The Orioles quickly scrapped their apology plans because Alomar and club officials were clearly shaken by Hirschbeck's wild outburst. Hirschbeck was so upset that he went back to his hotel room, and the crew umpired the game with just three umpires. Baltimore general manager Pat Gillick tried to smooth things over with an apology by the organization. "From the Orioles' point of view, we don't condone spitting on people," he said. "I apologize on behalf of the organization to John Hirschbeck and the umpiring crew."

Nothing would stop this runaway train now, however. As word spread of Alomar's post-game comments and Hirschbeck's reaction throughout the world of baseball and the sports media, the story mushroomed like an atomic bomb.

Only adding to this melodrama was the outcome of Saturday's game. The Orioles won 3–2 in the tenth inning on a solo home run by the hero of the game—Roberto Alomar. The win clinched the wild-card spot for Baltimore, and they celebrated in the clubhouse by pouring beer all over each other. "I feel good for myself and for the team," Alomar said. "I was struggling a little bit, so getting the hit makes it much better."

Nothing would make it better for Alomar, though, who had no clue what he was in for in the days ahead. American League president Gene Budig only compounded the mess by mishandling the penalty. He quickly gave Alomar a five-game suspension, to be served the next season, before he truly realized the scope of outrage over the incident.

Alomar became a national villain, a symbol for all of America of the spoiled, rich athlete and the loss of sportsmanship in our games. He was roasted not only on the sports pages, but the editorial pages as well. He was front-page and network news. Nothing could stop it—not even his eventual public apology and a $50,000 pledge to research for a cure for ALD, matched by the Orioles, an offer the umpire's union urged the charity to turn down. (It didn't.)

This was Alomar's written apology, issued three days after the spitting incident: "I wish to take this opportunity to apologize to John Hirschbeck and his family for any pain and embarrassment that my comments and actions may have caused them. I deeply regret my disrespectful conduct towards a man that I know always gives his utmost as an umpire. Certainly, he has worked at least as hard as I have to make it to the majors. Notwithstanding what occurred, I have great respect for him and his profession. I'm sincerely sorry that my actions deeply offended John, and, by engaging in indefensible conduct, I failed the game of baseball, the Orioles organization, and my fellow major leaguers. If umpire Hirschbeck will agree, I am prepared to extend my apologies to him personally at a time and place convenient to him. I take a great deal of pride in the fact that throughout my years in baseball, I've always demonstrated complete respect to everyone I have shared the field with. I can say with all sincerity an incident like this will never happen again.

"Today I have pledged a contribution of $50,000 to the Johns Hopkins University and the Kennedy Kreiger Institute for ALD Research, and I am gratified to learn that the Orioles organization has joined me in a similar commitment in order to help win the battle against this deadly disease, which has claimed the lives of so many innocent children. While I understand that this gesture in no way excuses or mitigates my conduct, I do hope that it demonstrates my honest concern and complete remorse for what has happened, and my hope is that some good can emerge from this unfortunate, and, for me, a most regrettable happening."

All the money and statements of apology in the world were not going to stop this public-relations nightmare. Alomar was public enemy number one with major league umpires, who were incensed about what he did, what he said about Hirschbeck's family, and the punishment Budig handed down—a suspension. Even though the suspension would not be carried out until next season, Alomar was appealing it, a typical reaction by the players' union, but another poor public-relations move. The umpires threatened to strike during the playoffs unless Alomar received a tougher punishment.

That brings us to Camden Yards, where the Orioles faced the Indians in the first playoff series to take place on this fall day, and the world waited to see whether or not the umpires—who had a contract that prohibited any such job action—would carry through on their threat. Major league baseball prepared to go to court that morning to get an injunction forcing the umpires back to work. They hired crews of replacement umpires, one of which was secreted away in the auxiliary clubhouse within the bowels of Camden Yards, waiting to be called on. About forty minutes before the scheduled game time, Marty Springstead, supervisor of umpires for the league, came out of the umpires' room, but they were not there. The regular umpires were sitting in a hotel room, watching ESPN, waiting for a call from their attorney, as the sports world wondered if the Alomar incident would cause baseball's showcase fall season to unravel.

About twenty minutes later, Springstead came out of the umpires' room and told reporters that the regular umpires would work this day. The umpiring crew arrived at the ballpark like rock stars, with cameras running and reporters jostling to get a glimpse. An agreement had been reached that they would hold off on their threat to walk out, and Budig, instead of waiting for next year to hold a hearing on Alomar's appeal, would hold it the next day. That plan became moot, however, because Alomar realized how foolish it was to appeal a penalty that most people thought was not far severe enough. He dropped his appeal, and though the umpires would continue to make threats to walk out, ultimately a court injunction would stop them. But the heat on Roberto Alomar would continue.

The Orioles actually played some baseball in this 1996 postseason, and Camden Yards saw the best and worst of it. The best of it, when it finally began, came in Games 1 and 2 of the Division Series against the Indians. This team had fallen short of winning a World Series the year before against the Atlanta Braves, although with powerful hitters like Albert Belle, Jim Thome, and Manny Ramirez, the Indians had every intention of going back for a second try. But the first at bat for the Orioles in the bottom of the first inning set the tone for the entire game. In fact, that leadoff batter for the Orioles may have carried them the entire season—Brady Anderson.

Anderson had been emerging for several years as a star player, after struggling for several seasons as a prospect after coming to Baltimore from Boston in a 1988 trade for Baltimore pitcher Mike Boddicker. Anderson's breakthrough season came in 1992, when he had one of the all-time seasons for a leadoff hitter: .271 average, one hundred runs scored, twenty-eight doubles, ten triples, twenty-one home runs, eighty RBIs, ninety-eight walks, and fifty-three steals. He didn't approach those numbers for the next three seasons, but he played solid offense and excellent defense, developing into one of the best outfielders in the league.

There was no seeing 1996 coming for Anderson, though, no explaining the remarkable season he would have. He would hit an astonishing fifty home runs, second only to Mark McGwire's fifty-two, hitting number fifty on the last day of the season against Toronto, and breaking Frank Robinson's club record of forty-nine. Anderson drove in 110 runs and scored 117, with thirty-seven doubles, twenty-one steals, and a .297 batting average. He set an all-time record for most times in a single season leading off a game with a home run with twelve. In Game 1 of the Division Series against Cleveland, he did it again, leading off the bottom of the first with a home run off Cleveland starter Charles Nagy.

Anderson's teammates followed him. B. J. Surhoff hit two home runs, and Bobby Bonilla blasted a grand slam for a 10–4 win over the Indians. For Bonilla, this was a particularly sweet moment in a difficult season. Bonilla came to Baltimore on July 28, 1995, from the New York Mets for minor league prospects Alex Ochoa and Damon Buford. Bonilla came with a reputation as a malcontent, a troublemaker who failed to live up to his big contract in New York, and he was a target for the wrath of New York fans.

Baltimore fans and Orioles players, though, saw a different Bobby Bonilla. His enthusiasm and smile made him a fan favorite, and in a clubhouse with little life, Bonilla picked up the atmosphere. He organized a fantasy football league and just stood out for his lively approach to the game, surrounded by stoic teammates with quiet personalities. He also played well during his time with Baltimore in the second half of 1995, batting .333 with ten home runs and forty-six RBIs in sixty-one games. While always considered a defensive liability, he played well enough at third base, benefiting from playing next to Ripken at shortstop.

But Bonilla's good times ended when Davey Johnson arrived. Johnson didn't have much regard for Bonilla. On Johnson's first day, during the press conference for his hiring, Johnson said that Bonilla "was no Gold Glove," no matter where you played him. Bonilla reported to spring training one week early, but he went nearly the entire spring training before Johnson lowered the boom and surprised Bonilla by telling him he would be the full-time designated hitter (DH). Bonilla balked at first, saying he would not be the DH. Then he reluctantly—and vocally—did so under protest. It was a disaster, as Bonilla hit just .221 with two home runs in forty-four games as the DH. After he was moved back to the outfield, Bonilla batted .346 with twenty-five home runs and eighty-nine RBIs.

Bonilla was criticized for his battle against being the DH, but what Johnson did was unfair and one of several mistakes the manager made in his first American League managing season. He underestimated the psychological impact of being the DH, and never gave Bonilla enough time to prepare. This miscalculation was the primary reason for the Orioles' poor start and held them back until Johnson finally relented and moved Bonilla out of the DH role.

Bonilla lit up Camden Yards during the ballpark's first playoff game, making it a memorable one, a 10–4 win behind the solid pitching of David Wells. The second game also pleased the hometown crowd when the Orioles came away with a much closer 7–4 win over Cleveland. Cal Ripken provided the turning point in the game.

With Scott Erickson on the mound, the Orioles took a 1–0 lead in the bottom of the first off Cleveland starter Orel Hershiser on a throwing error by third baseman Kevin Seitzer, allowing Roberto Alomar to score from third. They extended it to a 4–0 lead in the bottom of the fifth inning on another home run by Brady Anderson and RBI hits by Ripken and Eddie Murray. The Indians immediately bounced back with three runs in the top of the sixth when Kenny Lofton singled, stole second, stole third, and scored on a ground ball by Seitzer. Jim Thome singled to right-center field, and Albert Belle blasted a home run into the left-field seats. The Orioles tied the game in the top of the eighth but missed an opportunity to blow the game open. With left-handed reliever Jesse Orosco starting the eighth, Seitzer singled to center and was replaced by pinch runner Jeff Kent. Thome singled to center, and hard-throwing but volatile reliever Armando Benitez came in to pitch to perhaps the most feared hitter in the American League, Albert Belle. Benitez was very careful with Belle, walking him.

The bases were loaded with nobody out, and Benitez came up big, saving the game and perhaps the short five-game series for Baltimore. He allowed a sacrifice fly by Julio Franco to score Kent, to tie the game at 4–4. But it would end there. Benitez struck out Manny Ramirez and got Sandy Alomar to pop up to his brother, Roberto, for the final out. Benitez's performance pumped up the Orioles. "If somehow we get through this series, you've got to look at what that kid did at the key moment," Bonilla said after the game.

Bonilla walked to lead off the bottom of the eighth, and Mike Devereaux came in to pinch run for him. Ripken doubled to right-center field, and Devereaux moved on to third. With first base open, the Indians intentionally walked Eddie Murray, and Indians manager Mike Hargrove replaced Eric Plunk with lefty reliever Paul Assenmacher to face the left-handed hitter Surhoff. With the infield in, Surhoff hit a bouncer back to Assenmacher, a double-play ball. He threw home to Sandy Alomar, who stepped on home to get the force on Devereaux, and then threw to first to try to get Surhoff. But the ball got past Kent at first, allowing Ripken to score what would be the winning run. The Indians argued that Surhoff tried to block the path of the play, but that plea fell on deaf ears.

The Orioles scored two more runs on a sacrifice fly by Anderson and a single by Roberto Alomar for a 7–4 lead. Closer Randy Myers shut down the Indians in the top of the ninth to preserve the win, putting Baltimore up 2–0 in the series and giving Camden Yards fans two memorable playoff games.

The series went to Cleveland and another Camden Yards offspring, Jacobs Field, with the Alomar incident still capturing headlines. The umpires' union was going to make as much political hay of this as they could to convince fans that they suffered too much abuse at the hands of players. Much of the time, however, the abuse is triggered by the aggressive combativeness of the umpires themselves, who seem to bait players in arguments. Many believe that is what happened to Alomar in Toronto. The umpiring crew shamelessly called a press conference before Game 3 at Jacobs Field, and nearly each one had something to say about the incident.

"In my twenty-eight years of umpiring professional baseball," said Jim Evans, "I've never seen anything like it. I have a nine-year-old daughter, and I would not be any more offended if someone spit in my daughter's face. So it is something we have taken personally and as an association. There has been another black mark on baseball. Irreparable damage to the game."

Ken Kaiser remarked, "If you've watched professional sports through the years, if you've watched what happened in the NBA last year with the officials being attacked, then this situation here . . . pretty soon we're going to be like English soccer, where if you don't like the game, you shoot the official."

Larry Young commented, "I think it should be stressed that the only reason we are working today is to abide by the judge's orders. We are not lawbreakers. We do defend our colleague John Hirschbeck, and, I might add, a very close personal friend. We feel that he has been wronged and also the memory of his son. We were willing to walk out not only of this series, but also the American League Championship Series and the World Series."

On the field, the Orioles suffered a setback in Game 3, with Benitez this time being the goat of the game. In the bottom of the seventh, he gave up a grand-slam home run to Belle with the score tied at 4–4—the Indians reached starter Mike Mussina for four runs on seven hits in six innings. This gave Cleveland an 8–4 lead, which ended with a 9–4 win.

But what was unnerving for the Orioles was the hostile reception that Alomar got from the rabid Indian fans. The Orioles knew they were in for a rough time, but they could not have anticipated the depth of the abuse he received at Jacobs Field. "It really shook him," said Davey Johnson. "It has worn on him big time." It got so bad that in Game 4 at Jacobs Field, Orioles general manager Pat Gillick and assistant general manager Kevin Malone nearly got into a fistfight in the stands with Indians fans attacking Alomar. "We started out in the seats, but we almost got into a fight, so we moved to higher ground," said Malone, as the two moved to a private box to watch the rest of the game.

What a game it was—a bizarre, dysfunctional game for the dysfunctional Orioles, with as ironic an ending as you would find in any melodrama. Baltimore did nearly everything it could to lose the game, striking out a record twenty-three times. "I wrote the game off so many times," said starter David Wells. The Orioles took a 2–0 lead in the top of the second on solo back-to-back home runs by Palmeiro and Bonilla. Cleveland came back to score two in the bottom of the fourth on a two-run single by Sandy Alomar to tie the game at 2–2, and took the lead by adding a run in the bottom of the fifth on an RBI single by Omar Vizquel. Baltimore hitters seemed helpless at the plate, a cakewalk back and forth from the plate to the dugout, and were losing 3–2. But in the top of the ninth, pinch runner Manny Alexander scored on an RBI single by Roberto Alomar, tying the game at 3–3.

The Orioles nearly lost it in the bottom of the ninth, however, when Palmeiro and Todd Zeile collided on an infield pop up, almost costing them a run and giving the Indians runners on first and second with just one out. The Orioles nearly won the game in the tenth inning, but Cal Ripken stumbled while rounding second after Eddie Murray singled to right, and Ripken was thrown out trying to go back. If he had been safe at second, the Orioles would have had runners at first and second with just one out.

The game remained tied until the top of the twelfth, when, with a sold-out crowd of 44,280 at Jacobs Field calling for his head, Roberto Alomar lined a 1–1 fastball from Jose Mesa over the center-field wall for a solo home run, giving Baltimore a 4–3 lead. The ballpark went silent. Fans were stunned that the target of their wrath had just gotten even by stopping the Indians from reaching the World Series again—something that appeared to be a given going into the postseason. Randy Myers closed out the bottom of the twelfth, and the Orioles were moving on to the American League Championship Series.

The Baltimore clubhouse was bedlam, with players shouting, hugging, and spraying champagne. They were releasing the pressure of the Alomar incident as much as celebrating winning the Division Series. "You almost knew the script was already written that when we had a chance to win it, he was going to win it," Davey Johnson said of Alomar.

Ripken called the win "one of the most gratifying of my career." But he knew that the Alomar incident still hung over his team. "It's hard for any of us to be in Robbie's shoes," he said. "It's a very difficult situation, and one that I know he regrets as a person and a baseball player. He admits that he made a mistake, he admits all of this right out in the open, and now it's time for him to go on. That hit against Mesa," Ripken said, "it blew life back into our team. I'm glad he hit it, or else I'd be explaining why I made a base-running blunder around second base."

Some more frustration was released when Eddie Murray credited owner Peter Angelos for refusing to trade players like Bobby Bonilla and David Wells during the season, as Gillick and Malone wanted to do, and also pushed for the mid-season trade to acquire Murray from Cleveland. "We'd like nothing better than to win this for Peter," Murray said. "He took a stand, and I'd like to see us win this for him." Imagine that, a player dedicating his effort to winning for the owner, with no labor agreement still reached by that time and the taste of the bitter baseball strike still hanging around. There was nothing typical about the Orioles.

There was certainly nothing typical about Eddie Murray. His return to the Orioles in July 1996 in a trade with Cleveland was one of the brightest spots of the season for Orioles fans. Murray was one of the franchise's all-time players, and, though difficult for reporters to deal with, is considered one of the best clubhouse leaders of his time. He was the heart and soul of the Orioles from 1977 through 1988, driving in more than one hundred runs in five of those seasons. But he got into a battle with owner Edward Bennett Williams and the local media, as he was made a scapegoat for the Orioles' worst season in club history in 1988, when they went 54–107. Murray wanted out, and the Orioles were forced to trade him on December 4, 1988, to the Los Angeles Dodgers for Juan Bell, Brian Holton, and Ken Howell—none of whom ever turned out to be worthy of such a trade. Murray played three seasons with Los Angeles and two years with the New York Mets before coming to the Indians in 1994. He was a fan favorite whenever the Indians came to Camden Yards, and the crowds would chant "Eddie, Eddie" when he came up to the plate. He was also a favorite of Angelos, and the owner lobbied hard to get Murray back to Baltimore when Cleveland made him available.

Murray made a triumphant return, filling in the troubled DH spot for Baltimore. He enjoyed one of the finest moments of his career when, on September 6, 1996, in a rain-delayed, extra-inning game against the Detroit Tigers, Murray blasted his 500th career home run—the exact same day that Cal Ripken had broken Lou Gehrig's record the year before. Murray ended his career after the 1997 season with the Anaheim Angels and the Los Angeles Dodgers, retiring with 504 home runs, 1,917 RBIs, and 3,255 hits. He is only one of three players in baseball history to have 500 home runs and 3,000 hits; the other two are Hank Aaron and Willie Mays. Murray remains part of the show at Camden Yards as a coach for the Orioles.

While Murray dedicated the series win to the owner, Roberto Alomar sat in front of his locker, overwhelmed by what he had been through, contrasting it with the joy of hitting the game-winning home run. "I was just trying to get a hit," he said, smiling. Then, through the sea of writers surrounding his locker, a familiar face burst through. It was his brother Sandy, who came over from the Cleveland clubhouse to congratulate Roberto, who burst into tears upon seeing his brother as the two men hugged. "I love my brother," Roberto said later. "I am sorry for what I did. I made a mistake."

Alomar would be forgiven the very same day by Hirschbeck, who released a statement from his home in Poland, Ohio. "I wish to state publicly that I forgive Roberto Alomar for his actions," Hirschbeck said. "I am sure that he wishes as much as I do that this incident had never occurred. Denise [Hirschbeck's wife] and I speak today with the hope of putting the events of this past week to rest and to begin the process of healing and restoration. It is time to bring closure to this matter. . . . I ask that everyone who loves baseball—umpires and players, fans and journalists, unions and owners—will join us in reconciling our differences and in restoring our mutual respect in and for the great game of baseball."

Learning of Hirschbeck's statement after the game, Alomar said, "I hope I can meet with him and his family to tell him how sorry I was that this happened. I hope this puts everything behind us." That wasn't going to happen, though. A lot of people who were still angry—umpires, journalists, fans, unions, and owners—had no intention of forgiving Alomar. In addition, he was heading for the most unforgiving place in America, New York City, where the fans and tabloid media were licking their chops at a chance to get at him.

The papers were full of articles about Alomar, with columnists urging fans to let him know what they thought of him, and talk-show hosts delivering venomous attacks against the second baseman. There were death threats, and New York police and major league and Orioles officials feared for Alomar's safety. After all, there is no more dangerous place to play in baseball than Yankee

Stadium, where fans often throw objects—sometimes dangerous projectiles—at players. Before Game 1 of the series, Yankees manager Joe Torre urged fans not to get out of hand. "Let them voice any opinion they want to voice, but leave it at that," he said. "Throwing any type of object on the field would be a disgrace to me."

The Orioles-Yankees rivalry didn't need anything to fuel it. During the regular season, New York, winners of the American League East, defeated the Orioles in ten of the thirteen times they played. The Alomar incident was only gasoline on the fire. But in this Twilight Zone year for the Orioles, the strangest thing was yet to come.

The day started with the continuing war of words between baseball officials and the umpires' union about Alomar, but no one mentioned Alomar after the game. There would be a new name on everyone's lips, and he would be the toast of New York. Fast forward to the bottom of the eighth inning. The Orioles were leading 4–3 and had a chance to win at Yankee Stadium and negate the Yankees' home-field advantage. Benitez was in the game for Baltimore, facing Derek Jeter. The Yankees shortstop lofted a high fly ball to right field, and Tony Tarasco backed up against the wall, put his glove up in the air, and waited for the ball to fall into it.

It never did. Before Tarasco could make the catch, a twelve-year-old boy from Old Tappan, New Jersey—Jeffrey Maier, a name that will live in infamy among Orioles fans—stopped it, reaching his glove out over the fence and trying to catch the ball. He didn't get the prize. The ball was snatched away by another fan. No one ever found out that other fan's name, but by the next day, everyone knew who Jeffrey Maier was.

This was clearly fan interference, but umpire Rich Garcia entered the Hall of Fame for blown calls when he called it a home run, sending the Yankees crowd into a frenzy and Orioles manager Davey Johnson out of the dugout and into right field. Johnson, Tarasco, and other Orioles surrounded the umpire, and the fans responded by throwing all sorts of debris at Johnson, who was thrown out of the game, and the others. Television replays clearly showed that it was fan interference, but that didn't help the Orioles. Garcia was not going to change his mind.

The score was tied at 4–4 until the bottom of the twelfth inning, when Bernie Williams led off with a home run to give the Yankees a 5–4 win in Game 1. Maier, interviewed during the game, was proud of his role in the win. "I was just trying to catch the ball," he said. "It bounced right out of my glove and bounced on the floor. I feel bad for the Baltimore fans, but as a Yankee fan, if I helped the team, I feel pretty good."

The Orioles felt robbed, and the controversy was only made worse when, after watching the replay after the game, Garcia admitted he blew the call. "When I look at it on the replay, no, it obviously was not a home run. But I still don't think he could have caught the ball," he said of Tarasco. "I probably could have called fan interference. But I would not have called Jeter out from what I saw, and I only saw the replay once." When asked what he thought the crowd reaction would have been if he had changed the call and called Jeter out, Garcia replied jokingly, "Do I have to answer that?"

This was an embarrassing post-game performance by Garcia, given the stakes of the game. To say that Tarasco would not have caught the ball was another bad call. Tarasco had the ball in his sights and was making no attempt to jump for the ball. "There's no way I would not have caught that ball," Tarasco said. "It was a magic trick, because the ball disappeared out of thin air. Merlin must have been in the house. It was a routine fly ball that just happened to be back on the warning track. The kid just reached over and grabbed it. We almost touched gloves."

Garcia's goof came on the heels of umpires union chief Richie Phillips's proclamation at a press conference earlier in the day attacking Alomar and the league's disciplinary action against the second baseman. Phillips described the crew at Yankee Stadium as part of an umpiring corps that was "the finest in the world." That seemed a hollow claim after the blown interference call, since no umpire tried to overturn it. Furthermore, for the playoffs, the major leagues use six umpires instead of the four normally used during regular-season games. When Davey Johnson pointed that out after the game, he sarcastically wondered, "How many do they need, nine, one for each player?"

It seemed as if the fate of the Orioles was being decided by some power with a sense of the absurd. Consider this: Before the start of Game 1, the Orioles management, Gillick and Malone, met with the Yankees management and the umpires to go over the ground rules at Yankee Stadium. The number one topic of discussion? Fans reaching over and interfering with balls. "It was like it was almost spoken into existence," Malone said.

The wildness continued. The Orioles filed a protest with acting commissioner Bud Selig, actually going to the commissioner's office the next morning with a legal brief put together by Angelos's law offices and baseball people to try to get the outcome of the game overturned. Here is an excerpt from that document, under the section of "Basis of Protest":

"This is an extraordinary protest based on extraordinary events. A human error by the umpire, making a mistaken call, would not justify the attention of the commissioner and league president. A fan impulsively interfering with the play would not justify your attention. This protest, however, strikes at the very essence of Major League Baseball: integrity and consistent application of the rules.

"To Mr. Garcia's credit, upon his reflection and further review after the game, what appeared to him to have been a home run at the moment was now clearly something else. By his own explanation, Jeter's fly was 'not a home run,' likely a 'missed call,' 'probably interference,' and at most a ball that would have 'only hit the wall.' Without question, the outcome of the game would have been different."

The appeal concluded that "the best interest of baseball fans is not served by the silence on the part of those who have a responsibility to speak. Here, millions of fans, the national media, and umpire himself have already spoken. It is time for the commissioner to safeguard the integrity and restore public confidence in baseball. The Orioles respectfully request that the commissioner direct the league president to reverse the umpire's decision."

That was not going to happen. American League president Gene Budig wrote in response that "the best interests power of the commissioner does not apply in this case. It is not intended to be used to circumvent the on-field judgement of the umpires or the express authority of the league presidents to decide game-related protests. This is consistent with precedents throughout baseball history in which judgements made by umpires on the field have been given deference."

Jeffrey Maier was given his share of deference, becoming the biggest celebrity of the city. His parents took him out of school the next day so he could ride in a limousine from television show to television show, starting with *Good Morning America* and ending with David Letterman, with stops at radio shows and lunch at the All-Star Cafe in between. Maier was given box seats for himself and his family for Game 2 by the *New York Daily News*.

Baltimore would somehow come back to win Game 2 by a score of 5–3 behind the pitching of Wells, with home runs by Palmiero and Zeile. In between innings, Garcia signed autographs for fans in the stands, another example of the absurdity of what had taken place, though Garcia said he was not trying to make light of the situation. "Some kids asked me to sign their tickets, and one of them had a picture," he said of the autographs. "Trust me, I took it seriously, and I still take it seriously. The last two days have not been the greatest days of my life, but I'm not going to walk out there with my head down. I'm a proud man. I've worked hard every day of the last twenty-two years, and I'm not going to put my head down after twenty-two years because of one play."

Maier, on the other hand, showed some humility. He indicated that the players still had something to do with the win in Game

1. "I'm not as famous as the Yankees," he said. "The players go out there every day. They deserve the credit." But even with the Game 2 victory, the damage appeared to have been done. There was something about this series as it returned to Camden Yards for Game 3. Even with the series tied at 1–1, the feeling was that the momentum was with New York.

"That kid could have changed everything" assistant general manger Kevin Malone said, looking back on the series. "You don't want to say one game or one incident, but it very well may have. Baseball is a game of tempo, a game of rhythm. It does have a flow to it. I think if we come out of there 2–0, they have to come down here and sweep and still have to go back to New York and win one, so we really felt we would have been in the catbird seat. But that changed the atmosphere of the series."

Several years later, Gillick felt that baseball missed a chance to show some courage by not granting the Orioles' appeal. "I was disappointed that it was denied, not so much for the team, but more so for the industry, from the standpoint that I believe there were millions of people watching this game on television," Gillick said. "They saw someone reach over the fence and interfere with play. This was something that wasn't right. It was absolutely wrong, and baseball could have done something about it. They could have said, no, that's not what should have happened, and put the runner back on second base. I thought baseball could make a statement that they want to do the right thing.

"Instead, the Yankees won the game, and this kid was a hero in New York, on television, on the back pages of the newspapers," Gillick said. "I thought it was ridiculous."

Baltimore fans flocked to Camden Yards for Game 3, but they appeared as shell-shocked as the Orioles were, expecting that something would go wrong. It did. Mussina was brilliant on the mound through seven innings. Baltimore led 2–1 going into the top of the eighth, having scored two runs in the bottom of the first on a two-run home run by Zeile, who would go from hero to goat in the same game.

Mussina had retired ten in a row going into the top of the eighth. But with two outs, Jeter doubled down the right-field line. Bernie Williams brought him home with a single to left, tying the game at 2–2. Tino Martinez followed with a drive to left field that B.J. Surhoff ran down. Surhoff made the throw home, but Zeile cut it off. Williams stopped at third, and Zeile turned to try to throw to second to get Martinez. When he saw he had no chance, he tried to stop his throw. But the ball slipped out of his hands and rolled away. Williams then bolted for home to give New York a 3–2 lead. "It was a bizarre play," Zeile said. "I felt it slipping out of my hands. I couldn't stop it."

Mussina had already been in trouble, but the Zeile play seemed to unnerve him further. Johnson, however, elected to keep him in the game to face Cecil Fielder, who had little success against Mussina in the past, with just six hits in thirty-nine career at bats. But Fielder chose this moment to deliver his seventh hit, a two-run home run over the left-center-field fence. This was a huge blow to the Orioles, giving the Yankees a 5–2 lead in the game and a 2–1 lead in the championship series. As glorious as the first two playoff games were at Camden Yards, these three were dark days for the ballpark and its fans.

New York thumped Baltimore in Game 4, thanks to the slugging of Bernie Williams and Darryl Strawberry, who each hit two home runs to lead the Yankees to an 8–4 victory over rookie Rocky Coppinger. The crowd of 48,974 sat numbed by the realization that for all intents and purposes, their season at Camden Yards would most likely end tomorrow.

Strawberry's two home runs provided the Orioles with a look at what might have been. Strawberry had once been one of the most feared hitters in baseball during his younger days with the New York Mets—and Davey Johnson—setting the Mets club record for home runs in one season with thirty-nine. But after signing as a free agent with the Los Angeles Dodgers in 1991, Strawberry fell on hard times, with physical problems adding to his personal struggles of dealing with alcohol and drug addictions. His troubles drove him out of Los Angeles and then later out of San Francisco, as his erratic behavior resulted in instances where he simply disappeared from the team on both clubs. He also faced income tax woes and seemed finished as a ballplayer by the end of the 1994 season.

But Yankees owner George Steinbrenner took a chance on him in 1995. After playing thirty-one minor league games, Strawberry was called up late in the season and showed some promise, batting .276 with three home runs and thirteen RBIs in thirty-two games. This wasn't enough, though, for Steinbrenner to bring Strawberry back in 1996, so the slugger began his season playing for the independent minor league St. Paul Saints, where he put up big numbers, with eighteen home runs and thirty-nine RBIs in twenty-nine games. He eventually wound up back with the Yankees, but the deal was engineered by *New York Post* columnist Tom Keegan, who believed Strawberry was good copy, and he played Peter Angelos and Steinbrenner against each other.

Keegan wanted the Yankees to sign Strawberry, but Steinbrenner was dragging his heels. So Keegan, who knew Angelos from covering the Orioles in 1994, spoke to Angelos and told him how great Strawberry was doing in St. Paul. Angelos then directed Gillick to look into signing Strawberry, and Gillick dispatched a scout to watch Strawberry play. When Steinbrenner learned from Keegan that the Orioles were sending a scout to see Strawberry, the Yankees owner moved quickly to sign the slugger before the Orioles could.

Now, in Game 5 of the championship series, Strawberry was delivering yet more ironic pain to the Orioles, a team that was drowning in painful ironies during this postseason. Game 6, though, would provide the ultimate irony. Some would say that Roberto Alomar got his due in the top of the third. After Jim Leyritz led off with a home run off Baltimore starter Scott Erickson, Jeter followed with a single, then Wade Boggs reached on an infield hit.

Bases loaded. Nobody out. Bernie Williams hit a ground ball toward second. The Orioles had a chance for a double play to minimize the damage. But as Alomar reached down for the ball, it went through his legs and into right center field, allowing Jeter to score. The error wound up costing Baltimore three more runs, as Fielder blasted a three-run home run to give New York a 5–0 lead. This was followed by a tremendous solo blast by Strawberry—448 feet into the Yankees bullpen beyond the left-center-field wall, one of the longest home runs ever hit at Camden Yards. The Yankees ended the inning with a 6–0 lead.

Baltimore closed the gap to 6–4 with solo home runs by Zeile and Murray and a ninth-inning two-run home run by Bonilla, who had a horrible series, going one for twenty. But with two outs in the bottom of the ninth, Ripken grounded out to Jeter to end the game and the Orioles' season.

For Roberto Alomar's critics, justice was served when the six-time Gold Glove second baseman became the goat of the game. But he hardly admitted as much in a post-game interview. "I don't think that we lost the game because of the error," he said. "They just played better baseball than us. They took advantage of some pitches up in the zone."

Baltimore fans quietly filed out of Camden Yards for the last time in 1996. It was a roller-coaster postseason. They nearly saw an umpires' boycott of the Orioles' first playoff game there. They celebrated two Camden Yards wins in the Division Series, and mourned three straight losses to the Yankees. They stood by Alomar and cheered him while the crowds on the road vented their rage at him. But they, like so many others, would debate the Alomar-Hirschbeck incident for months to come. It changed Alomar's career, and it is forever etched into the American sports landscape. Two years later, the Alomar incident and the penalty he received was used by Latrell Sprewell in his efforts to get his NBA suspension reduced for choking Golden State Warriors coach P. J. Carlisimo.

What happened on that September 27 night in Toronto? Hirschbeck has denied that he provoked Alomar, and Alomar has refused to reveal publicly what transpired. But to this day, the Orioles organization continues to argue that, although they don't condone what Alomar did, his behavior was not without provocation, and that Hirschbeck has never taken responsibility for his role in the controversy. "I watched as the whole spitting incident took place that night and knew that there was this provocation that had to be very intense for this man who I knew was very kind and gentle," said Orioles vice chairman Joe Foss. "I learned afterwards the profanity and the names that Hirschbeck had called Robbie that not only provoked him but that were so culturally enraging for a Latin player. . . . it didn't excuse Robbie for what he did, but it certainly explained it.

"But what frustrates me today beyond words that I can express is that the next day Hirschbeck comes into our clubhouse threatening to kill Robbie," Foss said. "That seems to have been lost sight of by the public. John Hirschbeck was reacting to comments that he had read that Robbie had said that he must have changed because of the loss of his son. Well, as difficult as that was for John Hirschbeck to accept, as traumatic as those comments were on his family, isn't it traumatic for Robbie to be insulted, his mother to be insulted, through some vicious comments in front of 46,000 people in the heat of competition?"

Agreeing with this comparison might be difficult, since obscenities are part of the language among ballplayers, and since Alomar's comments revolved around such a personal tragedy. But they are comparable on this level: What Hirschbeck said triggered the spitting, and what Alomar said triggered Hirschbeck's threat and scuttled any chance to end the controversy that next day. They were both key, volatile moments in this furor.

Gillick also believes that Hirschbeck was guilty of the sin that seems to plague so many of the game's umpires today: baiting players. "Robbie went back to the dugout, and I think the umpire was just looking for trouble," Gillick said. "It was one of those situations where the umpire didn't let it go away, and they got into an argument, and the incident occurred. I think there is blame on both sides."

This controversy punctuated what had been a wild and dramatic season at Camden Yards in 1996, the year the ballpark took center stage in the postseason for the first time.

CHAPTER NINE

Manager of the Year

Davey Johnson landed at Baltimore-Washington International Airport with a knot in his stomach on this particular Saturday in August 1998. This was the first time he was back in Baltimore since leaving shortly after the Orioles lost Game 6 of the American League Championship Series 1–0 to the Cleveland Indians at Camden Yards in October 1997.

It was a disappointing loss. After all, the Orioles had won ninety-eight games and led the American League East from the first day of the season to the last, only the third team in league history to do so. The Orioles had defeated the powerful Seattle Mariners and Randy Johnson 3–1 in the best of five series. But they were shocked by the underdog Indians in the Championship Series and missed a trip to the World Series for the second straight season. Still, it was hardly a season after which the Orioles manager should be leaving town in fear of losing his job. But in the Camden Yards soap-opera atmosphere, Johnson left Baltimore not sure if he would be returning.

But now here he was, eleven months later, coming back, with his pitching coach, Ray Miller, now managing a floundering Orioles team that wouldn't get anywhere near the playoffs. "It was tough to come back," Johnson said. "I won't be going to the park." Then he smiled and said, "I'm in exile."

Johnson came back for an appearance and autograph signing in Baltimore County. Nearly 300 people paid $18 to get the former Oriole manager's signature. Nearly all of those who waited on line at the Tall Cedars of Lebanon Hall felt the same as many Orioles fans did when Johnson resigned in November: angry that he was gone. "It's a shame he's still not with the Orioles," said Ed Banayat of Falls Church, Virginia. "He's won everywhere he has been."

The story of the 1997 playoffs at Camden Yards is more proof that nothing simple seems to happen at this ballpark. Everything is a drama, and the main one going into the postseason was the feud between Johnson and owner Peter Angelos. But other, far more inspiring dramas than the bitter battle between the owner and the manager were also going on. For example, Mike Mussina, having beaten Randy Johnson twice in the Division Series, was certainly an important story.

But the real story of the playoffs was the remarkable return of Eric Davis, the Baltimore right fielder who was in the starting lineup for the Division-Series-clinching Game 4 and went one for four. Davis in the lineup in the playoffs at Camden Yards was a triumph of the human spirit.

Davis was out of baseball for the entire 1995 season, having retired after a brilliant career marred by injuries. The game got to be too much for Davis, whose body was breaking down. He couldn't take being the kind of ballplayer who could play just thirty-seven games for the Detroit Tigers in 1994, suffering from a herniated disk in his neck, or batting just .183—hardly the sort of numbers expected for someone who was once touted as the next Willie Mays. After visiting with his former Reds teammate Barry Larkin during the 1995 playoffs, however, Davis became convinced he could come back. So he worked out, preparing in the off season for his comeback with the Cincinnati Reds. Davis wound up as one of the best comeback stories of the year: out of baseball in 1995, batting .287 with twenty-six home runs, eighty-three runs batted in, and twenty-three steals in 129 games in 1996.

In 1997, Davis signed a $2.2 million, one-year contract with the Orioles, and it looked like a bargain at the start of the season. Davis was the most electrifying player on the team, starting off with a .302 average with seven home runs, twenty-one RBIs, and twenty-seven runs scored in just thirty-four games. But on May 24, Davis left a game in Cleveland with severe stomach pain. He played the next night against the Indians and went with the Orioles for their series with New York, but he flew back to Baltimore and checked into the University of Maryland Medical Center for tests.

Davis was originally diagnosed with a stomach abscess and then a perforated bowel and was put on antibiotics. When his condition didn't improve, there were concerns that he had an even more serious problem, and further tests confirmed those fears. Davis, thirty-five years old, with the body of a Greek god, had cancer of the colon.

While the Orioles opened their first interleague series—three games with the National League champion Atlanta Braves at Turner Field—Davis was under the knife on June 13, getting the tumor and part of his colon removed. "He has a favorable prognosis," said Dr. Keith Lillemoe, professor of surgery at Johns Hopkins University and the surgeon who performed the operation. "We're very optimistic."

Lillemoe was talking about living, recovering from the disease. He wasn't talking about playing baseball again, particularly this year. Such a prospect seemed remote, almost ridiculous to consider. After all, he would have to undergo chemotherapy treatments that would last well into the end of the season and beyond. No one had ever tested the possibility of taking chemotherapy treatments—a physically demanding program with sometimes severe side effects—and playing baseball at the same time.

After coming out of the hospital, Davis returned home to Los Angeles to recover, but that recovery, in his mind, included returning to play with his teammates before the season was over. His fight helped inspire the Orioles, and his mere presence in Oakland to see his teammates when the Orioles went on a West Coast trip at the beginning of August gave the team an emotional lift. Davis sat on the bench and cheered them on to a 13–3 win, their highest run production in three months. "All it took was to have him in uniform for our offense to perk up," Johnson said of Davis's presence in Oakland. "Everyone enjoyed having him around, that's for sure. I might just kidnap him."

Johnson wouldn't have to. Soon, to everyone's amazement, Davis was back in Baltimore, working out to get ready to return to the lineup. Unknown to Orioles fans, one of the biggest dramatic moments in Orioles history nearly took place on this road trip to Oakland: the end of Cal Ripken's consecutive-game streak. Ripken had been struggling with back spasms that were getting worse as the season went on. After the All-Star break, he was batting just .190 (sixteen for eighty-four), and on August 1, he had to leave the game in the eighth inning because the back spasms were so severe. The next day, Ripken thought he wasn't going to be able to play, but he did, and would suffer for much of the season until therapy and exercise improved his condition going into the postseason.

Not long after the Oakland road trip, Davis began taking batting practice in Baltimore. He anticipated being activated after September 1, when the rosters were expanded to forty players. "I didn't have any expectations of myself going into this," he said. "But everything's been real positive so far." He had not been hurt too bad by the first round of chemotherapy, and said he was dealing with the treatments "as best as I can."

Davis's was such a remarkably inspirational story that all he would have to do really to make it such was simply show up for one game and take one at bat. That alone would have been considered a triumph. The day he finally was back in the lineup—September 15, the first game of a day-night doubleheader against the Cleveland Indians—touched everyone who witnessed it. "This is something I've never seen before," said bullpen coach Elrod Hendricks, who has seen just about everything in his thirty-seven years in professional baseball. "And it's something I hope I never see again."

There is no inspiration without misfortune, and Hendricks was saying that he hoped he never saw another ballplayer have to go through what Davis did. In addition to dealing with his illness, Davis also had to bury his older brother Jimmy several weeks earlier, after he was struck down by a heart attack. This was a tough year for the Orioles family, struck hard by this disease. Orioles legend Boog Powell was also diagnosed with colon cancer, as was one of the Orioles minor league players, Joel Stephens.

Davis's name in the lineup card that day also hit home with Davey Johnson. His father had been diagnosed with bone marrow cancer, and five days later he was dead. "When they said Eric had cancer, I thought he was going to die," Johnson said. "This is such a personal thing, and yet I don't know anyone who hasn't been touched by it. To me, it's a sign of victory for him just to be able to play again at the highest level of baseball."

Every one of the 48,262 people at Camden Yards that day seemed to be touched by yet another remarkable drama unfolding at the ballpark. The crowd stood and roared for several minutes when Davis came out of the dugout and took the field in the top of the first inning. They cheered again when he came up to hit in the bottom of the inning. "It made me a little teary-eyed," Davis said. "I stepped back and tipped my hat to let them know I appreciated what they were giving me. It was an emotional gift to my heart."

Davis beat out a ground ball in the bottom of the fifth, and then Johnson took him out of the game. That would have been a fine ending for this story, but there was more. The Orioles were faced with a difficult decision. While Davis's story was a source of inspiration, they could not afford to carry him on their postseason roster unless he could contribute on the field, at the same time he was undergoing a second round of chemotherapy. Davis managed to sustain enough offense to show he could help the team, and it paid off in Game 1 of the Division Series against the Seattle Mariners, when Davis went one for three, driving in two runs in a 9–3 Seattle victory. When the Orioles came home for Game 3 at Camden Yards, Davis could not play because he was undergoing a chemotherapy treatment. But his place in the lineup in Game 4—a 3–1 Orioles win, with Davis going one for four—brought the fans to their feet once again, honoring the man for his courage and spirit.

Davis's return to play in the postseason was one of the biggest stories for the Orioles in the 1997 playoffs, but far from the only subplot in the melodrama of Camden Yards. There was, as always, the saga of Cal Ripken. While Ripken's consecutive-game streak was glorified by the media two years before, when he broke Lou Gehrig's record of 2,130 straight games, it had become a target of criticism since then. In fact, everything that involved Ripken seemed to be a dramatic crisis. He had reached such stature in sports, and particularly in baseball, that anything out of the norm was big news. When Johnson took him out of a close game against the New York Yankees the year before for a pinch runner, it was big news. When Johnson moved Ripken to third for six games—the first time Ripken had not been the Orioles shortstop since 1982—in place of Manny Alexander, it was bigger news.

So on opening day 1997, when Mike Bordick was Baltimore's starting shortstop and Ripken was at third base, it was very big news. Ripken was thirty-six years old on opening day, and his critics maintained he had lost his range at short. The Orioles' front office believed so, too, and wanted to shore up the entire infield defense with someone new at short and Ripken at third. The year before, B. J. Surhoff, Todd Zeile, and others played a forgettable third base for Baltimore.

This was no small feat. It required delicate meetings and phone calls and greasing the public-relations wheel to make sure this did not appear to be an affront to Ripken. General manager Pat Gillick spoke with Ripken to discuss the move with him, with the Orioles' plans to sign highly respected Oakland shortstop Mike Bordick to a three-year contract the key to the move.

"Cal's position was that he would move to third if there was someone that in Cal's mind that he thought was a proven shortstop, someone who could play the position," Gillick said. "I don't think he really liked moving off of short. But I think he thought it was for the good of the club, and that was the way we were going to go, that he would do it. The only way you could have moved Cal off short and on to third was between seasons. Give him a spring training to get comfortable at a new position, even though he is a great player. He likes to think things through. He doesn't like to be embarrassed. He would have preferred to have been at short, I think. That's only natural. But I think he recognized that for the good of the team, that was the way to go."

The move was so delicate that in a well-publicized phone call Bordick spoke to Ripken before Bordick signed with Baltimore, to make sure that Ripken was indeed agreeable to the move. "Mike was a bit apprehensive about coming over here and taking Cal's spot until he had a chance to talk to Cal about it," Gillick said. "That gave Bordy a good sense of coming here."

Ripken seemed to accept the move and even enjoy the challenge of the new position. "It's been very motivating for me," he said before opening day. "It's been invigorating. I've actually really enjoyed the process," he commented, adding, "the mindset is not so much coming into spring training and knowing you're going to be playing a different position. The mindset is that when you're out on the field, you have to react. So, of course, you have to train yourself to think like a third baseman."

Ripken may have been invigorated, but Bordick was hardly feeling relaxed. He knew he was facing a potential no-win situation, even with Ripken's blessing, and was feeling the pressure before taking his position at shortstop for the first time at Camden Yards as an Oriole. "I know that's hallowed ground out there," Bordick said. "Being in an Orioles uniform at that position, I will do whatever I can to do it proud." Bordick played a solid shortstop, but never really got untracked at the plate, batting just .236, with the pressure of replacing Ripken weighing on his mind much of the season.

Ripken, who signed a two-year contract extension with a club option for a third that virtually ensured Ripken would finish his career as an Oriole, may have enjoyed the challenge, but soon he was debilitated with back spasms. He slumped terribly in September, batting just .156, fueling the cries and demands that he sit down. Like so many times before, Ripken lashed back on the field in the playoffs as the Orioles' best player, batting .438 (seven for sixteen) in the Division Series against Seattle and .348 (eight for twenty-three) against Cleveland in the AL Championship Series.

But the glory of Davis and the struggles of Ripken were subplots in the story of the 1997 playoffs at Camden Yards. The central characters in this drama were Orioles owner Peter Angelos and manager Davey Johnson, and the animosity between the two that clouded what should have been a very successful season.

The two had clashed since Angelos hired Johnson in November 1995. But with his three-year contract and taking the Orioles to the playoffs for the first time in thirteen years in 1996, Johnson's job status was relatively secure. This was particularly true after the 1997 season began; the team started out in first place after the first game of the season and never lost that position. It appeared that Johnson was on solid ground and would survive another year. But when you have Davey Johnson, you get not only the confident and intelligent baseball man; you also get the arrogant and impatient man who will, sooner or later, clash with authority. He did so in New York with Mets general manager Frank Cashen, and he did so in Cincinnati with Marge Schott, although it's hard to find fault with anyone who had a difference of opinion with the bigoted Reds owner. Johnson committed the same sort of sin in Baltimore under the most bizarre circumstances, involving, of all things, a mid-season exhibition game against the Orioles' minor league Class AAA team, the Rochester Red Wings.

Roberto Alomar had played in his eighth All-Star Game on July 7, surprisingly voted by the fans as the AL starter even though he continued to be booed in ballparks on the road for his role in the Hirschbeck controversy the season before. The next day, the Orioles were scheduled to play in Rochester against the Red Wings, a practice major league clubs employed as a boost to their minor league systems. Often at these games, the star players either don't play, or they play for an inning or two and then sit down, giving the local fans just a taste of what they came for.

But Alomar didn't make the trip. His grandmother had passed away, and he wanted to be with his family in Puerto Rico. So he went without Johnson's permission, and the manager was livid. He wanted to make an example of Alomar, to ensure that his other stars would not try the same thing. He fined the All-Star second baseman $10,000, on top of a $500 fine he handed Alomar for missing an April banquet.

This, though, is where Johnson made his mistake, on two counts. First, he fined Alomar without telling Angelos. Second, and the most bizarre part of this controversy, Johnson instructed Alomar to write the check for the fine to a charity called the Benjamin Carson Scholars Fund, which, it turns out, Johnson's wife, Susan, directed in a volunteer role. Whether Johnson's intentions were good, there was a conflict of interest in his actions. Angelos, who already had a strong dislike for his manager, was livid, particularly when he found out about the fine from the Players Association, which was planning to fight the disciplinary action.

So the tension between Johnson and Angelos was at an all-time high as the Orioles were finishing their excellent ninety-eight-win season and heading into the playoffs. It was so bad, in fact, that on the eve of the Orioles' Division Series opener against the Seattle Mariners, Angelos found himself forced to respond to questions from reporters about his manager's job security. Some speculated that Johnson would have to lead his team to a World Series victory to save his job. Angelos denied that. "Nobody can demand of a manager that he win a World Series or lose his job," Angelos said. "It doesn't work that way. I don't know of anyone in his right state of mind who would make such a demand. It doesn't happen that way, and that's not the case with Davey. That is not my position at all.

"They won the division, and hopefully they will go further," Angelos continued. "Obviously, in every relationship there are differences, but I think he has done a good job. You can't argue with success. I think this year has been a good year for him, a good year for the team, and I'm pleased with where we are." Angelos said all this with his teeth grinding with anger. Privately, he was obsessed with what he believed was Johnson's style of arrogance and deceit, and it killed him that he was paying this man he despised $750,000 a year.

Angelos went on to say that in 1997, "there has been less friction between management and the professional baseball people whose job it is to compose the team and then direct it on the field." It would have been difficult to outdo the turmoil of the preceding year. But before this year was over, Angelos and Johnson would come very close to the chaos of the 1996 postseason.

Despite Angelos's statements about his manager doing a "good job," Johnson never heard anything from Angelos privately along those lines. In fact, when he won the American League East, he got a telegram from, of all people, New York Yankees owner George Steinbrenner.

Before Angelos and Johnson had their dramatic clash, though, the manager would have his moment in the sun. He rolled the dice and took a remarkable gamble against the Mariners ace left-hander Randy Johnson by sitting down three of his best hitters—all lefties—for Game 1 at the Kingdome. Rafael Palmeiro led the team with thirty-eight home runs and 110 RBIs during the season. But Jerome Walton, who missed much of the season with leg injuries, started at first base. Roberto Alomar, normally a switch-hitter but reduced to a left-handed batter this year because of a shoulder injury, still batted .333 in 112 games, but sat down in favor of utility infielder Jeff Reboulet, who batted just .237 in ninety-nine games. B. J. Surhoff, one of the better left fielders in the league, who hit .284 with eighty-eight RBIs in 147 games, was benched in favor of the fragile Jeffrey Hammonds, who managed to have his best year in an injury-plagued career, with twenty-one home runs and fifty-five RBIs in 118 games. All three replace-ments were right-handed hitters.

On paper, the changes made sense. After all, Palmeiro was one for twenty-one lifetime against the Big Unit; Surhoff, two for twelve; and Alomar, eight for thirty-seven. But it still required a remarkable amount of the same arrogance that Angelos hated in Davey Johnson for him to make such a move, benching his best hitters in the first game of a best-of-five-game series, numbers or not. "I'll bet no one in history has ever started a playoff series by sitting down their leading home-run hitter and RBI guy," said general manager Pat Gillick. "But it's the logical thing to do."

Davey Johnson was willing to take on all the doubters. "Randy Johnson is the most intimidating pitcher in baseball, par-ticularly to left-handers, so I'm going with my right-handers," he said before the game. "It's a decision I can live with. That's why they pay me the big money to make these kinds of decisions. If it doesn't work, then I'll take the fall."

Davey Johnson would be proved right. Hammonds walked twice and scored twice. Reboulet delivered a key two-strike sacri-fice bunt that put runners in position for Eric Davis, the inspira-tional leader of this team now, to drive two runs home with a single in the top of the fifth that gave Baltimore a 4–1 lead. Walton went hitless in two at bats, but the overall idea worked. Randy Johnson seemed like the intimidated one. He left the game after just five innings, having thrown 100 pitches, giving up five runs on seven hits and four walks.

In fact, Davey Johnson's plan worked even better than he could have hoped for. After reliever Mike Timlin came in for Randy Johnson, the Orioles manager brought in Palmeiro for Walton, and he hit a double to center. Johnson brought in Alomar for Reboulet, and he received an intentional walk and later scored when Johnson brought in Surhoff, who drove a two-run double down the right-field line in the top of the sixth inning.

By this time, the only noise coming from the crowd of 59,979—the largest ever for a baseball game at the Kingdome—was booing at their home team. Not only had Davey Johnson handled Randy Johnson, but he had turned the usually frenzied Seattle crowd against the Mariners. Orioles starter Mike Mussina did his part, holding the Mariners to two runs on five hits in seven innings pitched in a 9–3 win for the Orioles, who took a 1–0 lead in the best-of-five-game series.

There would be no sleight of hand in Game 2 in Seattle. The Orioles would benefit from an injury to Seattle starter Jamie Moyer, a former Oriole, who left the game in the fifth inning with a strained elbow. At that point, Seattle was leading 2–1 when Moyer gave up a two-out single to Mike Bordick and then walked Brady Anderson on four pitches. He left the game after throwing one pitch to Alomar. Mariners manager Lou Piniella had to go to his flammable bullpen, bringing in Paul Spoljaric, who gave up a double to Alomar, scoring two runs and giving Baltimore a 3–2 lead. The Orioles then demolished Seattle reliever Bobby Ayala, scoring six runs on their way to a second straight 9–3 win, with Scott Erickson getting the win.

Despite their ninety-eight-win season, Baltimore had limped into the playoffs in the final weeks, playing .500 ball, and were considered the underdogs against a Mariners team with such big names as Ken Griffey, Randy Johnson, and Alex Rodriguez. But the Orioles were dominating the series. "People forgot how good we really are," said assistant general manager Kevin Malone. "People got caught up in the Seattle stars, and we didn't play very well at the end of the season. But this team has shown the ability all year to turn on the intensity when it has been needed, and we showed it loud and clear in these first two games."

Camden Yards hosted the Division Series for the second straight season, as Game 3 was back in Baltimore. Piniella was looking forward to the trip. "I'm going to have some crabcakes and Chardonnay," he said.

The Orioles felt good about their chances to wrap up the Division Series before the hometown fans in Game 3. They sent Jimmy Key, who had pitched in two clinching World Series games for the New York Yankees and the Toronto Blue Jays, to the mound. "I can't think of anyone else I would want out there," Davey Johnson said.

Seattle managed to stay alive, though, as Jeff Fassero defeated the Orioles 4–2, disappointing the sold-out crowd of 49,137 who packed Camden Yards in anticipation of celebrating a series victory. The Orioles were disappointed because now they would have to face Randy Johnson, and there are only so many times you can tug on Superman's cape. The Big Unit was pumped up for another chance to redeem himself. "This game means a lot to me and to my teammates," Randy Johnson said after Fassero's win. "It gives me a chance to redeem myself."

This might have been the most uncomfortable 2–1 lead in playoff history. The most dominant pitcher in baseball—43–6 over three years—felt that he had to redeem himself. He did, to some extent, in Game 4. But his opponent on the mound for the Orioles, Mike Mussina, felt that he had more at stake: his reputation as a big-game pitcher.

Mussina was one of the top five pitchers in all of baseball. Over five seasons, he had a record of 90–41, the highest winning percentage (.687) of any active pitcher in the game with fifty or more decisions, and had come within two outs of pitching a perfect game during the season against the powerful Cleveland Indians. But he had gained a reputation of not being a big-game pitcher, after giving up four runs in six innings in a Division Series game against Cleveland in 1996, followed by a five-run beating in eight innings against the New York Yankees in an American League Championship Series game. Mussina had pitched well in Game 1 of the Division Series against Randy Johnson, but it was a 9–3 game, hardly a test of his spirit. This one, Game 4, would prove differently, and would give Camden Yards one of its most memorable games.

Johnson pitched great, throwing 137 pitches and allowing three runs in nine innings, good enough to win, especially with the powerful Mariners lineup, with the likes of Griffey, Rodriguez, Jay Buhner, and Edgar Martinez. But Mussina stepped up and pitched the game of his life, on one day short of the normal four days rest. He held the Seattle hitters to one run on just two hits, striking out seven.

"My guy pitched his heart out today," Piniella said of Randy Johnson. "He pitched like a champion, and he went out and battled. He pitched an outstanding game. The other man on the other side pitched better."

The other man. The Moose. With two wins in a five-game series against Randy Johnson, Mussina buried all the talk of coming up short in big games. "These are probably two of the biggest games he has ever won," said his catcher, Chris Hoiles. "Especially when you consider the guy he was facing."

Mussina and his teammates celebrated with a clubhouse full of champagne spraying everywhere, and music blaring. Davey Johnson lit up a victory cigar in his office. He, too, was the toast of the town, going again with his remarkable right-handed lineup gamble against Randy Johnson. Reboulet, of all people, put the Orioles in front early with a solo home run on a 3–2 Randy Johnson fastball. Of Reboulet's five home runs in 1997, two came against Randy Johnson.

"You have to give credit to Davey's lineup," Piniella said. "I've never seen a team do this to Randy before." Davey Johnson was more than willing to take the credit. He basked in the spotlight, and was already setting the stage for the Championship Series, boasting, "I think it's only fitting that we eliminate the Yankees," the team that defeated the Orioles in the 1996 championship series. "They won ninety-six ballgames and were the second-best team in the American League. If Cleveland doesn't do it first, it'll be left to us."

Cleveland did it first, surprisingly. They upset the Yankees in the fifth game in their Division Series, behind the pitching of twenty-one-year-old rookie Jaret Wright. The Orioles would be wishing it had been the Yankees instead.

In the midst of all the celebration at Camden Yards, the tension between Davey Johnson and Angelos was never far from the surface. Some within the Orioles organization were convinced that if Baltimore did not make it to the World Series, Johnson would be fired. Yet again, a remarkable drama was unfolding behind the scenes.

The way it began for the Orioles in Game 1, Davey Johnson appeared to be secure. In the opening game at Camden Yards, Scott Erickson held the tough Cleveland hitters to just four hits in eight innings for a 3–0 win, on a solo home run by Brady Anderson—Cleveland pitcher Chad Ogea's first pitch of the game. Roberto Alomar added to the lead with a two-run home run in the bottom of the third inning.

One is all Erickson would need. "We were ready, but we just ran into a buzzsaw by the name of Scott Erickson," said Indians manager Mike Hargrove. The next night, the Indians seemed to suffer the same fate, though Jimmy Key was no buzzsaw. He labored through four innings, giving up two runs in the first, and after seventy-seven pitches was relieved by Scott Kamieniecki in the fifth inning. Fortunately for the Orioles, Cal Ripken, continuing his remarkable postseason play, hit a two-run home run in the second inning to tie the game at 2–2. Mike Bordick then gave Baltimore a 4–2 lead with a two-run single off Cleveland starter Charles Nagy in the sixth inning.

Kamieniecki did his job, pitching three scoreless innings. Baltimore was on the verge of going up 2–0 in the best-of-seven series, a seemingly insurmountable lead for a team that had already run through the American League from the first day of the season and disposed of the Mariners easily in the first round of the playoffs.

In fact, it seemed like a lock in the top of the eighth inning. Perhaps the hardest thrower in the league, Armando Benitez, who loved to watch the radar gun hit 100 miles per hour at Camden Yards, was about to pitch. He had been one of the top setup men in baseball that year, holding the lead in forty-three of the forty-four games he had entered with Baltimore in front. In seventy-one appearances, Benitez had given up just twenty runs and struck out 106 batters in just seventy-three innings pitched. With a 4–2 lead, the fans at Camden Yards were convinced that they were on their way to seeing the first World Series at the ballpark—the only jewel missing so far in the crown of the Home of the Game.

"He's been my guy in the eighth inning all year," Davey Johnson said. "He has been one of the best setup men in baseball. He's been nearly perfect in that situation." But one pitch—one hanging slider—ended it all. That one pitch finished the Orioles' season. "It felt like we were running uphill after that," said assistant general manager Kevin Malone. This sent the organization into a spiral that it still hasn't recovered from. That one pitch may have cost Davey Johnson his job.

Benitez was a twenty-five-year-old from the Dominican Republic with a massive 6-foot-4, 230-pound body, and a child-like attitude. He had remarkable talent but was also remarkably immature. Two years before, after giving up a grand-slam home run to Edgar Martinez to lose a game in the ninth inning against Seattle, he intentionally hit the next batter, Tino Martinez, setting off a near brawl. When Benitez got into the clubhouse, he packed his clothes and was heading back to his homeland. Pitching coach Mike Flanagan had to talk him out of it. But he plunked Martinez again, this time after a Bernie Williams home run against the New York Yankees, setting off an ugly brawl that resulted in Benitez being shunned by his own teammates and an eight-game suspension for Benitez.

But that one pitch in that second game of the 1996 championship series sealed Benitez's place in Camden Yards history. He started the top of the eighth by striking out pinch hitter Jeff Branson. Next, he walked Sandy Alomar but struck out Tony Fernandez. Two outs, and Baltimore was just four outs away from a 2–0 lead in the series. If Benitez could get just one more out, the Orioles would bring in the best closer in baseball that year, Randy Myers, who had saved forty-five of forty-six games.

But then Benitez walked Jim Thome on a controversial ball four by umpire Jim Joyce. This angered Benitez, who now had two runners on base with two outs and Marquis Grissom coming to the plate. Still, everyone felt confident. Opponents had batted just .125 that year against Benitez with runners on base, and on the only two occasions Grissom faced Benitez in his career, he struck out both times.

After running the count to 1–1, Grissom went around on a hanging slider, blasting the pitch over the center-field wall for a three-run home run, giving the Indians a 5–4 lead that they held in the ninth inning for the win. This tied the series at 1–1 before the teams went back to Cleveland for the next three games.

The next day, Benitez watched the tape of Thome's ball four over and over again. "He swung the bat," the reliever said. "The umpire missed it." The Orioles tried to shrug it off during the off day. Eric Davis stayed in Baltimore, recovering from a late-night chemotherapy session after Game 2. He would start in Game 3. No one was too upset. After all, Mussina was pitching.

Mussina gave another memorable performance, but the outcome at Jacobs Field was all wrong. The Orioles right-hander struck out fifteen Cleveland hitters, a league championship record, over seven innings, giving up just one run on three hits. The twilight-sky backdrop made it tough for everyone to hit, and the Orioles were as helpless against Cleveland starter Orel Hershiser as the Indians were against Mussina—maybe more so. Hershiser shut out Baltimore hitters through seven innings, striking out seven. It appeared that Cleveland would hang on to a 1–0 victory when in the top of the ninth, Indians second baseman Tony Fernandez failed to tag Jeff Reboulet on a grounder by Jeffrey Hammonds. Reboulet scored when Grissom, the hero of Game 2, lost a pop fly by Brady Anderson in the lights. The score remained 1–1 until the bottom of the twelfth, and ended there in a bizarre and ironic fashion. These Baltimore Orioles never seem to do anything without a fair amount of drama and intrigue.

Randy Myers had walked Grissom and given up a one-out single to Fernandez, moving Grissom to third. Omar Vizquel came up to the plate, and, with the count 2–1, Vizquel came around to bunt on a suicide squeeze. The hard-breaking slider from Myers bounced off catcher Lenny Webster's glove. What happened next, though, was a source of controversy. Webster claimed Vizquel tipped the ball, and it should have been a foul ball, for strike two. Vizquel claimed he never touched it.

Unfortunately for the Orioles, the home-plate umpire agreed with Vizquel, calling the run safe and giving Cleveland a heartbreaking 2–1 win. The umpire? John Hirschbeck, who turned the Orioles' postseason upside down last year as a result of the Alomar spitting incident.

"It definitely tipped off his bat before it hit my glove," Webster said. "I've seen the replay several times, and it clearly shows it was foul." Hirschbeck sat in the umpires' dressing room wondering if indeed he had made the right call. He made the call he saw, and he was relieved when a reporter told him the replays appeared to show that Vizquel didn't tip the ball with his bat, despite what Webster claimed he saw on the tape. "I was very surprised that [Webster] wasn't going after the ball," Hirschbeck said. "If it had been a foul, I would have signaled and yelled loudly, and it would have been emphatic."

Cleveland now had a 2–1 lead in the playoffs, and for the first time all season, the Orioles were chasing someone. It turned out they weren't ready for it, with another bizarre home-plate play involving backup catcher Lenny Webster burying them in an 8–7 loss in Game 4 and giving the Indians a 3–1 lead. Webster failed to block Arthur Rhodes's wild pitch in the bottom of the fifth at Jacobs Field with the score tied at 5–5. David Justice came in from third, and Webster, after running down the ball, made a pathetic shovel pass to Rhodes to try to get Justice, who scored to put Cleveland ahead 6–5. Webster then froze as the ball rolled away from Rhodes, who was pinned down by Justice in the home-plate play. This enabled Sandy Alomar to score as well, for a 7–5 Indians lead.

Also, for the first time all year, the comfort level of winning that protected manager Davey Johnson was no longer there. Angelos was steaming about the team's collapse. Furthermore, the battle over the Alomar fine was still unresolved and became more of a sore point as the team fell behind in the Championship Series. Even before Game 4, Baltimore general manager Pat Gillick said he thought there was a fifty-fifty chance that Johnson would get fired. Speculation was also running high in the Baltimore media that Johnson's job was in jeopardy.

The speculation was so bad that Cal Ripken and Brady Anderson stepped forward and, on the verge of Game 5, publicly supported their manager. Ripken said it would be a real setback if Johnson were fired. "If you're looking for stability in a franchise, making changes is not the answer," Ripken commented. "We had a great season, and actually a great couple of years. There's a lot of credit to be given to a lot of people for our success this year, but you also have to credit the people in charge. Davey deserves that credit."

"For him to be fired would be very unjust," Anderson said. "I think he deserves a contract extension. We have a good thing going here. Last year we made it to the postseason for the first time in thirteen years, and now we have made it two years in a row. If we want to build something here, there is a better chance of doing it by having the same manager.

"If he got fired, the feeling around here would be awful," Anderson continued. "There have been some controversies in the past, but we've gotten to know each other better and better. It takes a little while for some people to get to know each other. I think he deserves to be here as long as he wants. He has a great record, and he has been a great leader."

Maybe the team responded to all the talk about their manager's job in jeopardy. They came through with a 4–2 win in Game 5 in Cleveland, behind the pitching of Scott Kamieniecki and the bat of Eric Davis, who capped off his remarkable comeback with a leadoff pinch-hit home run in the top of the ninth. Under his uniform when he came up to hit, Davis was wearing a T-shirt that read "Chemo Sucks" on the front and "But It Works" on the back.

The Orioles went back to Camden Yards for Game 6, down 3–2 in the series, but feeling pretty confident they could force a Game 7, with the pitching star of the postseason, Mike Mussina, the Game 6 starter for Baltimore. Unbelievably, Mussina turned in another gem of a performance, allowing no runs on just one hit in eight innings. And unbelievably, just like his last start against Hershiser, Charles Nagy, his opponent on the mound, matched him, shutting out the Orioles for nearly eight innings.

Both bullpens continued the shutout pitching until the twelfth inning. In the top of the twelfth, with Benitez on the mound again, Tony Fernandez slammed a two-out solo home run over the left-field wall for a 1–0 series-clinching victory. Baltimore hitters could not give Mussina the support he needed. In Game 6, for instance, cleanup hitter Rafael Palmeiro, the team's top RBI man, stranded five runners in the first five innings alone. But it's hard to believe that things would not have been different if Benitez had not given up that Game 2 home run to Grissom. Like Jeffrey Maier in 1996, it was the one play that turned the series against the Orioles.

The series was particularly tough for Mussina, who had a historic performance during the postseason, setting a major league record with forty-one strikeouts in twenty-nine innings pitched, with several of those starts on short rest. In that span, he allowed just twelve hits while compiling a 1.24 earned run average. Yet in fifteen league Championship Series innings against the Indians, the Orioles failed to score one run for Mussina. "Mike was unbelievable," pitching coach Ray Miller said. "He rose to the occasion and was outstanding. The next person who ever questions Mike Mussina's ability to pitch in a big game is going to have to fight me."

No one was going to do that. But there would be a fight, all right—an all-out brawl between Davey Johnson and Angelos, one that rivaled the George Steinbrenner–Billy Martin wars, except there was little chance of Angelos hiring Johnson over and over again. The bad blood between the two began in Johnson's first press conference at the end of October 1995. Angelos and his associates passed over Johnson when they were looking for a manager to replace Johnny Oates, the first manager Angelos fired. Angelos hired Phil Regan, who had no major league managing experience, over Johnson, who had been interviewed for the job.

One of the controversies that led to Oates's firing was his failure to play an Angelos favorite, Leo Gomez, at third base on a daily basis as the owner told him to. So in his interview—conducted by a committee consisting of Orioles vice chairman Joe Foss, team lawyer Russell Smouse, general manager Roland Hemond, and assistant general manager Frank Robinson— Johnson was asked what he would do if someone in management told him to play a certain player. Johnson said he would ask the individual if he wanted to be the manager and would let him know in no uncertain terms that Johnson would decide who played and who didn't. When asked the same question, Regan told the committee about how when his team in winter ball in Venezuela was going through a losing streak, he let the owners make up the lineup card. That was the right answer.

Johnson led the Cincinnati Reds to the National League Central Division title in 1995, while Regan was a disaster. Even though Johnson was successful with the Reds, he was being forced out there by owner Marge Schott. So Johnson was looking for work after the 1995 season, and this time Angelos, who first tried to hire Tony LaRussa but balked at his salary demands, jumped at the chance to get Johnson, the former Oriole All-Star second baseman and a member of two Baltimore World Series championship teams.

When Johnson met with reporters after Angelos hired him, he was asked what he thought about being passed over the first time the year before. Johnson laughed and said, "I didn't think there were too many smart people up here." The comment angered Angelos, and from there the relationship grew to be acrimonious. It appeared to hit rock bottom after the 1996 playoffs when Angelos fired Johnson's pitching coach, Pat Dobson, over the manager's objections, and hired former Orioles pitching coach Ray Miller, who was available after leaving Pittsburgh when Jim Leyland took the managing job in Florida.

Angelos made the right decision. Dobson had lost the respect of his pitchers. Mike Mussina ordered him off the mound late in the season when Dobson came out to talk to the pitcher. During a press conference in the playoffs, when Scott Erickson was asked how much Dobson had helped him this season, Erickson replied coldly, "Next question." But even though it was the right decision, it was a blow to Johnson, and only served to fuel the feud between the two men.

After losing to Cleveland in the league championship series, Johnson went home to Florida. He was steaming because instead of getting plaudits for the fine season his team had, he was getting the cold shoulder from Angelos, and was still feeling the heat for the Alomar fine. Johnson was fuming when, after the Game 6 loss to Cleveland, Angelos declared that he would be meeting with Johnson to determine his future.

Sitting at his home in Florida, Johnson decided that he would not twist in the wind and let Angelos play him when the owner declared that Johnson's job status was "under review." He had one year left on his three-year, $2.25 million contract, and, faced with a $750,000 salary to pay Johnson in 1998, Angelos was not likely to fire the manager. But it was clear that he would make life more difficult than ever for Johnson, who wasn't prepared to live through a season of uncertainty. Moreover, his anger grew, rather than subsided, over the attacks on his wife, even though what he did was clearly a mistake and a conflict of interest.

So at the end of October, Johnson asked the Orioles to either extend his contract or buy it out, rather than create a lame-duck status for 1998. At the time, the manager was laying low from the media. His attorney, Skip Dalton, was doing the talking for him. "I was joking with someone the other day that the Yankees used to be the only team where you can have a successful season, the manager can have a long-term contract, and the team still has to announce that the manager is going to come back at the end of each year," Dalton said.

According to Dalton, Angelos and Johnson were scheduled to talk in a teleconference call, but the owner begged off, asking to reschedule it. Nothing happened, so Dalton sent a fax to Angelos asking for the contract extension. Dalton said he sent the fax in response to Pat Gillick's comments that Johnson's chances of returning in 1998 "were no better than fifty-fifty."

Dalton said when they learned of general manager Gillick's comments, "it was unsettling. If Mr. Angelos is unhappy with the managing situation, we don't question that. He's the owner. But if he is unhappy, we would hope he would take a business-type approach and put everything on the table. If the Orioles are going to want Davey to move on, we would hope they would allow him to do it now so he can look into other opportunities. But don't get me wrong—that's not what Davey wants to do. We did this just to open up discussion about the future."

If that was the case—if Johnson really wanted stay—then he made a huge mistake by sending this fax for an extension. It was a cannon shot at Angelos. A week later, Angelos met with Gillick and Malone, who were trying to salvage the relationship and keep their management team intact for at least one more season. But for Gillick, the problem was Johnson, who was not willing to stay the course for one more year, even under the duress of an owner who despised him. "I met with Peter and tried to make a case," Gillick said. "I talked to Davey, too, and asked them to patch this up. It was a little bit ridiculous. We had a great year. We went wire to wire. I think it was two guys who are very competitive and very strong willed. But I thought they ought to get together and work things out."

A ninety-minute telephone conversation set up between Angelos and Johnson turned into a shouting match. Gillick went to Florida to try to convince Johnson to return for his final year, but was unsuccessful. The feud frustrated Gillick because Johnson was the one who convinced Gillick to take the general manager's job when everyone else was telling him not to go work for Angelos. Now Gillick would be here, and Johnson might be gone. "I was upset about it from the standpoint that we had two good years and all of a sudden it was gone," he said. "Everybody has to do what they have to do, but I would have liked to have seen him try to work his way through that one year he had left on his contract."

Shortly after that, on November 5, the argument was over. Johnson submitted his resignation—on the same day he was named American League Manager of the Year. "I felt like we needed to resolve this one way or the other in the best interests of the organization," Johnson said the day he resigned. "I wrestled with this decision for two weeks because I kept thinking it would be worked out, and that I would get the support I needed to win a championship in Baltimore." So he resigned by fax, and Angelos accepted by fax. Here is the text of Johnson's resignation:

Dear Peter,

Since I have been unable to contact you by telephone, I am writing to let you know that Susan and I will be out of town for the next two weeks on a vacation planned long ago.

Despite our differences, I hope you realize the depth of my commitment to the Baltimore Orioles and the City of Baltimore. While I believe that your position relative to the Alomar fine and the Carson Scholars Fund is intended more for public relations than true disapproval, I nonetheless respect the fact that you were not apprised of my desire to direct the Alomar fine to the Carson Scholars.

As I would hope you realize, the only reason which I, as manager of the club, issue fines to players for failure to conform to club rules and policies is for the ultimate benefit of you, as an owner. It has always been my belief that players must respect the authority of the manager and ownership and recognize that, regardless of their status as a player, their behavior must comport with certain standards.

While I do not believe that there was any conflict of interest or impropriety in requesting the fine proceeds be directed to a charity with which my wife was involved, I recognize in retrospect that such direction could create the appearance of impropriety and that the better practice would dictate leaving decisions related to directing such funds to you as the Chief Executive Officer of the Orioles.

Notwithstanding our differences related to this issue, I must say that your indifference to the work I have performed over the last two years in guiding the Orioles to the playoffs and in delivering a wire-to-wire Division Championship is discouraging, to say the least. Your apparent lack of regard for my management skills and for me as a person is reflected in your statements to the press and the front office staff that my status as manager is "under review."

My only wish is to help you and the other owners do what is best for the Baltimore Orioles and the City of Baltimore. If, in your judgement, the best course of action for the Orioles is to replace me as manager, then I would be willing to offer my resignation and forfeit my entitlement to compensation pursuant to the terms of my contract in 1998, provided you accept my resignation today so as to allow me to pursue other opportunities. In return, I ask that my outstanding expenses be paid in a timely fashion together with your commitment to not block the efforts of any other clubs who might have an interest in my services as field manager.

The uncertainty related to my status, coupled with the intense media interest has been difficult for me and my family. Although I can appreciate that you have many important matters which occupy your time and attention, I do feel I am entitled to be treated with a modicum of respect and that this matter should be resolved promptly.

Please let me know by day's end whether you wish to accept my offer of resignation. If not for my interest, then for the club and the fans, it's time to put this matter to bed.

Very truly yours,

David A. Johnson

P.S. Susan and I will be leaving at approximately 3 p.m. After that time, please feel free to leave word for me with Skip Dalton. Thanks.

Angelos was more than willing to accommodate his manager. The following is the text of Angelos's fax to Johnson:

Dear Davey,

In my considered judgement, it would clearly be in the best interests of the Orioles organization for a change of field manager for 1998. Therefore I accept your letter of resignation, faxed to me today, and the conditions therein set forth in which you offer your immediate resignation and offer to forfeit any compensation, pursuant to the terms of your contract, for 1998.

In doing so, you request payment of outstanding expenses in a timely fashion and my commitment not to "block the efforts of any clubs who might have interest in (your) services as a field manager." All of the conditions in your fax are, accordingly, agreeable and accepted by the Orioles. You are absolutely free to pursue any baseball position as a field manager or otherwise, with any team in either league.

Regretfully, your letter fails to recognize the real issue posed by your imposition and handling of the Alomar fine and your divisive statement to the press in July that unless the Orioles got to the World Series, you would not be permitted to return for the final year of your contract. Such a statement, during a pennant drive, was ill-advised and potentially a harmful distraction. Your own actions and conduct—not mine—have produced the fulfillment of your prophesy.

I absolutely reject your contention that my strongly held objection to your directing the Alomar fine be paid to a charity by which your wife is employed was intended "more for public relations than mere disapproval." I can assure you that my disapproval is deeply felt and consistent with what I insist be appropriate conduct on the part of all Orioles' employees. It strikes me, as field manager, you should have been much more sensitive to such situations and to have avoided even what you concede "could create the appearance of impropriety."

While this is a regrettable ending of our relationship, I wish you the best in the future.

Very truly yours,

Peter Angelos

That was the end of the Peter Angelos–Davey Johnson soap opera, played out on the field at Camden Yards and in the B&O Warehouse for two years, ending long distance, via fax.

Angelos was vilified by the local media and the sports talk shows, and may never be able to mend those fences with Orioles fans. He did quickly hire Ray Miller as Johnson's replacement, but the team's dismal play in 1998, with a 79–83 record, only served to convince Angelos's critics that he was the villain in this drama.

For Johnson, the situation will forever haunt and confuse him. "It should have been the best time of my life," he said. "Here I was coming back to Baltimore, the place where I played, and it turned out to be the worst time. It was a battle from day one.

"I couldn't have continued like that," he added. "Lord knows I wanted to do well and do the right thing. If I could have written my own script, it would not have come out that way. But the stuff with Susan was just too personal. That was the last straw.

"My downfall was that I assumed the general manager was really my boss," Johnson said. "I guess I didn't have enough contact with the owner, but I felt it was wrong for me to go around my boss. Maybe that's the new deal in ownership now, but I'm from the old school, where there was a chain of command, and the general manager was your boss. And we had Pat Gillick there, the best baseball man in the game."

The Orioles had made it to the American League Championship Series for the second straight season in 1997. After all the faxes, it didn't seem to matter anymore.

CHAPTER TEN

The Angelos Era

The sweat poured off everyone in the courtroom on this hot August New York day. The only thing hotter than the temperature, though, was the tension in the courtroom, as staggering sums of money were being thrown around like $20 bills. One side said $152 million, the other $153 million. It kept going—$154 million, $155 million, $160 million, $165 million.

Nobody was sweating more than Joe Foss, the Washington banker who had put together the financing package for Peter Angelos to bid on the Baltimore Orioles. But those plans didn't take into account where this auction to buy this major league baseball franchise was going. Every time Angelos upped his bid, art dealer Jeff Loria would do the same.

Georgia Angelos turned to Foss and said, "Peter is going to buy this baseball team."

Foss nervously replied, "I hope so, but I don't know for sure."

Mrs. Angelos said, "You don't know my husband. When he wants something and sets his mind to it, he is going to get it. I've been at auctions with him before."

Foss didn't like the sound of that. "There is a price where economically we should stop," he said.

"I know that," Mrs. Angelos replied. "But you don't know my husband. We're going to buy this baseball team."

She was on the money—a lot of it, in this case. Loria went to $166 million, Angelos to $167 million. Loria, $168 million; Angelos, $170 million. Loria, $171 million; Angelos, $172 million. Loria, $173 million; Angelos, $174 million. Loria . . .

Sold to the son of a Greek bar owner from Baltimore for $174 million (actually the price was adjusted to $173 million because the Angelos group was given a $1 million credit for legal work in drawing up the contract). "If he had gone to $200 million, I would have gone to $201 million," Angelos said. "There was no way I wasn't coming back to Baltimore without a baseball team."

The Baltimore Orioles would never be the same. Just as Larry Lucchino was the main player behind the creation of Camden Yards, Peter Angelos was the director of much of the drama that took place at the ballpark after he purchased the team on at this August, 2, 1993, bankruptcy auction. He paid a record amount for this sports franchise, but then, this was no ordinary franchise. Camden Yards had changed the rules for everything. With a ballpark like Camden Yards, you could spend $173 million and still expect to at least pay your bills and make some money as well.

When all this took place, the questions were: Who is Peter Angelos, and how did he build a $300 million fortune? Angelos—like Larry Lucchino—was born in Pittsburgh, on the Fourth of July in 1929, the year of the stock-market crash. He was the son of a Greek immigrant tavern owner whose family moved to the Highlandtown section of Baltimore in 1941. He was a neighborhood kid, playing baseball and doing some boxing as well. He would go on to serve in the United States Army, and while running the family restaurant, he earned his law degree at the University of Baltimore. He quickly became a well-known figure around Baltimore and got heavily involved in politics. Angelos was elected to the Baltimore city council at the age of twenty-nine and was a high-profile politician. He was ambitious as well, running for mayor at the age of thirty-seven—and losing—in 1967. After that loss, Angelos disappeared from the public eye and the news pages, concentrating instead on building a law practice.

Angelos's break came in 1978, when a local union asked him to talk to some of its members who had contracted asbestosis to see if they had a case against their employer, Bethlehem Steel. That began a process in which Angelos would eventually wind up representing nearly 9,000 steelworkers, shipyard employees, and other workers who were damaged as a result of the use of asbestos on the job. When the suits were finally settled, manufacturers wound up paying about $1 billion to these asbestos victims, with Angelos getting $300 million of that money as his fee. His law firm is now one of the largest and most powerful in Maryland, and he stands to make another fortune because his firm has been representing Maryland in its suit against tobacco companies.

Angelos had never shown any interest in becoming a major league baseball club owner until he began reading in early 1993 that Cincinnati businessman William DeWitt was close to a deal to buy the Orioles from Eli Jacobs. Baltimore has been wary of out-of-town ownership ever since Bob Irsay left with the Colts football team in 1984. DeWitt had not indicated any plans to move the team—with a thirty-year lease and a money-maker like Camden Yards, he couldn't or most likely would not want to anyway. If he was successful in purchasing the Orioles, that would have meant three generations, dating back to Edward Bennett Williams, of out-of-town owners for the franchise. Angelos believed that the Orioles should have local ownership, and he and real-estate developer Wayne Gioioso met with Lucchino at his Washington office. They got the cold shoulder. After all, Lucchino, already part owner of the team, would be part of the new DeWitt ownership group. Everywhere that Angelos inquired—including talks with Governor William Donald Schaefer—he was told that he was far too late in the process and that the DeWitt purchase was a done deal.

But Jacobs's finances were collapsing quickly, and on March 29, his creditors forced him into involuntary bankruptcy. This put the Orioles, Jacobs's most valuable asset, up for open bidding in bankruptcy court. Angelos certainly had the most interesting group: novelist Tom Clancy, filmmaker Barry Levinson, sports announcer Jim McKay, and tennis star Pam Shriver were among his investors. For the next four months, the top prospective bidders—Angelos, DeWitt, Loria, and former NFL tight end Gene Fugett, now the chief executive officer of the Beatrice Corporation—talked and jockeyed with one another to try to convince each other to join up, without losing their status as the controlling partner. The morning of the auction, DeWitt agreed to join Angelos's group, and they prevailed at the auction.

In an interview with *The Baltimore Sun* weeks after the auction, Angelos predicted what his role would be with the club: "I understand that Edward Bennett Williams really got into this, that he attended as many games as he could and raised holy hell when things weren't going well. I have said to people who related that to me, 'That's not going to happen to me.' I really don't think it will. I can be pretty detached."

It's hard to imagine those words coming out of Peter Angelos's mouth. His role couldn't possibly be less detached. He is involved in all major baseball decisions and quickly made his presence felt. First, he wanted to change Camden Yards. Angelos wanted to add about 5,000 seats in center field, which he said would be used as part of a program to make games more accessible to school-age children. Even his friends reacted in horror at the idea of tinkering with a ballpark that had been so successful. "He was hell bent on it," Governor Schaefer said. "You had to talk him out of it. I think he thought that he wasn't going to do any damage to it. But he would have ruined it. He would have wrecked the place."

DeWitt found out quickly that his partnership meant he would merely own a piece of the team, nothing more. He had believed he would be the main baseball person in the group, the one making the key decisions. But it soon became apparent to him that his role would be very limited in the organization. Although Angelos offered Lucchino a chance to stay on with the Orioles, after discussions with Angelos it also became clear to Lucchino that he would not have the same authority under Angelos that he did under Jacobs as president and CEO. "We spent a couple of weeks sorting out what our respective roles would be, and it became clear to me that he was going to be the pilot of the ship," Lucchino said.

It was clear to everyone that Angelos was going to be the pilot, although no one knew how deeply he would be involved, even before he officially took over control of the team in October 1993. The Orioles were still in a division race toward the end of the season, and Angelos made it clear in the press that he would have liked the team to be more aggressive in making deals. For example, he wanted to go after Fred McGriff, who wound up moving from San Diego during the Padres' fire sale to the Atlanta Braves. Baltimore general manager Roland Hemond didn't like what he was reading and was concerned about what the future would hold for him in Baltimore. He had reason to be.

That prediction of being "detached" seemed ludicrous pretty quickly. Angelos jumped feet first into the baseball decisions. To his credit, it turned out that he had pretty good instincts and in some cases made better decisions than his baseball braintrust of Hemond and assistant general managers Doug Melvin and Frank Robinson. Angelos was committed to investing large sums of money for a winning team, something his predecessor Jacobs would not do. He was also determined to make the Orioles a championship team.

The Orioles had a choice between two high-priced free agents for first base, Will Clark and Rafael Palmeiro, who had been teammates at Mississippi State. Clark had been a star with the San Francisco Giants, and the Orioles' front office and manager Johnny Oates wanted him badly. Clark had a reputation as a strong clubhouse leader, in addition to being a quality hitter. His best season was 1991, when he hit .301 with twenty-nine home runs and 116 RBIs in 148 games. But he had a long history of physical problems. He had missed thirty-nine games in 1993 and fifty-two games the year before because of knee, back, and other chronic injuries. Still, the Orioles wanted him and brought him to Baltimore to sign him to a $30 million, five-year deal.

Angelos stopped the deal dead in its tracks. He demanded that Clark undergo an extensive physical and that the Orioles examine his medical records before committing to that much money. "They were going to sign him without getting a look at his medical reports," Angelos said. Those reports were not very encouraging, but the Texas Rangers moved in quickly and surprisingly signed Clark to the five-year contract he was seeking. What was shocking about the signing was that Palmeiro had been the Rangers' first baseman for five years and was coming off his best season: thirty-seven home runs, 105 RBIs, 124 runs scored, and a .295 average. Yet the Rangers didn't want Palmeiro back. This caused a personal grudge between the former teammates when Clark signed with Texas. Palmeiro was in the midst of building a new home in Texas and fully expected to continue his career there. The Orioles signed Palmeiro instead to the same deal—five years, $30 million.

Angelos turned out to be right. Palmeiro has been by far the better buy of the two players. Clark has missed 140 games over his five-year contract; Palmeiro, six. Clark has hit seventy-seven home runs; Palmeiro, 182. Clark has driven in 397 runs; Palmeiro, 512.

Angelos, not Hemond, Melvin, or Robinson, called most of the shots for the 1994 roster. He told them to sign left-handed pitcher Sid Fernandez, who got a $9 million, three-year contract. Angelos says he told them to sign closer Lee Smith, who got a one-year deal. But Angelos had some help. He was getting advice from a very close source—his sons, John and Lou Angelos. John had graduated from law school, and Lou was still going to law school, but both were rabid baseball fans. When their father purchased the team, they, and not the front office, became his advisors on baseball personnel matters.

Many people wondered where Angelos was getting his information when he would cite stats and argue with Hemond, Melvin, and Robinson. After all, Angelos was not the sort to read the box scores every day, at least not before he bought the team. But everyone found out how much of a role his sons played in the business of the Baltimore Orioles in an interview John did with me that was published in *The Washington Times*. It was a revealing interview that would have long-lasting implications for the perception of this franchise under its new ownership.

In the August 1994 interview, John Angelos said he was angry about comments in *The New York Times* and *The Orioles Gazette* that credited Melvin for signing Lee Smith. "That's ridiculous," John said. "That's just Monday-morning quarterbacking. At least keep quiet about it. Don't go taking credit for something that you didn't do. That really bothered me. They wanted Steve Farr. They brought him up here for a workout. We were down in Florida visiting my brother Lou, and my father is on the phone talking to the Orioles' front office. They're trying to convince him to sign Farr, and we're almost yelling at him, waving a stat book in his face, saying 46 saves, 46 saves," which was Smith's number with the St. Louis Cardinals and the New York Yankees in 1993. "My father told them to call his agent, and they finally did, and we got him. Think of where we would be if we didn't have Lee Smith."

John also credited his father with the decision on Gregg Olson; the Orioles opted not to resign their career-saves leader because of a torn ligament in his pitching elbow. "Every baseball person in this organization told him that we should tender a contract to Olson," John recounted, "but he looked at the medical reports and said no way. Then their second choice was Alan Mills. We almost went into the season without a closer. You sign Sid Fernandez and then experiment with a closer?" Smith would go on to save thirty-three games in thirty-nine opportunities during the strike-shortened 1994 season.

But John and Lou Angelos also pushed the Orioles to sign Fernandez, who turned out to be a bust, injured throughout much of the 1994 season and into 1995 as well. This forced Peter Angelos to trade him to Philadelphia and eat about $2 million of his remaining salary. "They didn't want to sign Sid," John Angelos said. "My father called them and said he wanted him signed—tomorrow. Here was a pitcher with a proven track record," which was 98–79 over ten seasons, "and there wasn't a lot out there this year in pitchers in the free-agent market. So do you sign Mark Portugal, who comes up with one good year, or a guy who had pitched well for ten years?"

In defense of John and Lou Angelos, there is a lot of resentment in baseball when those considered outsiders to the game have some influence. Yet the fact remains that selecting established major league talent in this day and age is not rocket science. A tremendous amount of information is available to anyone with a knowledge of the game, from scouting reports to detailed statistics on how every major league player performs in nearly every possible scenario. Years ago that information was known only to baseball executives. Now it can be purchased at Barnes and Noble. But the information-age explosion and the growth of fantasy baseball has threatened the domain of baseball insiders—which includes many baseball writers. Let's face it, the baseball expertise of Roland Hemond and Doug Melvin prompted the trade of Glenn Davis for Curt Schilling, Pete Harnisch, and Steve Finley.

In addition, the Orioles are far from the only franchise where people other than baseball executives have input into baseball decisions. Neither general manager was involved in the trade that sent Mike Piazza and Todd Zeile to the Florida Marlins for Bobby Bonilla and Gary Sheffield. That trade was made solely by the owners of each team. Former Orioles general manager Kevin Malone, soon after he took the GM's job with the Los Angeles Dodgers, found out quickly that the autonomy he said he would have with the Dodgers that he never had with the Orioles was not to be. According to reports in *The Long Beach Press Telegram*, Malone wanted to hire Kevin Kennedy as his new manager, but he was ordered by Fox point man Bob Graziano to hire Davey Johnson instead.

The Angelos sons are out in the open now in their roles in the Orioles organization, as was witnessed by their appearance at the press conference last fall to hire new GM Frank Wren. Perhaps they should have been all along. The stories of their behind-the-scenes involvement only helped to feed the image of fantasy baseball fanatics playing with a major league team.

The Washington Times interview caused a lot of ripples in the B&O Warehouse. Although both Hemond and Melvin were very diplomatic in their answers for the story, it created even more tension in an already difficult situation. According to Melvin, he suggested to Hemond after Olson signed with the Atlanta Braves that the Orioles move quickly to sign Smith. "When we didn't sign Olson, I saw all this money that we spent on the offensive part of the club would be going to waste if we didn't have a closer," he said. "I took Lee Smith's name to Roland and said he was available, but that it was the eleventh hour of negotiations and that if we wanted to respond, we should do it quickly. We entered negotiations and got him signed. It doesn't matter to me who gets the credit. We work as a team. If John Angelos wants to take credit for it, he can. . . . I haven't seen him in any of our meetings, so I don't know how involved he is in baseball decisions."

This is the way Hemond tells the Lee Smith story: "We were looking at Farr as a setup man. At the time we had not abandoned the possibility of signing Olson. But then when Olson went, we pursued Smith. . . . The Olson scenario had not concluded itself, and we knew that Smith would not have an interest in signing with us if we still had Olson. The sequence of events sometimes dictates the action you take."

Here was the sequence of events that followed shortly after this article was published. Melvin was gone two months later, resigning to take the general manager's job with the Texas Rangers. Hemond stayed on for one more season, but he knew his time was up in June when he failed to sign Ron Gant, who was recovering from a broken leg incurred in a motorcycle accident. Angelos was adamant in his desire to sign Gant, who wouldn't be ready to play until 1996. But the Reds beat him to it, which infuriated Angelos. He criticized Hemond for not signing the outfielder.

Hemond said he had been talking to Gant's agent and let him know that when his client had worked his way back enough to run or swing a bat, to let the Orioles know. But Gant's friend, Deion Sanders, who was with the Reds, talked him into coming to Cincinnati for a visit, where general manager Jim Bowden quickly made a deal with him. "We were blindsided by circumstances," Hemond said. "The writers went to Peter, and he said our front office wasn't aggressive enough. That was when I lost my cool and said I guess I'll sign Joe DiMaggio and Bruce Hurst. Hurst had just retired with a bad back, and I figured DiMaggio couldn't have much left as a player, right? That was uncharacteristic of me." Hemond knew the situation was bad. "That night I figure this might be the beginning of the end," he said. "The end was in sight. It was a no-win situation."

The end was in sight for another member of the Orioles hierarchy—manager Johnny Oates. Angelos was leery about bringing Oates back as manager after he took over the team, but Oates had been named American League Manager of the Year by *The Sporting News*, and the local media were heavily lobbying Angelos to keep Oates. He did, but another personnel recommendation by his sons signaled the end for Oates.

The Orioles manager did not want his third baseman, Leo Gomez, back for the 1994 season. He pushed to sign free agent Chris Sabo, which the Orioles did, and he wanted Gomez off the roster when the season opened. But Angelos, acting on the advice of his sons, wouldn't let them trade Gomez. "The front office was ready to either trade him for Paul Quantrill," the Boston Red Sox reliever, "or release him," John Angelos said. "My brother and I didn't think he had a fair chance, for whatever reason. After all, how many ballplayers hit sixteen home runs in their first major league season and seventeen the next?" Gomez hit only ten home runs in 1993, when he was handicapped by an injured wrist.

So Gomez stayed. Instead of being the guy least likely to have a job, he became one of the most powerful players on the team—all because Peter Angelos had taken a liking to him, treating him like a family member. "I guess I sort of adopted him," Angelos said. "He's like my nephew." Gomez would then refer to the owner as "Uncle Angelos" in the clubhouse.

Sabo proved to be a medical disaster, with back problems so bad he could barely stand up. Three weeks into the season, he was sidelined with back problems, and Gomez got his chance to play. He made the most of it, hitting above .300—during one eleven-game stretch he batted .432—and driving in runs. He was playing well enough that when Sabo came back on May 22, Gomez was still starting. Five days later, Sabo launched into a tirade over sitting behind Gomez. "I'm the third baseman when I'm healthy," he said. "I'm not the one who hit .190 last year," which was Gomez's 1993 batting average. "Nothing against Leo, he's a good guy," Sabo continued, adding, "he's swinging the bat well right now, but he's no Mike Schmidt or anything." Sabo seethed but he sat.

Angelos then suggested to the front office that perhaps Sabo could be tried in left field. "I'm not a baseball expert, but I played ball when I was a young man," Angelos said. "And if you could play third base, you could play left field. It wasn't that hard." Sure enough, on June 11, Sabo played his first major league game in left field, at Fenway Park in Boston. He continued to play occasionally in the outfield until Gomez began slumping in July. As Gomez slumped, Sabo began seeing more time at third base.

Little did Sabo know, though, that he was playing his last game at third base for the Orioles in the second game of a doubleheader against the Cleveland Indians on July 28. Angelos had been telling Oates that he wanted Gomez to play third, and the owner was furious when Sabo played in that July 28 game. Angelos called Oates into his office the next morning and ordered him to use Gomez as his everyday third baseman, or risk being fired. The next day, Gomez hit a two-run home run to give Baltimore a 7–5 win over the Toronto Blue Jays, and Angelos leaped out of his chair in his private luxury suite at the ballpark, raising his arms in triumph. When asked about his meeting with Oates, Angelos said, "I thought Leo should be our regular third baseman. When Sabo was hurt this year, Leo got the opportunity to play and made the most of it, performing in a manner that was nothing less than superb. I and others in the organization felt that Leo should continue at third base until he couldn't perform at the level that was needed and expected. As far as I'm concerned, he never reached that level to be taken out."

After the game, Oates, alone in his office, responded to Angelos's comments like a man desperately trying to save his job. "I concur with Mr. Angelos wholeheartedly," he said. "I think that Leo should be playing third base. He deserves to be playing third base, and he will be playing third base." There was no saving Oates's job though. The season ended on August 11 with the players going out on strike, and Oates was fired by the end of September, although it was handled poorly by Angelos. It was reported that the owner was seeking permission to talk to Oakland Athletics manager Tony LaRussa while Oates was still officially the Orioles manager.

This was the first season of the "detached" reign of Peter Angelos. Ironically, his finest moments as the Orioles owner—his day in the sun as a hero to baseball fans—came when his team wasn't playing baseball, during the bitter baseball strike.

Angelos clashed repeatedly with his fellow owners during the baseball strike over strategy, particularly their planned use of replacement players. When the owners voted to unilaterally impose a salary cap, Angelos voted against it. (The move, in fact, eventually backfired on them in a National Labor Relations

Board charge that effectively gave the players a court victory and forced the owners to back down, ending the strike.) When the owners voted to use replacement players during the strike, Angelos was the lone owner against the idea. His famous line at one of the owners meetings was, "Let's pass out the Kool Aid," comparing his colleagues to the followers of the Reverend Jim Jones at the Jonestown massacre.

Angelos's maverick, outspoken positions made him the target of his fellow owners' wrath, and they ostracized him from their business dealings. Angelos, though, had extensive experience in labor issues and still operated behind the scenes with union chief Don Fehr, powerful player agent Ron Shapiro, and federal mediator William Usery to try to resolve the labor dispute. Angelos had something to offer, and something to say. "I didn't sign on to be silent, to be acquiescent," Angelos told *The Baltimore Sun* in October 1994. "I am no schoolboy, and I'm not a Boy Scout who just joined the troop. If I have something to say, I'll say it."

His stance against replacement players made him a national hero. He was profiled in *The New York Times* and appeared on *Nightline*. He was named *The New York Daily News* Sportsman of the Year. Baseball fans saw him as the only owner looking out for the interests of the game, and he was also heralded for refusing to endanger Cal Ripken's consecutive-game streak when the shortstop was within 121 games of Lou Gehrig's 2,130 mark. "The product the Orioles deliver to the fans is major league baseball," Angelos said. "Not minor league baseball, not a pickup team or a scrub team or rookie team or a combination of people who are thrown together, and offer it up to the fans as major league baseball. There is only one major league baseball, and that in Baltimore consists of the team that we have at present."

While all other teams opened spring training with replacement players, the Orioles ran a camp consisting of just minor leaguers already in their system, none of whom was eligible to be players' union members yet. American League president Gene Budig threatened Angelos with a fine of $250,000 for each missed game during the regular season, and his franchise could be taken away from him if he failed to field a replacement team on opening day. But Maryland politicians rallied around Angelos, and both city and state legislators passed bills opposing the use of replacement ballplayers at Camden Yards as a show of support for the Orioles owner. A federal court ruling against the owners just before opening day brought about the end of the strike, and the confrontation between Angelos and his fellow owners was avoided.

Given the owners' disastrous strategy during the labor dispute, it appears that Angelos was right in his view that the use of replacement players was a huge mistake. In fact, years later, he said he believed the owners would have triumphed if they had stayed away from using the replacement players. "That only galvanized the players, made them stronger," he explained.

While Angelos was battling his fellow major league owners, he was also waging war with the NFL and raised yet again his status as a savior for the city of Baltimore by trying to acquire a pro-football franchise for the city. He led the fight for an expansion team, and then conducted talks with both the Los Angeles Rams and the Tampa Bay Buccaneers to try to purchase those franchises and move them to Baltimore. But he failed on both counts and later became an enemy of new Maryland Stadium Authority chairman John Moag, who engineered the deal to bring the Cleveland Browns to Baltimore.

When the 1995 season opened, the new Orioles manager was Phil Regan, who was hand-picked by a so-called "committee" selected by Angelos. But Regan was in over his head. Moreover, he alienated the players. After the 1995 season, Angelos fired Regan and Hemond and then quickly hired Davey Johnson to manage the Orioles. Angelos had passed over Johnson the year before when he hired Regan because he had reservations about Johnson's ability to get along with management. This time Angelos chose Johnson over Tony LaRussa, who he felt was asking for too much money—$1 million, plus bringing along pitching coach Dave Duncan for another $250,000.

Johnson seemed like a great choice. He was the winningest active manager in baseball, he had led the New York Mets to two Division titles and a World Series championship, and he had led the Cincinnati Reds to two straight first-place finishes in the National League Central Division. But he had a conflict with Reds owner Marge Schott and was being replaced by Ray Knight. So now Johnson would be coming home to Baltimore, where he had been a star second baseman on those great Orioles championship teams of 1966 and 1970.

Meanwhile, Angelos still had to find a general manager. He had been considering a group of mediocre candidates, but he was feeling the pressure from fellow investors to hire someone of note after firing Hemond. So he tried to convince Pat Gillick, who had brought the Toronto Blue Jays two world championships as its GM but was now in semi-retirement with the club, to take the Baltimore job. At first, Gillick wanted no part of it, and he was being warned by many people in baseball, including Hemond, not to go work for Angelos. "There were a lot of people that told me not to come here, some people who I have a lot of respect for who told me not to come here," Gillick said. "Consequently I had to take that into consideration, and that was part of my reluctance initially to come here. Some people didn't think it was a situation that I wanted to get involved with."

It took Johnson, Gillick's former minor league teammate in Elmira, to convince him to come to Baltimore. Johnson lobbied Gillick hard at the 1995 winter meetings in Phoenix, and Gillick finally agreed to come to Baltimore to talk to Angelos. He, like Johnson, signed a three-year contract worth $2.25 million. Angelos now had two of the best in the business, Johnson and Gillick, to run his team. He then added Kevin Malone, who had been the Montreal general manager and a candidate for the Orioles job, as an assistant general manager. It was a star-studded management team, and Angelos, whose hiring of Regan in 1995 had slightly tarnished his status, had redeemed himself and then some by pulling off this coup.

The glory soon faded, though, when Angelos clashed with Gillick and Johnson. For Gillick, the worst of it came when the Orioles were struggling with a record of 51–52 at the end of July, eleven games behind the first-place New York Yankees, but just five and a half games out of the wild-card position. Gillick wanted to make some deals for the future and proposed trading away veterans Bobby Bonilla and David Wells for young players and minor league prospects. One of those prospects was Jeromy Burnitz, who hit thirty-seven home runs the preceding year. But Angelos refused to let him, which caused some heated arguments between the two men, creating a rift that lasted until Gillick left when his contract was up at the end of the 1998 season.

Gillick, considered by many to be the best general manager in baseball, with thirty-seven years in professional baseball as a player, scout, and front-office executive, said Angelos's refusal to let him make a trade was difficult for him. "I thought it was the direction I would have liked to have gone at that time," Gillick said later. "He had another perspective on it. In a situation now where there is a lot of money invested, everyone has to listen to everyone else's side of the story. In this particular situation, his position was that the fans are very important, the fans that purchased tickets and anticipated a certain quality to the team, and to really take that team and to dismantle that team, it really wasn't fair to the fans. I think he was thinking on behalf of the fans. I was thinking of an overall standpoint for now and in the future, what is the best thing for the baseball team. But sometimes there has to be someone else who is basically an advocate for the public and do what they think is best in the eyes of the public. I think that is what Mr. Angelos was trying to do."

Angelos said the team was too close to a wild-card spot to make such a trade. "It would have had to been so substantial and dramatic a trade that fans would be willing to live with giving up the rest of the season for the future," he said. "Our pitching rotation was intact; our bullpen was intact. We were just five games out. I didn't understand why this was being insisted upon."

Angelos turned out to be right. The Orioles bounced back to win the wild-card position and reached the American League Championship Series before losing in five games to the Yankees. It was a tough time for Gillick, though. He had to live with the articles being written about how Angelos stepped in and saved the team, and the general manager kept a very low profile during the 1996 playoffs. Now, though, some writers have taken Angelos to task for not making those 1996 deals, as well as for the losing 1998 team and the lack of prospects in the minor league system. But that is unfair hindsight. The fact is that with the high ticket prices today, the stakes and the expectations of fans are higher as well. If you had polled the fans at Camden Yards in 1996 and asked them if they were willing to give up their shot at the playoffs for the future, it's unlikely they would have gone along. The Orioles had not reached the playoffs since 1983. It was important for them to be there in 1996, even if it meant mortgaging the future.

The accolades Angelos received for the Orioles playoff appearance were short-lived. First, he was criticized for defending Roberto Alomar in the John Hirschbeck spitting incident. Angelos said he did not defend what Alomar did, but he insisted the second baseman was provoked. Then, Angelos got into a battle with popular Orioles announcer Jon Miller. Angelos was unhappy with Miller's radio calling of Game 5 of the Championship Series. He thought that Miller was taking the Orioles loss—which put them out of the playoffs—a little too lightly. He also was not happy with Miller's absence when he did ESPN work, and a contract dispute resulted in Miller leaving the Orioles after fourteen seasons to be an announcer with the San Francisco Giants in his hometown. Angelos was widely criticized for letting Miller go, although the owner claimed that Miller wanted to go to San Francisco all along. "I think the most decisive factor was his wife wanted to go back where her family was," Angelos said on a Baltimore radio show. In his book, *Confessions of a Baseball Purist*, Miller said he wanted to stay in Baltimore.

Then, Angelos and Johnson got into an off-season battle over Johnson's pitching coach, Pat Dobson. Angelos wanted to fire him and bring in former Orioles pitching coach Ray Miller, who was leaving Pittsburgh, where he had worked with Jim Leyland for ten seasons. Angelos claims that Johnson suggested he might quit if Dobson was fired. Angelos said he would accept Johnson's resignation. And that is how the 1997 season started off.

Again, you have to credit Angelos for making the right move. Miller was considered among the best pitching coaches in the game, and he clearly had a positive effect on the Orioles' 1997 pitching, which carried the club to a wire-to-wire first-place year in the AL East, with a 98–64 record. The Orioles went on to defeat the Seattle Mariners in the Division Series but were upset by the Cleveland Indians in the Championship Series.

But throughout the season, the battle between Angelos and Johnson raged on, fueled even more by the $10,000 fine that Johnson levied against Alomar and then ordered paid to a charity that Johnson's wife directed. The grievance Alomar filed with the players union was an additional embarrassment. Angelos called Johnson's actions "insubordinate," and this resulted in a war of words that eventually ended with Johnson's resignation, readily accepted by Angelos, on the same day Johnson was named AL Manager of the Year.

The perception was that Angelos forced Johnson out, and the Orioles owner was savaged nationally in the media. He had now gained a reputation as the new Steinbrenner. It was a long fall from his hero status as the voice of the fan during the baseball strike to the villain of Baltimore baseball. The talks shows in Baltimore were filled with angry diatribes from fans who blamed Angelos for driving Johnson away, and it got very ugly.

Johnson is gone. Gillick is gone. Malone is gone. And Angelos has gone into his bunker, his twenty-second-floor office in the Charles Center in downtown Baltimore. In an interview in those offices, Angelos talked about the wars he has fought and his conspiracy-theory view that includes the national sports media.

"Stopping those trades," the 1996 Bonilla and Wells deals, "certainly didn't do me any good. I think it earned me the enmity of the pros [Gillick and Malone], especially when it turned out I was right. I assured the pros back then that they shouldn't feel aggrieved because they could classify my decision as a business decision and not a baseball decision, where non-pros should never indulge themselves, according to the sportswriters. If the public really knew the truth, they would really be unhappy with the sportswriting profession. You all bullshit the public. I've been right a lot of times, but you never read it in the newspapers," he said.

Angelos asserts that he took the position he did in those trades because "this team hadn't been to the playoffs in thirteen years, and it was important for us to get there. We were only five games out of the wild card. The pros, the infallible pros, were saying let's trade this one, let's trade that one. They were saying this is a team that didn't know how to win. They were knocking the team. We had a manager who every day was taking shots at his players in the newspaper, alienating a couple of our key players. I ordered him to shut up. I told him if he wanted to criticize the players, he ought to take them into his office, as I would with a lawyer I had a difference with, quietly, privately, telling him what I thought was wrong and don't bring it out in public."

Angelos insists that Johnson wasn't forced out. "Didn't he insist on a three-year extension publicly? I said he had one year to go and his contract would be honored, and then we would talk about a renewal after the 1998 season. Why was it so distorted by the writers?" Angelos thinks that the groundwork was laid for the media's misperceptions. "The writers had been prepared by the distortions and representations that were coming from certain baseball pros to writers." His position is that the writers were lied to. "Unfortunately, they believed it, because there is a tendency to believe anything negative about an owner, and to believe something positive about the pros."

Angelos believes that press coverage about him has been

unjustly negative and even irresponsible. Among the misrepresentations he cites is a widely reported criticism about his sons. "What was written about my sons calling the dugout and telling the manager how to run the team during the course of a game. . . . I couldn't believe anybody would believe that," Angelos said, adding, "no one asked me about it."

Angered by this story, Angelos lashed out at people who would have known the truth but did not speak out to set the record straight in the media. "Isn't it incumbent on you, if you have personal knowledge that something didn't happen, to speak? Maybe I'm just glad that it's being said. On the other hand, it seems that if it is not true, even if I dislike you, morally I have an obligation to speak."

About the Johnson episode, Angelos blasted the former manager for saying he'd be fired without a World Series win. "That was ridiculous. He was out of line, simple as that. He started talking about getting fired in July. People were asking me, and I said, 'What are you talking about?' They said Davey said that. I said, 'Talk to Davey. I don't know what he is talking about.'" Angelos says such stories "made me appear unreasonable. . . . Steinbrennerish, and all the rest of the negatives. I never said anything like that. But Davey kept saying it. That was reason enough for me to fire him right there. I didn't, but I should have, since I was going to get tagged for it anyway. You ask people today what happened, and people will say Angelos fired him. But he quit, and then they will say I made him quit. What he did was so transparent. When he got the Manager of the Year award, that's when he played his aces. He thought, either give me three years or I'll quit. I said your resignation is accepted. He didn't think I would do that, because he thought I was concerned about being savaged in the press. When he got that award, he thought for sure that it wasn't going to happen, that I wouldn't have the guts or the foolishness, take your pick. Davey figured I wouldn't take all that heat."

Angelos faulted Johnson for the Alomar fine—"If I had known about it, the whole thing would have gone away. There would have been no fine, no controversy"—and for implying he'd quit if Dobson left. "When I got rid of Dobson, he resented that," Angelos said of Johnson. "What the hell do I care what he resents? I have enough intelligence to make a judgment that Dobson couldn't cut it. We don't get to the playoffs in 1997 with Dobson," Angelos said. Of the subsequent face-off with Johnson, Angelos recalled, "He said, 'Well, maybe I won't be back.' I said, 'That's your decision, my friend.'"

"I didn't fire him at all," Angelos repeated. "In fact, I put up with him despite all these things he was doing, or not doing. I had certain reservations about him. That's why I didn't hire him the first time when we hired Regan. Davey was the obvious choice, but I knew of some of these other problems. Davey did a good job. I can't complain. If only these other things hadn't been going on, one after the other. Even then I wasn't going to fire him. He was very much liked here. He was remembered as the second baseman here on some of those great Orioles teams."

This is Peter Angelos's view of these events. It is the view of an angry, bitter man, and in some aspects, his bitterness is warranted. The Orioles are not the first organization that Johnson managed himself out of. He was fired from the New York Mets and forced out in Cincinnati. The fact is that after Johnson resigned from Baltimore, he was passed over for jobs in Chicago, Toronto, and Tampa Bay before the 1998 season, and in Detroit and Colorado after the season. When he was finally hired as the manager of the Los Angeles Dodgers, he was far from their first choice. The Dodgers officials privately expressed reservations about Johnson's ability to work with management, and news accounts reported that Malone wanted Kevin Kennedy, not Johnson, as his manager but was overruled by the Fox owners. So, obviously, others in baseball besides Angelos had serious concerns about Johnson.

Furthermore, the Johnson who resigned conflicts with the Johnson who made the following statement during an interview before the start of the 1997 season: "If you have a contract, you live up to it. But I'm learning that in this day and time, people have contracts, but that doesn't mean they're committed. I've learned that, but it's hard for me to learn that. I've always thought that if you signed a contract, it's more than a piece of paper. You've given your word that's what you are going to do for that amount of time. You didn't have any more right to walk away or resign than they could fire you."

But not all of Johnson's transgressions were quite what Angelos made them out to be. The comments the owner referred to about Johnson saying he would be fired if he didn't win the World Series were blown way out of proportion and were similar to comments he had made numerous times before, as he did in an interview before the start of the 1997 season. "I always feel I have to win, no matter what the circumstances," Johnson said. "That's the pressure I put on myself. I expect it. I don't know any other way."

While Angelos claims that he had no intention of firing Johnson and that he didn't force him out, his words after the season make those claims ring hollow. After the Orioles exited the 1997 playoffs, Angelos said he planned to meet with Johnson to discuss his future and later said that the manager's status was "under review." These are hardly the sort of signals that a manager can take comfort in that his job is secure.

Angelos may have made the right call on not trading Bonilla and Wells, but he never gave Pat Gillick the opportunity to build his organization. He hired Gillick, one of the most respected baseball men in the game, to gain respect for having such a name as general manager. Yet Gillick couldn't choose his own director of player personnel, inheriting Syd Thrift when he was hired. If you hire Pat Gillick, it is to run your organization. Gillick was thwarted by Angelos on a number of moves that would have helped the team, such as during the expansion draft for the

Tampa Bay Devil Rays and the Arizona Diamondbacks after the 1997 season. The general manager worked out a deal to trade young prospect Estaban Yan for established left-hander Al Leiter, but this required protecting Yan during the draft and putting high-priced first baseman Rafael Palmeiro on the expansion list. No one was going to take Palmeiro, with his $6 million salary, but Angelos wouldn't let Gillick do it. So while the Orioles starters were dropping like flies with injuries last year, Leiter was winning seventeen games for the New York Mets.

There is no denying Angelos's commitment to the Orioles. They had the highest payroll in baseball in 1997—$77 million— and he has made it clear he will continue to spend the rewards they reap from Camden Yards on the team. He is also a leader in community and charitable efforts. He sits on the board of four colleges and such organizations as the University of Maryland Foundation and the Grant-A-Wish Foundation. He has donated $1 million to the Babe Ruth Museum to develop its Camden Station museum project. He has been recognized with the Ellis Island Medal of Honor and the AFL-CIO Social Justice Award.

But Angelos sits in his office overlooking the city of Baltimore like a man under siege, convinced he is right, and so many others are wrong. "I deal in truth," he said. "I don't deal in misrepresentations and distortions. My game is truth."

Index